Warring Factions

*Interest Groups, Money,
and the New Politics
of Senate Confirmation*

Warring Factions

Interest Groups, Money,
and the New Politics
of Senate Confirmation

LAUREN COHEN BELL

The Ohio State University Press
Columbus

Copyright © 2002 by The Ohio State University.
All rights reserved.

Library of Congress Cataloging-in-Publication Data

Bell, Lauren Cohen, 1973–
    Warring factions : interest groups, money, and the new politics of senate confirmation / Lauren Cohen Bell.
        p. cm.
    Includes bibliographical references and index.
    ISBN 0-8142-0891-6 (cloth : alk. paper) — ISBN 0-8142-5088-2 (pbk : alk. paper)
    1. United States—Officials and employees—Selection and appointment—History.   2. Pressure groups—United States.   I. Title.
    JK731 .B37 2002
    328.73'07455—dc21
                                                            2001008345

Cover design by Dan O'Dair
Text design by Bookcomp Inc.
Type set in Adobe Caslon by Bookcomp Inc.
Printed by Thomson-Shore Inc.

9 8 7 6 5 4 3 2 1

This book is dedicated to all current, former, and future presidential nominees and scholars of the confirmation process.

Contents

Preface

Political scientists know more about the American Congress than they do about other institutions of government largely because of the excellent work of a number of scholars who have devoted their lives to understanding the processes and procedures used by Congress. Today, we understand well the complexities of lawmaking, the burdens of representation, and the politics of governing a country of nearly 300 million people.

Despite our understanding of the national legislature, one aspect of its business remains understudied. That aspect, the Senate's confirmation process, is the general subject of this book. Although a spate of recent studies has begun to peer into the Senate's process for approving or rejecting presidential nominees, none to date has comprehensively explored the changing dynamics of the confirmation process or the role that interest groups have played in transforming Senate confirmation politics in the 1990s. My goal in writing this book is to illuminate the Senate's work in this important area and to offer insights into the ways in which the Senate's confirmation process has become little more than an extension of its legislative work. What was once a process free from outside influence and, quite frankly, above partisan politics has now become an arena for competition among warring factions of interest groups and senators. This book tells the story of the transformation.

I could not have completed this study without the help, guidance, and support of a number of people. The roots of the project extend back to a graduate research seminar at the University of Oklahoma and to the wisdom and guidance of the leader of that seminar, Dr. Gary Copeland, who helped me to refine my interest in the Senate confirmation process over a period of several months in 1996 and 1997. I am grateful to Dr. Copeland for his support of this research endeavor, and to the Carl Albert Congressional Research and Studies Center at the University of Oklahoma for its financial support of the initial draft of this project. In addition, the research opportunities provided by the American Political Science Association's Congressional Fellowship Program, under the direction of Mr. Jeffrey

Biggs, were invaluable. So too was the support of the staff of the United States Senate Committee on Judiciary, where I was fortunate to work as a fellow during the 1997–98 academic year. Finally, the support of my faculty colleagues at Randolph-Macon College, especially Bruce Unger, Brian Turner, and Tom Badey, has been unwavering, and I am grateful to have such dedicated, talented, and supportive colleagues.

Pieces of this research have been presented and reviewed in a number of different venues and by a number of different people. I am grateful for the wise comments of University of Oklahoma faculty members R. Keith Gaddie, Cindy Simon Rosenthal, Jill Irvine, and Wil Scott. Steven Wasby at SUNY Albany, Glen Krutz at Arizona State University, David Richert at *Judicature*, Jeffrey Segal at SUNY Stony Brook, Jeffrey Yates, Christopher Kelleher at Congressional Quarterly Press, Kevin Scott at The Ohio State University, G. Calvin Mackenzie at Colby College, and several anonymous reviewers for their suggestions and constructive criticisms.

I am also grateful to the many interview subjects and experts who added their expertise to this project. In particular, I wish to thank the staff of the Senate Judiciary Committee with whom I worked for ten months in 1997 and 1998, especially Melody Barnes, Michael Carrasco, Mary De-Oreo, and Bruce Cohen. I also wish to thank former U.S. Senators David L. Boren (D-OK), Warren Rudman (R-NH), and Paul Simon (D-IL) for taking time away from their new endeavors to discuss their experiences with me. Further, my heartfelt thanks extend to several anonymous interview subjects, including several sitting U.S. senators and their staffs, and to Michael and Mary Ellen Schattman, Nan Aron of the Alliance for Justice, Tom Jipping of the Judicial Selection Monitoring Project, Alex Acosta of the Project on the Judiciary, Tracy Hahn-Burkett and Eliot Mincberg from People for the American Way, Scott Olson from Common Cause, and Steve Schwalm of the Family Research Council. In addition, I wish to thank the editorial board and staff of The Ohio State University Press, including Malcolm Litchfield, Jean Matter, and Laurie Avery. I truly could not have completed this project without them.

Finally, I am also deeply honored by the support and commitment of my family and friends: Arnold, Celeste, and Faith Cohen, Frances Collins, Bea Cohen, Trudy Goodkin, Jane Koerner, Christina Foell, Molly Carlson, Lesli McCollum, Malissa Heldreth, Deonna Woolard, Elizabeth Gill, Wendy Closterman, Adrian Rice, Craig Williams, Jon and Kim Mott, Karen Click, and the entire Bell family. My thanks and love extend especially to my husband, John, whose support and love made this book possible.

Introduction: The Decline of the Confirmation Process

> Here's a bipartisan program that is saving taxpayers millions every year: Nearly 250 of the government's 726 most senior jobs are going unfilled.
>
> *Time Magazine,* May 26, 1997

The United States Senate divides its work into two categories: legislative business and executive business. Legislative business consumes the vast majority of the Senate's time. When the Senate is engaged in legislative work, it is doing the nation's business—debating and passing laws, representing citizens of each of the states, legitimating the American federal government. Executive business, including the consideration of proposed treaties and presidential nominations, traditionally has been less controversial than legislative business. In contrast to "the nation's business," it is the business of making the government itself run, and because of its more bureaucratic nature, it has never been considered as important or significant as the Senate's legislative work. Through the early 1990s the Senate's consideration of executive business also was less controversial than its work on legislative business. Presidents expected Senate support for their initiatives—including their nominations—and with few exceptions, the Senate complied. Today, however, the Senate's process for considering executive business, especially its consideration of presidential nominations, has changed dramatically.

This is a book about the Senate's confirmation process—the constitutional process the Senate uses to approve or reject presidents' choices to fill federal government positions. It is a book about the history, the evolution, and, arguably, the downfall of the process. Most significantly, it is a book that demonstrates the extent to which interest groups and money have transformed the Senate's confirmation process into a virtual circus. Today's

1

confirmation process looks very different from the process envisioned by the original framers. Broad political forces have transformed the confirmation process. Political, legal, and financial wrangling has transformed the Senate's once-secret consideration of presidential nominations into a public arena for the articulation and advancement of political interests.

Every year, the president nominates and the Senate confirms thousands of individuals to posts in the executive branch, the federal judiciary, and the military. For nearly two hundred years, the vast majority of these appointments to the highest positions in the federal government were routine, and conventional wisdom on the appointment process suggested that the Senate acted only as a "rubber stamp" on presidential selections.[1] Professor G. Calvin Mackenzie, a longtime observer of confirmation politics, noted in 1996: "In the vast majority of cases, confirmation occurs routinely after the Senate has reviewed the credentials of nominees submitted by the president."[2] A 1999 textbook on the relationship between the president and the Congress concurred, adding: "All evidence suggests that the Senate generally defers to presidential nominations."[3] Regarding judicial nominations, constitutional scholar David O'Brien has noted: "[T]he vast majority of nominees are routinely approved by the Senate Judiciary Committee after only perfunctory investigation and according to no fixed standards."[4] Indeed, since 1931, the Senate has confirmed over 97 percent of presidential nominees.[5]

It is not surprising that scholars continue to profess the notion that the Senate acts as a rubber stamp on presidential nominations. This conventional wisdom accurately reflects the fact that the vast majority of presidential nominees are eventually confirmed. But the numbers are deceiving. The focus on confirmation outcomes as a measure of the health and stability of the confirmation process has misled scholars into a false sense of security that the process still works well. Nearly perfect confirmation rates for presidential nominees tell us nothing about the *process* of confirming the president's choices. All they reveal is that most nominees are eventually confirmed. These rates do not differentiate those nominees who were confirmed in a day from those confirmed in a month from those confirmed after a year or more. Nor do raw confirmation rates indicate the many factors that might cause nominees' confirmation processes to vary.

In recent years, the Senate has intensified its scrutiny of presidential nominees. For a small but growing group of individuals nominated to positions at the highest levels of the federal government, the conventional wisdom is just plain wrong. The confirmation process for these presidential nominees has undergone significant changes in the last few decades. It is no longer characterized by senatorial deference to the president, and it is no longer so swift or certain. Rather, nominees to top positions in the executive and judicial branches now face a lengthy confirmation process characterized by partisan bickering, animosity, struggles for power, and rancor never before witnessed by confirmation observers.

Change in the Senate's confirmation process has been driven by two factors. First, changes to the external political environment have constrained the behavior of U.S. senators. Senators are no longer insulated from media attention, nor are they immune from national political trends, including the increasing prevalence of interest groups in American society in general and in the legislative process more specifically. Further, divided control of the White House and Congress has coupled with the increasingly partisan environment on Capitol Hill during the 1990s to create new stresses in the confirmation process. Moreover, changes to Senate rules and norms have permitted changes in the political environment to intervene in the confirmation process. As the Senate changed from being the hierarchical, inner-directed institution it was at mid-century to becoming a collection of one hundred coequal individuals, each of whom possesses complete autonomy, the incentive structures for interest groups to engage in senatorial lobbying have changed as well. Interest groups and the money that they have injected into the legislative process are now fixtures in the Senate's confirmation process. Today's confirmation process is a system in which interest groups and their financial resources can dominate. Just over forty years ago, Richard Fenno observed: "Although the president does operate in the appointment process with a free hand, he does so at the sufferance of the United States Senate."[6] Fenno could not have been more prescient. As Senate norms have changed generally, the confirmation process has been changed as well. This introductory chapter illustrates the ways in which the confirmation process has unraveled in the 1990s and sets the stage on which the rest of the story will be played out in the chapters that follow.

Why Study the Confirmation Process?

With the exception of litigants in federal lawsuits, few people care very much about vacant seats on the federal bench. Even fewer care about the jobless rate among high-paid federal bureaucrats or wealthy campaign contributors seeking ambassadorships to foreign countries. By and large, the erosion of the confirmation process for top federal jobs is not a salient issue to the vast majority of American people. But it should be. The choices that a president makes in nominating people to fill up vacancies and the process that the Senate uses to determine the integrity, fitness, and qualifications of these nominees have direct consequences for the quality of governance in the United States. Understanding the confirmation process can help individuals to evaluate more fully the health, stability, and direction of the American system of government. There is no other governmental process that brings together as many political actors as the confirmation process for federal officials. Taken in its entirety, the appointment process assembles actors from the executive, legislative, and judicial branches; from the federal bureaucracy; and from outside organizations such as interest groups and the media.

Examining the dynamics of the confirmation process can also yield important clues about the political system. As Rogelio Garcia, a Congressional Research Service (CRS) specialist in confirmation politics notes: "The [confirmation] process is just a microcosm of the political process."[7] In addition, studying the confirmation process for major appointments is especially important because each set of nominees exists within its own web of political interests. As Richard Fenno notes in his seminal study of presidential cabinets: "Since the network of relationships which affects the cabinet includes the president, the executive branch of government, the Congress, political parties, and pressure groups, a study of the cabinet becomes in its broadest sense a study of American politics in general."[8] Regarding ambassadors, Dayton Mak and Charles Kennedy note in *American Ambassadors in a Troubled World: Interviews with Senior Diplomats:* "The selection and appointment of American ambassadors is a unique process involving presidential preferences, domestic policies, professional abilities from within the foreign service and special qualifications from without."[9] With regard to the Supreme Court, constitutional law scholar Lawrence Tribe has written that "there is hardly an aspect of American life that has not been touched by the hands of our highest tribunal."[10] The lower federal courts also exist at the nexus of competing legal, social, and political interests, each vying for the upper hand in pending litigation.

The changes to the confirmation process that have occurred in the last few decades indicate that the system for staffing the American federal government is in need of repair. The slowing of the confirmation process and the increasing number of vacancies in top federal jobs suggests that our political system is no longer functioning as it once did, thus keeping federal judgeships vacant and agencies and embassies understaffed. This, in turn, has important consequences for the functioning of government. As United States Supreme Court Chief Justice William Rehnquist wrote in his *1997 Year-End Report on the Federal Judiciary*, "Vacancies cannot remain at such high levels indefinitely without eroding the quality of justice that traditionally has been associated with the federal judiciary."[11]

Studying the confirmation process is the only way to ascertain the true dynamics of the appointment process more generally. The confirmation process gives a full picture of the competing interests involved since it is much more open to public scrutiny and involvement than is the president's nomination process. While the president's selection of a nominee primarily takes place behind closed doors, the Senate confirmation process—conducted through public hearings—provides an open forum for senators, members of Congress, staff, interest groups, and even members of the public to make known their concerns about a nominee. The contemporary Senate's norms and procedures also provide ample room for interest groups who oppose a nominee to slow or prevent confirmation.

The Changed Nature of the Confirmation Process

Throughout much of American history, presidential nominees could expect little opposition from the Senate. With just a handful of notable exceptions, the Senate routinely deferred to the president when making its confirmation decisions. Unless a nominee was being considered for a Supreme Court justiceship (in which case he or she would be more carefully scrutinized because of the seriousness and lifetime nature of the appointment), he or she could expect to be confirmed quickly and without controversy. In the mid-1990s, however, evidence that the Senate would no longer defer to the president began to surface. Nominees to even the lowest levels of the federal courts are now carefully scrutinized. Unlike in the past, when virtually all nominees were confirmed, today no nominee to a major position is assured of confirmation.

The nomination of Michael Schattman to fill a vacancy on the U.S. District Court for the District of North Texas illustrates this point. The Senate had never perceived district court judgeships as worthy of much scrutiny, and such nominations certainly were not often subjected to interest group mobilization. Thus, when Mike Schattman was nominated in December 1995 to fill a vacancy on the North Texas District Court, he assumed that it was the beginning of a process that would lead to the fulfillment of a lifelong dream. At the time of his nomination, Schattman had served nearly fourteen years as judge in the 348th Judicial District of Tarrant County, Texas, and he had always wanted to serve his country from the federal bench. Initially, Schattman's confirmation prospects looked good. He had sailed through his White House background check, and he had the support of his home-state senators. On April 15, 1996, Texas senator Phil Gramm declared: "I have communicated my satisfaction with Judge Schattman's credentials and qualifications to the [Senate] Judiciary Committee."[12] Less than two weeks later, Texas junior senator Kay Bailey Hutchison also noted that she was supportive of Schattman's nomination: "I have spoken directly to the chairman of the [Senate Judiciary] committee, Senator Orrin Hatch, to reiterate my support for Mr. Schattman's nomination."[13] With the support of both his home state senators, Schattman had no reason to believe that his confirmation would be anything more than a formality.

But Schattman's nomination did not proceed as he expected. The Senate Judiciary Committee took no action on his nomination in 1996. Upon his renomination in March 1997, at the beginning of the 105th Congress, his prospects for confirmation again seemed good. Both Senators Gramm and Hutchison continued to express their support for him, and North Texas newspapers began calling for his confirmation. Then, in July 1997, both Texas senators suddenly withdrew their support. Gramm claimed that concerns over Schattman's appearance at a prayer vigil had led him to abandon the nominee, while Hutchison cited concerns "raised by attornies [sic] whose views I respect."[14] Because of the Senate's long-standing tradition of deferring to home state senators when making confirmation decisions about federal judges, Schattman's nomination was effectively dead. Even as Schattman continued to work for confirmation, Texas newspapers declared that the process was over.[15]

In June 1998, Schattman withdrew his name from consideration. It was a frustrating end to both partisan and personal attacks on his credentials. Even more frustrating to Schattman was the fact that he was never provided with any information about his nomination, nor was he given an explanation for why his home state senators suddenly removed their support. After he withdrew, friends in the North Texas legal community told Schattman that a rumor was circulating that Senators Gramm and Hutchison had come under fire from conservative lawyers and wealthy contributors in North Texas whose preference it was to have a more conservative nominee for the vacant position. Six months following the withdrawal of his nomination, Schattman offered current and future nominees this advice: "Go to bed with your senator. And watch your back."[16] It was the end of a dream for Schattman and for his wife, Mary Ellen. It also meant that the North Texas judgeship, which had been vacant since January 1, 1996, would remain vacant. By 1999, the North Texas judgeship had been vacant for more than three years.

The Schattman case illustrates the extent to which the Senate confirmation process has deteriorated from a process that was stable and predictable to one that is haphazard, irregular, and unpredictable. In 1994, Yale

Law School professor Stephen Carter declared that the country was facing a "confirmation mess." It has become even worse since then. One needs only to consider a smattering of recent commentary on the state of the contemporary appointment process to recognize that widespread changes have occurred. Political scientist Norman Ornstein writes: "Over the past 30 years, as distrust for the executive has become the norm in Congress and partisan divisions have become more prominent, tough battles over presidential appointments have become more frequent."[17] Another study concludes: "[I]n the first year of President Clinton's second term, the changed character and the consummate disarray of the appointment process have been fully revealed. The recent evolution of the presidential appointment process has become not only inadequate to its purposes but a festering national embarrassment."[18]

There is no question that the process has changed. The once conflict-free Senate confirmation process nearly ground to a halt during the 105th Congress (1997–98), and that congress was the backdrop for what many observers of confirmation politics claimed was an all-time low in comity and efficiency in the process. Although the president was sending nominations to the Senate, many nominations stalled in one of the Senate's committees or were held up on the Senate floor. On June 4, 1998—just four months before the 105th Congress was due to adjourn—Bob Nash, President Bill Clinton's Director of Presidential Personnel, sent Senate Majority Leader Trent Lott the following letter:[19]

Dear Senator Lott,

I appreciate the help you have provided in confirming nominees the President has submitted to the Senate during the 105th Congress, and I would like to ask for your assistance in expediting the remainder of our nominees. We have had 252 nominations pending before the Senate in 1998, only 33% of whom have been confirmed. Nearly 40% of our current nominees have been awaiting confirmation for more than six months. There are 24 nominees (14%) who have been pending before the Senate for between 6 and 9 months; 12 nominees, or 7%, pending for 9 to 12 months; 5 nominees, or 3%, pending for 12 to 18 months; and 26 nominees, or 15%, pending for more than 18 months. . . . Many have been nominated for positions that are important to the efficiency and effectiveness of both our federal agencies and our judicial system. I would therefore appreciate any assistance that you may be able to provide in confirming these nominees.

Sincerely,
Bob J. Nash
Assistant to the President and Director of Presidential Personnel

Despite Nash's letter, by the time the 105th Congress adjourned in October 1998, only 100 of the 160 nominees (62.5 percent) awaiting confirmation in July had been confirmed.[20] Several nominations were returned to President Clinton, including a number of judicial nominees whose nominations had been pending for more than three years. Not only were a number of high-profile nominees among those whose names were returned to the president, but several nominations to lower-level positions in government also were not confirmed. Related to this phenomenon is the fact that it is now difficult for presidents to find individuals who are willing to endure the grueling confirmation process. Fewer and fewer people are willing to put themselves, their families, and their careers on hold in order to endure an uncertain confirmation process.

The consequence of this difficulty is the high number of vacancies in top-level positions in the federal government. A 1998 report on the state of the confirmation process during the Clinton administration noted: "Despite the relative stability in positions at the highest level, the administration as a whole experienced a vacancy rate in appointed positions in the executive branch that frequently exceeded 25 percent. Many departments and agencies went through much of 1997 with a large percentage of their top positions in the hands of acting or temporary placeholders."[21]

Nearly all assessments of the contemporary appointment process are dismal. In today's confirmation climate, nominees to relatively obscure positions become household names, not because of their credentials or the importance of the jobs they have been nominated to fill, but because the Senate refuses to confirm them. Since 1995, nearly all indicators of efficiency in the confirmation process suggest that the process has become less efficient than ever before. In short, the "rubber stamp machine" has been replaced by the "confirmation mess."

Interest Groups, Money, and the New Politics of Senate Confirmation

In her excellent treatment of changes to legislative processes in the United States Senate, Barbara Sinclair explains: "In the contemporary Congress the textbook diagram [of how a bill becomes a law] describes the legislative process on fewer and fewer of the major bills."[22] The same can also be said for the confirmation process. Textbook diagrams and historical accounts of Senate confirmation no longer accurately capture the nature of the process, which today is lengthy, laborious, partisan, and vitriolic. What accounts for the altered nature of the confirmation process? I argue that increased interest group involvement in the legislative process (a phenomenon that began in the 1960s) has combined with the influx of money into all facets of American political life (a trend that began in earnest in the late 1970s) to create a new politics of Senate confirmation. This new politics represents a process divorced from civility and cooperation. Today's confirmation process is characterized by partisanship, delay, and bitter attacks on presidential nominees. It is a process increasingly implicated in electoral politics and connected to the financial fortunes of interest groups and senators.

American University law professor Thomas Sargentich has noted that "interest group involvement in nominations is inevitable because [the confirmation process] is an inherently political process involving both Congress and the president."[23] Although a handful of previous studies have shed some light on the causes of change in the confirmation process, none to date has focused on the role that interest groups have played in shaping confirmation dynamics. This is despite the fact that interest groups have long been blamed for the defeat of Robert Bork, one of Ronald Reagan's nominees to the Supreme Court.[24] Further, no study has explored the impact that money has had on changing confirmation dynamics. Although several studies have explored interest group participation and the role of money in the legislative process, none has focused on the confirmation process, despite the clear impact that interest groups and financial incentives have had on it.

The interest group explosion of the 1960s and 1970s had important ramifications for the confirmation process. Today, there are more than four thousand political action committees working to influence electoral outcomes, and many of these groups also work to influence confirmation outcomes. Kay Schlozman and John Tierney, in their 1986 study *Organized Interests and American Democracy*, found that 53 percent of the two hundred organizations they sampled engaged in "attempting to influence appointment to public office."[25] A greater percentage of interest groups in their study attempted to influence the appointment process than engaged in direct-mail fund-raising for their organization, made public endorsements of candidates in political campaigns, or engaged in public protests and demonstrations.

This is not to suggest that interest group participation is necessarily bad. The primary reason that interest groups are a part of the process is because their input and influence is sought by senators, nominees, and even the White House. Often, interest groups influence confirmation politics because of what they contribute to the process. They provide vast quantities of information about nominees to senators and assist Senate staffers with their research into nominees' personal and professional activities. Presidents rely on interest groups to help gather grassroots support for their nominees. Information collected and provided by such groups can assist both presidents and senators with making reasoned judgments about a nominee's background or likely activities once appointed. And interest groups provide important avenues for American citizens to express their views. As former U.S. Senator Warren Rudman (R-NH) points out: "A basic fundamental right in the Constitution is the right to redress grievances. That means everyone's an interest group. Teachers . . . auto workers . . . single mothers. Of course you listen to them. Any member of the Senate who doesn't isn't doing a good job of being a senator."[26]

Because interest groups are important as filters for broader public messages, their participation in confirmation politics can alter the confirmation process itself. Previous studies of the Supreme Court confirmation process have found that interest groups play an important role in shaping the dynamics of the process.[27] Scholars have documented the importance of interest groups in defeating Ronald Reagan's nomination of Robert Bork to the Supreme Court in 1987.[28] One study notes: "By the time the Bork nomination was decided, groups from every part of the political spectrum had spent millions of dollars and immeasurable effort to block Reagan's effort to ensure a conservative Supreme Court far after his term in office."[29] Groups sponsored television advertisements, testified at Bork's confirmation hearings, lobbied members of Congress, and used direct-mail campaigns to bring the public into the Bork debate. By one account: "According to the Senate postmaster, the Bork controversy drew more mail than any issue in recent memory."[30] In the end, the full Senate rejected Robert Bork's nomination by a vote of fifty-two to forty-eight.

Of course, interest groups cared about the process long before the Bork nomination was announced, and nearly twenty years after his defeat, they continue to try to affect who gets appointed to high-ranking federal offices. For the most part, interest groups target their attempts at influencing appointment outcomes at the United States Senate, primarily because the selection process tends to be much more closed to their participation. In *The Interest Group Society*, Jeffrey Berry writes of judicial nominees: "[T]he norm is that the Justice Department or administration officials do not meet with interest groups to discuss possible selections."[31] During recent congresses, interest groups have been frequent participants in Senate confirmation politics for presidential nominees. More than four hundred organizations took a position on one or more nominees during the 105th Congress alone. Clearly, many interest groups care about the appointment process and work to influence its outcomes. They bring the entire range of their resources to bear on trying to influence the confirmation process in much the same way that they try to influence other legislative processes.

Sometimes, however, interest groups engage in questionable tactics designed to bring about the defeat of one or more presidential nominees. Recent coverage of the appointment process in the popular press reinforces the view that the lack of Senate action on presidential nominees is the result of pressure from outside interest groups on key members of the Senate leadership. These studies suggest that beginning with the Republican takeover of the U.S. Senate in 1995, conservative interest groups sought to lessen the impact of a Democratic president on the direction of the federal government by encouraging Republicans in the Senate to stall confirmation on many of the president's nominees.[32] Groups attempting to defeat a nominee may distort an individual's background or may attempt to plant seeds of doubts about the nominee's integrity, ability, or qualifications. Consequently, interest groups not only participate in confirmation hearings for presidential nominees, but that they also work behind the scenes to see that nominees they approve of are confirmed, while nominees they disapprove of languish. And they are often successful.

It is the behind-the-scenes participation of such groups that has made it possible for another political phenomenon to influence the confirmation process. This phenomenon is the interjection of money into the confirmation process and the linkage of senators' confirmation actions with upcoming elections. The participation of interest groups in the process brings with it money—sometimes lots of money—as well as links to wealthy individuals with an interest in public policy. The result is that senators now view their confirmation votes strategically, and there is some evidence that their confirmation decisions now are influenced by their desire to appease wealthy interest groups and campaign contributors who have an interest in the outcome of particular confirmation decisions. Today, some senators use the confirmation process to generate political and financial support from interest groups.

No study has explored comprehensively the impact of interest group participation on confirmation outcomes for presidential nominees, nor has any investigated the ways in which the scramble for campaign dollars and the new link between confirmations and campaigns has affected the confirmation process. Thus, this book examines the changed nature of the confirmation process and ascertains the impact of interest groups on it. It examines whether the variety of ways that interest groups participate in the confirmation process and the money that these groups generate and bring with them to the bargaining table can explain the changed nature of the Senate confirmation process across three sets of nominees: cabinet secretaries, ambassadors, and lower federal court judges.

Using both quantitative and qualitative data, this study addresses five questions: (1) What is the nature of interest group participation in the confirmation process? (2) What prompts interest groups to participate in the confirmation process? (3) What are the consequences of interest group participation in the confirmation process? (4) What is the role of money in the confirmation process? and (5) Can the participation of interest groups and the interjection of money into the process explain the overwhelming changes to the process that have become evident in recent years? The evidence demonstrates that when they get involved, interest groups can indeed be successful at influencing confirmation outcomes and that they are greatly responsible for recent changes to the contemporary process. The evidence also suggests that some senators are swayed by the financial inducements these groups offer and that these senators' behaviors in the confirmation process are related to financial incentives provided by the interest groups.

Data for this study were gathered from three sources. First, all available confirmation hearings for nominees to the federal judiciary and the president's cabinet between 1977 and 1998 were consulted, and data on interest group participation were compiled. Two data sets were then created. The first set contains data compiled from 1,242 judicial nominations made between 1979 and 1998. The second set was compiled with data from the eighty-eight hearings held on nominees to the president's cabinet between 1977 and 1998. These data sets are used in chapters 4 and 5 to quantify interest group participation in Senate confirmation hearings. Appendix 2 provides a more detailed explanation of the coding of the variables in the data sets and the sources used to compile them.

In addition to the quantitative analysis, in-depth interviews were conducted in 1997, 1998, and 2000 with more than two-dozen individuals who are or who have been integrally involved in the Senate confirmation process. Finally, many of the observations included in this project came from ten months of participant observation of the confirmation process from the vantage point of the United States Senate Committee on Judiciary.[33] Data and information were gathered from conversations I had during and after that time with former senators, Senate staffers, and former appointees. All of these data sources were combined to provide a full picture of the ways in which interest groups and money have changed the Senate's confirmation process.

Background

In the chapters that follow, references are made to several groups of nominees and positions that must be filled by the advice and consent process. Three groups of nominees are explored in detail: nominees to fill vacancies on the lower federal courts, nominees to fill vacant cabinet secretary positions, and nominees to represent the president of the United States abroad as ambassadors. While these groups are similar in that they encompass important positions in the federal government, each group maintains a number of unique characteristics. This section identifies the unique aspects of the structure of each position and the dynamics of confirmation that surround them.

First, the federal judiciary represents the third branch of American government. Judges and justices are charged with hearing federal criminal and civil cases that are brought either under the United States Code or on appeal from a lower court. The federal courts are organized hierarchically. At the lowest level of the federal judiciary are the federal district courts (ninety-two in all) and courts of specialized jurisdiction. In the middle are the Circuit Courts of Appeals (eleven in all, plus one each for the District of Columbia and the federal circuit), and at the top is the Supreme Court. The president nominates, and the Senate must confirm, judges to serve at all levels of the federal judiciary.

Nominees to the lower federal courts—the Court of International Trade, district courts, and Circuit Courts of Appeals—are appointed for terms of good behavior, which are effectively lifetime terms. They represent the overwhelming majority of judges in the federal judicial branch. Circuit Court of Appeals (CCA) judges "review appeals from decisions of the Federal trial courts, and are empowered to review the orders of many administrative agencies."[34] CCA judges are considered the highest-ranking judges of all the lower courts. There are thirteen CCAs, with multiple judges serving on each court. There are 179 CCA judgeships authorized by federal law.[35]

Below the CCAs are the federal district courts. These are the federal trial courts and are the point of entry for most business before the federal courts. There are a total of 649 district court judgeships authorized.[36] Finally, the United States Court of Federal Trade "has original and exclusive jurisdiction over civil actions against the United States, its agencies and officers, and certain civil actions brought by the United States arising out of import transactions and federal statutes affecting international trade."[37] A total of nine judges make up the U.S. Court of Federal Trade. Interestingly, however, there is one caveat governing the selection of trade court judges. According to CRS specialist Steven Rutkus, "no more than five [sitting U.S. Court of Federal Trade judges] may belong to any one political party."[38] Judicial nominees also generally make up the largest group of nominees confirmed in a given congress.

Nominees to the federal courts have always been the most highly scrutinized of all presidential nominees, in large part because they are the only presidential appointees whose terms are not limited. The Senate is generally cautious about confirming individuals who not only will make decisions affecting nearly every aspect of society, but who also can be removed only through impeachment by the House of Representatives. However, the Senate's caution usually does not result in a rejection of a judicial nominee; the confirmation rate for judicial nominees is about 85 percent, which is somewhat lower than the overall confirmation rate (in the range of 95 percent or above) but which is still high. In general, the Senate applies stricter scrutiny to CCA nominees, but that pattern began to change in the 104th and 105th Congresses. Today, district court nominees are also carefully scrutinized, as the Schattman case indicates.

In contrast to judicial nominations, nominees to vacant seats in the president's cabinet and to vacant ambassadorships almost never serve terms that last longer than the length of the president's tenure in office. In fact, few cabinet secretaries or ambassadors serve for the entirety of a president's term in office. According to Mackenzie (1996), the average length of service for non–lifetime-appointed personnel is now just slightly longer than two years. Throughout his presidency, but especially upon assuming his duties at the beginning of his first term, the president must choose individuals to head the fourteen major government departments. The heads of these departments are responsible for helping the president carry out his job of enforcing the laws through the rule-making and program-monitoring functions their agencies perform.

Although nominees to top positions in the executive branch have traditionally come under heavy scrutiny from senators and interest groups, over time they too have almost always been confirmed quickly and without much controversy. Considered to be part of the president's "team," and thus given a strong presumption of confirmability, nominees to the president's cabinet were not generally scrutinized as carefully as were nominees to the federal bench. Senators typically use the confirmation process for cabinet secretaries-designate only to ensure that nominees possess appropriate educational and professional qualifications and that the nominee is willing to appear before the Congress on matters of public policy.

The last group of nominees explored in this book is ambassadorial nominees. Ambassadors are the highest-ranking diplomats in the foreign service. They are appointed by the president to act as the president's official representatives abroad. The choice of ambassadors may have foreign policy implications, as some countries measure their standing in the American esteem by evaluating the stature of the ambassador sent by the U.S. government. Like nominees to the president's cabinet, ambassadorial nominees have nearly always been confirmed without controversy. A CRS report notes that between 1987 and 1996, the Senate confirmed 91 percent of the president's nominees to ambassadorships.[39] Once appointed, ambassadors manage the U.S. embassy and its staff and act as foreign policy coordinators for the United States in embassies and consulates abroad.

An important difference has traditionally distinguished ambassadorial and cabinet confirmations from judicial confirmations. That difference is that the Senate usually grants the president the latitude to appoint whomever he wishes. Nominees to ambassadorships and cabinet posts are routinely confirmed without controversy. Typically, the Senate has viewed ambassadorships as patronage appointments to figurehead positions and has done little to block a president's choice.[40] Similarly, many senators believe that the president is entitled to his choice in choosing members of his cabinet.[41] There is evidence, however, that these attitudes have changed.

These brief descriptions of the three sets of nominees considered in this study demonstrate just how important these positions are to the functioning of the American government. Thus, decisions by the president and the Senate about whom to appoint to fill vacancies that occur have real consequences. For that reason, it is necessary to explore the confirmation process for each of the three groups of major appointments.

Organization of the Book

Despite evidence to suggest that interest groups desire to influence appointment to public office and that they now use financial inducements among their tools of influence, much remains unknown about the dynamics of their participation in the Senate confirmation process. Thus, the remainder of this project explores why and how interest groups participate in confirmation politics, as well as looking at the impact of money on the process.

The first chapter is a brief treatment of the contemporary confirmation process. It sets out the chronology of both the president's nominating process and the Senate's confirmation process in a way that reflects the changes that have occurred from the time the Constitution was adopted to today's contemporary process.

Chapter 2 addresses both the "how" and the "why" of changes in the confirmation process. With regard to how the process has changed, four major changes are identified: an increase in the number of positions requiring Senate confirmation, a reduced role for the president, increasingly more partisan and ideological battles over nominees, and the growing use of delaying tactics to stall confirmation or prevent nominees from being confirmed altogether. The chapter then turns to the causes of these changes and concludes that while changing conditions in the Senate contribute in part to the new politics of Senate confirmation, in the contemporary confirmation process interest groups create incentives for senators to support or oppose nominees by using their most powerful tool—money.

The contemporary confirmation process is a struggle among competing social interests. Relying on elite theories and theories of pluralism, chapter 3 sets out the crux of the book's argument about the role of interest groups and money in the confirmation process. It explores groups' gradual incorporation into the confirmation process and considers the techniques and strategies they use to accomplish their goal of directing confirmation outcomes. At the center of all their strategies is money. Today, interest groups use their financial resources to engage in "astroturfing" (that is, the instigation of grassroots campaigns), public education, and, when necessary, the strong-arming of senators who may need a little extra incentive to vote the group's way on a particular nominee. Frequently, these groups are acting not on behalf of their grassroots members (who often have little information about the individuals being considered for high-ranking federal jobs) but instead are acting at the behest of wealthy donors and benefactors. At least one group, the Judicial Selection Monitoring Project, even used the confirmation process as a revenue-generating enterprise, sending out fundraising letters to supporters asking for help to keep "Clinton judges" off the federal bench. This chapter documents these strategies and techniques and concludes that the contemporary confirmation process is now simply a microcosm of the legislative process more generally, where money and interest group participation may dominate outcomes.

Chapter 4 is the first of two tests of the hypotheses generated in chapters 2 and 3. It focuses on judicial confirmations and reports the results from several tests of the theories outlined in the first part of the book. The first test is a quantitative analysis of 1,242 judicial nominations made between 1979 and 1998. The second is a qualitative analysis of the role of interest groups based on interviews with interest group leaders, former senators, and Senate staffers. It is revealed that interest groups' formal participation in the confirmation process has declined, while at the same time they are pursuing behind-the-scenes strategies that make it impossible for them to be held accountable by the public.

Chapter 5 is the second test of the interest group/money hypotheses that are generated earlier in the work. This chapter focuses on two additional groups of nominees—cabinet secretaries-designate and ambassadorial nominees—to explore the impact of interest group participation and money politics on other types of appointed positions. This chapter finds that unlike judicial nominees, interest groups are important actors in the confirmation process for cabinet secretaries-designate, and that they use the confirmation hearings on these positions to further policy discussions. Interest groups are less involved in the confirmation process for ambassadorial nominees than they are for either of the other groups considered in this project. In all cases, however, interest groups view their participation in the confirmation process as a revenue-generating enterprise.

In the conclusion of this study, the focus returns to interest groups. In today's group-dominated political systems, senators no longer can afford to ignore interest groups' opinions on presidential nominees. Groups at both ends of the political spectrum have access to wealthy contributors and other resources that senators have come to rely upon as they seek to achieve their electoral and political goals. Interest groups provide direct, tangible incentives to senators to behave in certain ways. As the confirmation process has become more visible (thanks largely to the groups themselves) senators' incentives to pay attention to interest groups have increased. The concluding chapter expands on these ideas while tying together the entirety of the project.

1

The Senate Confirmation Process Falls Apart

Some think of appointees as morally neutral technicians whose personal probity and embodiment of the community's standards are irrelevant to the job at hand. But as far back as George Washington, who called 'fitness of character' the salient factor in the choice of appointees, Americans have looked to the president's appointees not only to get a job done, but to lead the nation by edifying example. In a nation of more than 250 million people, there are sufficient numbers of talented and experienced people of high moral standards available for public service. We ought not either to define our expectations down or evade the real and serious conflicts entailed in defining those expectations.

Constance Horner, "Dissent," in *Obstacle Course*, 1996

When the framers of the United States Constitution considered how best to appoint federal political executives, they agreed that only two actors should be involved: the president and the Senate. They settled on these actors after protracted debate; over the course of the Constitutional Convention, the framers considered a number of proposals for the appointment of federal judges and officials, from sole legislative appointment to the suggestion that the executives of each of the states should make appointments to the federal government.[1] In the end, however, they decided that the president and the Senate should each play a role in the appointment of judges and other officers. Article II, Section II of the United States Constitution reads: "The president . . . shall nominate, and by and with the advice and consent of the Senate, shall appoint Ambassadors, other public ministers and consuls, Judges of the Supreme Court, and all other Officers of the United States whose appointments are not herein otherwise provided for, and which shall be established by law."

Like most other political processes, the appointment process for federal officials has survived many changes. Despite the enduring nature of the United States Constitution, many of its processes have been changed over time by federal laws and by constitutional amendment. Popular election of senators, presidential term limits, and universal suffrage are just a few examples of changes to principles set out in the Constitution. Even among those processes and institutions that have not been revised by federal law or constitutional amendment, most have been subject to scrutiny and interpretation by the federal judiciary. Although the Constitution has never been amended on the subject of the appointment process, many aspects of today's appointment process are very different from the one established by the framers. No longer are the president and the Senate the only actors in the process. Instead, the president and the Senate, respectively, function as arenas in which the selection and confirmation processes are carried out. Just as the legislative process has changed, so too has the Senate confirmation process.

Today, interest groups, constituents, federal executives, and members of the House of Representatives are also important players in the appointment process. As scholar Louis Fisher notes: "The actual power of nominating officials has been parceled out to interest groups, legislators, judges and party leaders with the White House trying to coordinate and centralize the decisions."[2] The president and the Senate may constrain the ability of other actors to influence the process, but both have also come to rely on the assistance of outside authorities when making federal appointments.

This chapter examines the evolution of the federal appointment process from its genesis at the Constitutional Convention of 1787 to its contemporary character. Although the focus of this book is on the Senate's confirmation process, it is important to explore the changes that have taken place in the appointment process more broadly, since these changes have led to the contemporary confirmation climate. Beginning with the debates among the delegates at Philadelphia and concluding with an explanation of how the contemporary process works, this chapter aims to shed some light on what the contemporary appointment process looks like and how it evolved into its current form. After examining the creation of the appointment process during the Constitutional Convention of 1787, several different eras of the appointment process are discussed in the pages that follow. The last part of this chapter considers several theoretical explanations to account for recent changes in the appointment process.

Philadelphia, 1787

The call for a Constitutional Convention to address the shortcomings of the Articles of Confederation brought prominent men from each of the thirteen states to Philadelphia in May of 1787. The Convention marked the end of an experiment with the Articles of Confederation, the nation's first charter of government. The Articles had been adopted by all thirteen newly independent states following the Revolutionary War. Unfortunately, the Articles of Confederation did not adequately meet the needs of a growing nation. Individual states were not meeting their financial obligations to the Confederation, and the Articles provided no clear mechanism for enforcement of those obligations. Even more alarming to America's first statesmen was the fact that Britain refused to negotiate treaties with the full Confederation of states, saying that because the Articles provided no authority to uphold such treaties, it preferred to negotiate with each state separately.[3] By 1786, it had become clear that the Articles were in need of revision. In November 1786, a call for a convention to meet in May of the following year for the purpose of revising the Articles was issued.

When the delegates arrived in Philadelphia, the magnitude of their task was clear. They would need to make decisions about all aspects of the national government. Once the delegates had agreed on the rules of debate and procedure for the Convention, they turned to consideration of Virginia delegate Edmund Randolph's "Resolutions," known commonly as the Virginia Plan. On May 29, 1787, Randolph proposed fifteen resolutions, including: "(9) Resd. that a National Judiciary be established to consist of one or more supreme tribunals, and of inferior tribunals to be chosen by the National Legislature, to hold their offices during good behavior; and to receive punctually at stated times fixed compensation for their services."[4]

This proposal marked the first time that the question of how the nation's judiciary would be created and staffed was considered by the delegates at the Convention. More generally, it set the stage for the debate over the appointment of federal officials, more generally. While Randolph's resolutions were among the earliest proposals considered at the Convention, the Virginia Plan's proposal for the creation of the federal courts and for the appointment of federal judges was not universally acceptable to the delegates at Philadelphia. For the duration of the Convention—indeed, until its very end—the question of how best to appoint federal judges was taken up repeatedly.

The question of how best to select federal judges became complicated when the Convention passed a resolution on June 1, 1787, to institute a national executive "with power to carry into execution the national laws" and "to appoint officers in cases not otherwise provided for."[5] As a result, some delegates objected to Randolph's proposal to allow the National Legislature to appoint the federal judiciary, because they believed that the newly created executive should have some role in making such appointments. On June 5, 1787, the delegates resumed consideration of Randolph's original resolution of May 29, striking out the phrases "one or more" and "National Legislature."[6] By doing so, the delegates amended Randolph's proposal and settled on just one "Supreme Tribunal." Whether its judges would be appointed by the executive or by the legislature was far from decided, however.

Although a majority of delegates had voted early on June 5 to remove the legislature's authority to appoint federal judges, they did not specify just *who would* appoint them. Several delegates remained convinced that the legislature ought to appoint judges and other public officers, in part because of their lingering fears of a tyrannical executive. South Carolina delegate Charles Cotesworth Pinckney, for example, was particularly adamant that the national legislature be wholly responsible for the selection of judges and officers. Fellow statesman John Rutledge also believed that to vest the executive with any power of appointment was to lean too much toward a monarchy.[7] But opponents of giving the legislature the power to appoint judges argued that the legislature was too numerous to be entrusted with the power to appoint public officials. For example, James Wilson of Pennsylvania argued that "experience shewed the impropriety of such appointmnts by numerous bodies. Intrigue, partiality, and concealment were the necessary consequences."[8] Agreeing in part with colleagues from both sides of the debate, James Madison stated that he was inclined to vest the authority in the Senate—"as numerous eno' to be confided in—and not so numerous as to be governed by the motives of the other branch; and as being sufficiently independent and stable to follow their deliberate judgements."[9]

A breakthrough in the discussion of the appointment process for federal judges came later on June 5, when Alexander Hamilton proposed a compromise. He suggested that the executive should make nominations to the Senate, which would then have the right to approve or reject them.[10] However, no additional votes were taken on June 5 concerning the appropriate appointment of federal officers, and again the matter was far from settled. Eight days later, on June 13, Madison's proposal that the Senate be responsible for appointing federal judges was debated and approved by the Convention.[11] Appointment of federal judges by the Senate was acceptable to the majority of delegates, and it seemed that the issue had been settled. For much of the rest of the Convention, senatorial appointment of federal judges would remain intact.

By this point in the Convention, the delegates had amended and agreed to the original resolutions proposed by Edmund Randolph, and a skeleton constitution began to emerge. But two days later, on June 15, New Jersey delegate William Patterson offered a substitute plan to the Virginia Plan. Patterson's proposals—the New Jersey Plan—were similar to those proposed by Randolph in some respects but were vastly different in others. The matter of who should appoint federal judges was one issue on which the two plans diverged. Whereas Randolph had initially suggested that the National Legislature appoint federal judges and the Convention had agreed to allow the Senate to make the appointments, the New Jersey Plan called for executive appointment of federal judges.

Over the next three days, while the delegates to the Convention debated the merits and shortcomings of the Virginia and New Jersey Plans, Alexander Hamilton was growing uneasy about both of them. On June 18, Hamilton—who had been silent throughout much of the previous weeks' debates—stated that he was opposed to both the Virginia and New Jersey Plans. According to James Madison's notes:

> Mr. Hamilton, had been hitherto silent on the business before the Convention, partly from respect to others whose superior abilities age & experience rendered him unwilling to bring forward ideas dissimilar to theirs, and partly from his delicate situation with respect to his own State, to whose sentiments as expressed by his Colleagues, he could by no means accede. The crisis however which now marked our affairs was too serious to permit any scruples whatever to prevail over the duty imposed on every man to contribute his efforts for the public safety & happiness. He was obliged therefore to declare himself unfriendly to both plans.[12]

Hamilton then set out his views on the proper construction of the new American government. Like the other plans before the Convention, he also addressed the issue of appointing federal judges and other officials. Hamilton proposed the following: first, that the executive should have the sole power to appoint "the heads or chief officers of the departments of War and Foreign Affairs." Next, he proposed that the executive "have the nomination of all other officers (Ambassadors to foreign nations included) subject to the approbation or rejection of the Senate." Finally, Hamilton proposed "Supreme judicial officers to be appointed by the executive and the senate."[13] Thus, midway through the Constitutional Convention, four clearly articulated (and incompatible) views on the proper appointment of federal judges had emerged. First, the provision that already had been approved by the committee of the whole House provided for the appointment of judges by the Senate. However, those delegates who supported the Virginia Plan continued to seek a legislative appointment power, while those delegates who supported the New Jersey Plan remained supportive of an executive power. Finally, Hamilton's proposal provided the delegates with a fourth option, which was to institute a shared appointment power between the executive and legislative branches.

Over the remainder of the summer, a coherent appointment process began to emerge. On July 18, the Convention defeated the New Jersey Plan's executive appointment provision. Hamilton's compromise solution was also voted on that day. It fared somewhat better than the provision for executive appointment, which had been soundly defeated, but the Convention deadlocked on Hamilton's proposal.[14] James Madison proposed a modified compromise, which provided that the executive would nominate federal judges and that such nominations would become appointments unless two-thirds of the Senate disagreed. The Convention postponed consideration of Madison's proposal until July 21, when it was defeated.[15] With the impasse on Hamilton's compromise, the appointment of federal judges and other public officers by the Senate remained intact.

The first real opposition to senatorial appointment of federal judges and ambassadors was raised by Pennsylvania delegate Governour Morris on August 23. He was concerned that since the Convention had recently given the power to try impeachments to the Senate, it would be wrong "to let the Senate have the filling of vacancies which its own decrees were to create." The delegates continued to debate the appointment clause for the remainder of the day but to no avail. At the end of the day, they recommitted the clause to committee, and no further action was taken. On August 24 and August 25, the delegates made minor changes to the president's authority to appoint officers other than those provided for in the Constitution.[16]

On August 31, "it was moved and seconded to refer such parts of the Constitution as have been postponed . . . to a Committee of a Member from each State."[17] Among the items referred to this committee was the language dealing with the appointment of judges and high-ranking officers. The second report of this "Committee of Eleven" proposed a shared role for the president and the Senate in the appointment of "ambassadors and other public ministers, Judges of the Supreme Court, and all other officers of the U.S. whose appointments" were not otherwise provided for in the new Constitution.[18] According to historian Jack Rakove, on September 7 and 8: "On the matter of diplomatic and judicial appointments, the framers reached near consensus on the virtues of combining the 'responsibility' of executive nomination, with the 'security' of senatorial advice and consent."[19] By September 8, the issue of how appointments would be made had been settled by the Convention.

Putting the Framers' Wishes into Action

As we have seen, the question of how best to appoint federal judges and other important officers was the subject of considerable debate at the Constitutional Convention. The appointment process that ultimately became Article II, Section II of the United States Constitution resulted from compromise among the delegates at the Convention. Its language—"The president shall nominate . . . and by and with the advice and consent of the Senate, shall appoint"—has remained intact since September 8, 1787, and thousands of men and women have been appointed to the highest ranks of the federal government under the process it established. However, the dynamics of the appointment process have changed over time, even if the constitutional foundations underpinning it have not. Other than what is written in Article II, Section II, the Constitution says nothing else about how the appointment process is to be carried out. "Advice and consent" is not clearly defined, and the framers established no guidelines in the Constitution itself for how the process was supposed to work. Indeed, questions about the proper role of the president and the Senate in the appointment of judges and other public officials still plague politicians and scholars today.

The earliest clues about the role that the framers intended each branch to play come from the debates about ratification of the Constitution. On October 24, 1787, James McHenry told the Maryland House of Delegates: "[The president's] power when elected is check'd by the Consent of the Senate, to the appointment of Officers, and without endangering Liberty by the junction of the Executive and Legislative in this instance."[20] On November 29, 1787, Luther Martin told the Maryland delegates: "Some would gladly have given the appointment of Ambassadors and Judges to the Senate, some were for vesting this power in the Legislature by joint ballot, as being most likely to know the Merit of Individuals over this extended empire. But as the President is to nominate, the person chosen must be ultimately his choice and he will thus have an army of civil officers as well as Military."[21]

On December 4, 1787, James Wilson told the Pennsylvania Convention: "With regard to the appointment of officers, the President must nominate before [the Senate] can vote. So that if the powers of either branch are perverted, it must be with the approbation of some one of the other branches of government: thus checked on one side, they can do no one act of themselves."[22]

The Federalist Papers also give clues to the framers' intent with regard to the balance of power between the president and the Senate in the appointment process. Alexander Hamilton notes in *Federalist* 65: "As in the business of appointments the Executive will be the principal agent." Further, in *Federalist* 66, Hamilton asserted that in appointing federal officers, "[t]here will, of course, be no exertion of choice on the part of the Senate. They may defeat one choice of the executive, and oblige him to make another; but they themselves cannot choose—they can only ratify or reject a choice he has made." In *Federalist* 76, Hamilton makes his strongest statement on the appointment of federal officers and the shared power of the president and the Senate:

> The Senate could not be tempted by the preference they might feel to another to reject the one proposed; because they could not assure themselves that the person they might wish would be brought forward by any subsequent nomination. They could not even be certain that a future nomination would present a candidate in any degree more acceptable to them. . . . To what purpose then require the co-operation of the Senate? I answer that the necessity of their concurrence would have a powerful, though in general a silent operation. It would be an excellent check upon a spirit of favoritism in the president, and would tend to preventing the appointment of unfit characters from State prejudice, from family connection, from personal attachment, or from a view to popularity.

Thus, we learn from the ratification debates that the framers intended the Senate to be a "silent" check on the president for the purpose of preventing cronyism, favoritism, and nepotism from blocking the appointment of the best qualified individuals. It will soon be clear, however, that the Senate today plays a vastly greater role in the appointment of federal officials than was initially intended by the framers. This new role is a result of a gradual evolution away from the process designed by the framers to a new politics of Senate confirmation.

Early Appointments

As the nation's first president, George Washington was the first to appoint judges and other officials using the new Constitution's framework. By and large, the Senate gave Washington carte blanche to appoint whomever he felt best to vacancies in the federal government. His first nomination—William Short to be temporary ambassador to France—was made on June 15, 1789; Short was confirmed two days later.[23] Most of Washington's nominees were swiftly confirmed by the Senate. However, the early years of the confirmation process set precedents that would be followed far into the future. Like the presidents who would come after him, Washington struggled with the appointment process, and on occasion his nominees were rejected by the Senate. Under Washington, "senatorial courtesy" was invoked for the first time; when President Washington nominated Benjamin Fishburn to be naval officer of the Port of Savannah, the Senate "rejected the nomination as a courtesy to the two senators from Georgia, who had a candidate of their own."[24] Thus, pressures from members of Congress were a fact of life even for the nation's first president. But by and large the appointment process in Washington's time was amicable.

Compared with contemporary personnel decisions, Washington's task was considerably less daunting. But, according to Joseph Harris: "No President exercised greater care than Washington in selecting persons for federal office; he consulted widely and maintained exceptionally high standards for public office."[25] Washington filled the positions of his administration with close friends, including Thomas Jefferson, Henry Knox, Edmund Randolph, Alexander Hamilton, Thomas Pinckney, Governour Morris, and John Jay. Washington had far fewer nominations to make than do contemporary presidents, and none of his early nominees had to wait long to be consented to by the Senate.[26]

A good example of the process Washington used to select his nominees comes from a brief examination of his appointments to the federal judiciary. In September 1789, the First Congress completed its work on Senate Bill I, The Judiciary Act of 1789. The Act created district thirteen district courts and three circuit courts. The Act also provided that a United States Attorney and United States Marshal be appointed to serve in each district, and the Act set the number of Supreme Court justices at six. President Washington signed the Act on September 24, 1789, and immediately sent the Senate nominations for the new positions. United States Circuit Judge Richard Arnold explains: "[O]ne of the President's first tasks, upon the enactment of the Judiciary Act of 1789, was to nominate justices and judges. Obviously the president had given this a lot of thought, because the nominations of six Supreme Court Justices, eleven district judges, eleven United States Attorneys, and eleven United States Marshals were sent to the Senate on September 24, 1789, the same day that the Judiciary Act was signed."[27]

President Washington nominated the remaining two district judges, U.S. attorneys and U.S. marshals the next day. On September 26, 1787, all of President Washington's nominations were confirmed, including the nominations of Thomas Jefferson to be Secretary of State and Edmund Randolph to be Attorney General. These nominations also had been pending before the Senate for just one day.[28]

George Washington's own words provide clues to the criteria he used for selecting judges and other political officers. He was anxious to appoint "the fittest characters to expound the laws and dispense justice," and was even willing to appoint political enemies if those enemies were the most qualified for the job.[29] Washington also had clear procedures for considering an individual for a job. First, "Washington let it be known pretty early that people who wanted federal office should ask for it in writing and should obtain whatever letters of recommendation they could."[30] Second, according to Judge Arnold, President Washington gave preference to individuals who were friendly to the new Constitution and to the government it set up, although he did occasionally make exceptions.[31] Finally, Washington felt it was important to nominate men of standing in their communities and states. Judge Arnold sums up Washington's selection criteria as follows: "(1) support and advocacy of the Constitution; (2) distinguished service in the Revolution; (3) active participation in the political life of state or nation; (4) prior judicial experience on lower tribunals; (5) either a 'favorable reputation with his fellows' or personal ties to Washington himself; and (6) geographic 'suitability.'"[32]

Of course, federal judges were not the only appointments that Washington had to make. Washington also appointed numerous individuals to head the departments in his government, to serve in federal offices within the states, and to act as ambassadors to Britain and France. Evidence suggests that Washington used similar criteria to select individuals to serve in these offices. One scholar describes Washington's appointment process with regard to appointments within the state of Rhode Island: "Washington not only involved himself in the appointive process to insure that Federalists would gain all the key federal offices at his command, in one instance he also agreed to demote one incumbent Antifederalist customs officer as the transition from state to federal customs took place."[33] Presidential appointment scholar Henry Abraham adds: "Both judicious and secure in his pursuit of excellence, [Washington] knew what he wanted and readily admitted to staffing both the judicial and the executive branches with reliable, cautious, conservative adherents to the Federalist cause."[34] In general, however, Washington was most concerned about appointed qualified individuals to serve in the federal government.

John Adams "continued the policy of appointing only qualified persons," but more than his predecessor, Adams was concerned about a potential nominees' political views.[35] During Adams's presidency, the practice of deferring to senators with regard to appointments within their home states was institutionalized; Adams almost always consulted with the entire state congressional delegation before making a nomination.[36] Thomas Jefferson also relied heavily on information from congressional delegations but sought information from outside sources as well. Jefferson and his cabinet heads placed heavy weight on the recommendations of individuals who were not members of Congress, and as a result, he had little trouble getting his nominees confirmed by the Senate.[37]

James Madison, in contrast, had a difficult time securing confirmation for his nominees. According to one study: "James Madison found that even his freedom to nominate was often circumscribed by a determined clique of Senators."[38] A small group of senators was determined to direct Madison's appointments, and they often threatened to block a nomination unless the president did what they requested—usually they requested that he choose another nominee.[39]

The nominations of Presidents James Monroe and John Quincy Adams and the years between 1820 and 1828 have not received much attention, except with regard to passage of the Four Years Act. The Act, which limited the term of office for many federal officers to four years, was passed by Congress in 1820. It was designed to foster rotation in office, but neither President Monroe nor President John Quincy Adams adhered to the four years provision, and as a result, both men faced the consequence of strained relations with the Senate as a result.[40]

The early years of the appointment process fully fleshed out and made practicable the method of appointment designed by the framers. Although early presidents essentially had their way with regard to selection of the government's officers, by the early 1800s, senators had begun to assert their coequal role in the appointment process. These senators often were able to block the appointment of individuals they found objectionable and to force the president to nominate someone else. This early period also saw the development of the norm of senatorial courtesy—the practice of deferring to senators on nominations to fill vacancies within their states—which remains in use today.

1828 to 1883: Appointments as Rewards

Throughout the first period of American history, presidents normally could expect senatorial deference to their nominees, and nearly all presidential nominations were eventually confirmed. Presidents frequently consulted members of the Senate for their advice, but nominees generally were well known to the president and often were selected based on their allegiance to the new Constitution. Upon presentation to the Senate, presidential nominees were routinely confirmed. To be sure, some presidents had an easier time than others. James Madison, for example, sometimes had great difficulty convincing the Senate to confirm his nominees. But in general, the Senate usually deferred to the president's choices and fulfilled its role as a silent check on the his selections.

In 1828, the appointment process began to change as broader political changes swept the country. Voters became highly mobilized, as "a new political universe, America's second under the Constitution, replaced the existing one. Its driving impulses were deeply partisan in ways never before known."[41] As electoral politics began to shift, so too did the way in which presidents allocated important positions in the federal government. It was expected that jobs—from positions at the top, all the way down to the lowest level of appointed positions—would be given to loyal partisans. Beginning with Andrew Jackson, merit became a less important criterion for appointment to political office. As Mackenzie writes: "Success in presidential elections had come to require the mobilization of rank and file voters across a country that was rapidly moving westward. To sustain growing party organizations, presidents began to use appointments as patronage awards for political efforts on their behalf."[42]

The use of appointments as rewards could be problematic, however, especially when the president's allies were the Senate's enemies. For example, President Jackson did not have an easy time making appointments to public office. According to Harris: "No other President ever had as many contests with the Senate over appointments as Andrew Jackson."[43] But unlike President Madison, who had caved to pressure from a small cabal of senators, President Jackson stood his ground on behalf of his nominees.

For example, when the Senate rejected ten of Jackson's nominations early on in his administration, Jackson renominated them, and all but four were eventually confirmed.[44] On the other hand, Jackson bears the distinction of being the first president ever to have a nominee to his cabinet rejected by the Senate; on June 23, 1834, Jackson nominated Roger B. Taney to be Secretary of the Treasury. Taney's nomination was rejected by the Senate the following day.[45]

For forty years after Andrew Jackson's term expired, the appointment power of the president was used to reward individuals for their support of the president and the party in power. Between 1837 and 1877, the "spoils system" dominated presidential appointments to government positions. With the shift in electoral politics to a party-dominated, machine-controlled system, party leaders and members of Congress looked to the appointment process to reward loyal partisans. When Congress and the presidency were unified in their party affiliations, members of Congress could be particularly successful in securing the appointment of their friends and supporters. According to Harris: "Congressional patronage . . . was not limited to offices that were subject to senatorial confirmation; fourth-class postmasters, for example, whose nominations did not require confirmation were appointed on the recommendation of members of Congress."[46] By the end of President Ulysses S. Grant's term, the Congress wielded tremendous influence over the nominations phase of the appointment process.

But the spoils system was also a tremendous burden for presidents during this period. Presidents were required to spend lengthy periods of time interviewing job seekers, many of whom felt entitled to a federal appointment in return for their active support of the party in power. President James K. Polk commented in 1846:

> My office was crowded up to the hour of twelve o'clock with visitors, and I was greatly annoyed by the importunities of office-seekers. It is most disgusting to be compelled to spend hour after hour almost every day in hearing the applications made by loafers who congregate in Washington, and by members of Congress in their behalf, and yet I am compelled to submit to it or offend or insult the applicants and their friends. The people of the United States have no idea of the extent to which the president's time, which ought to be devoted to more important matters, is occupied by the voracious and often unprincipled persons who seek office.[47]

By the late 1800s, the demanding nature of the spoils system, and its common consequence of vacancies in the federal government being filled by mediocre appointees, led to calls for reform. An American government textbook sums up the problem this way: "By the latter part of the 19th Century, the spoils system had fallen into disrepute. Administration was often in the hands of political hacks, corruption was common, and fending off job seekers was a major burden for politicians."[48] Nonetheless, the period between 1828 and 1883 provides evidence of the relationships that exist between the appointment process and the political environment. As the political environment changed, so too did the process of selecting and confirming individuals to serve in the federal government.

1883 to 1952: The Civil Service and an Era of Change

Pressure for reform of the spoils system reached a fever pitch in 1881, when President James A. Garfield was assassinated by a disgruntled individual who had been rejected for a federal post. Garfield's assassination was the catalyst for a new system of staffing the government. In 1883, Congress passed the Pendleton Act, which established a civil service and required that appointments to low- and mid-level jobs in the federal bureaucracy be made based upon merit and be made regardless of political persuasion or affiliation.[49] Passage of this act significantly diminished the number of positions for which the president was required to submit a nomination to the Senate or to which the president was required to appoint an individual.

Passage of the Pendleton Act also diminished the influence of the Congress with regard to the selection of individuals to fill vacancies within the federal government. Once federal jobs began to be apportioned based on skill rather than political clout, members of the Senate became less active in scrutinizing presidential selections for appointed positions and less likely to eschew a presidential nominee in favor of a personal friend or political crony. As a result, presidents began to assert control over the nominating process.[50] Presidents William McKinley and Theodore Roosevelt had relatively little trouble getting their nominees confirmed in the early part of the twentieth century. Although Roosevelt deferred to members of the Senate with regard to local appointments, he also "insisted on suitable standards for federal officers and asserted the right of the president to nominate."[51] In 1910, President William Howard Taft, himself later a chief justice of the Supreme Court, moved additional classes of federal jobs into the civil service in order to further reduce patronage appointments and demands on his time.[52] President Woodrow Wilson was quite successful in navigating the Senate's confirmation process, although during the closing years of his administration, the Senate refused to confirm many of his nominees because Wilson did not always abide by the norm of deference to home state senators on local appointments.[53] But the peculiar nature of Wilson's election to the presidency after Theodore Roosevelt and William Howard Taft divided the Republican party in the election of 1912 meant that Wilson "had few political debts to pay and was able to pick his cabinet with great care, appointing the persons he believed to be best qualified."[54]

Presidents Warren G. Harding and Calvin Coolidge were respectful of senatorial courtesy, but both also held high standards for appointment to political office. President Herbert Hoover, however, faced great difficulty in navigating the confirmation process, especially for his Supreme Court nominations. In part, this was because Hoover was not as likely to use patronage and defer to members of the Senate as were some of his predecessors. Another reason for Hoover's difficulty in the confirmation process was the presence of interest groups in the confirmation process. With the ratification of the Seventeenth Amendment in 1913, which provided for the popular election of U.S. senators, interest groups (primarily labor organizations) found new avenues of access to the Senate confirmation process. Indeed, one of Hoover's nominees, John J. Parker, helped to set the tone for a new era of confirmation politics. Parker's confirmation was opposed by a number of organized interests, including labor unions and the National Association for the Advancement of Colored People (NAACP). His confirmation hearings marked the first time that interest groups were present and gave testimony with the hope of defeating the nomination.[55]

In 1929, another change to the Senate irrevocably altered the nature of its confirmation proceedings. That year, the Senate affirmed a change to its rules that opened up executive sessions (the time during which nominees are debated and discussed before the full chamber) to public scrutiny.[56] Prior to 1929, when the Senate entered an executive session, its galleries would be cleared and senators would debate nominations behind closed doors. The opening of the Senate's executive sessions coincided with another important milestone that had an important effect on the confirmation process; this milestone was the dramatic expansion of the federal government and, as a result, the extraordinary increase in the number of positions requiring presidential appointment.

Between 1933 and 1950, the size of the federal government expanded rapidly, in large part because of the policies of President Franklin D. Roosevelt. This led to growth in the number of offices to which the president was required to make appointments. With the growth in federal agencies and programs under Roosevelt's "New Deal" came significant opportunities for him to make appointments. Early in his presidency, Roosevelt faced little opposition to his appointments, but by his second and third terms, he faced animosity from some senators who felt he was not responsive enough to their suggestions of suitable nominees.[57] Roosevelt's administration is also remembered for its "court-packing" plan, in which Roosevelt sought to increase the number of justices on the Supreme Court. Congress rejected his plan, but by the time of his death in 1945, Roosevelt had appointed all but one justice on the Supreme Court.[58] In addition, the famous "switch in time that saved nine" (Justice Owen Roberts's switch from voting against the president's New Deal proposals to voting in favor of them) demonstrates the power of the Roosevelt administration.

President Harry S Truman, the last president to appoint individuals during the period between 1883 and 1952, was also among the least successful at courting Senate approval. According to one report: "President Truman incurred more contests over his nominations in the Senate than perhaps any other president. Instead of being deferential to the wishes of individual senators, at times he nominated persons known to be highly offensive to them, and occasionally he made nominations in the face of their almost certain defeat."[59]

Truman had two main criteria for selection to federal office: first, the nominee had to be loyal to him and to his policies; second, the nominee had to possess prior experience in government. As a result, a higher percentage of his nominees came from the ranks of the federal bureaucracy at the time of nomination than that of any other president who came after him.[60] But despite his predilection to appoint individuals with experience in government, Truman was criticized for several things, including nominating his friends to important positions, nominating individuals who were too liberal or too loyal to the New Deal, and for nominating individuals to local office who had not been recommended by their home state senators.[61]

While the Senate's role in the appointment process waned between 1883 and 1929, changes to the institution and an increase in the number of positions requiring its consent led the Senate to engage in its constitutional role in the appointment process more vigorously after 1930. This is not to suggest, however, that the president was unimportant after 1930. As the "switch in time that saved nine" demonstrates, presidents wielded an enormous amount of power as a result of their appointment responsibilities. But where the advent of the civil service reduced senatorial scrutiny of presidential nominees, changes to the Senate in the first thirty years of the twentieth century allowed the pendulum to swing back the other way. By 1950, presidents and senates shared power in the confirmation process almost completely.

Another important phenomenon emerged between 1883 and 1952. With the initiation of the civil service under the Pendleton Act, a bureaucratic apparatus developed that allowed presidents and their staffs to monitor the training, performance, and evaluation of federal workers. This, in turn, led to a general bureaucratization of the appointment process. By the time of the Truman administration, the White House had begun to institutionalize its selection process. Truman was the first president to have a staff aide whose primary responsibility was to review candidates for federal jobs.[62] This was another important step in the development of the appointment process.

In general, three important trends developed during this third period of change in the confirmation process. First, more and more jobs were turned into civil service positions. This freed presidents from the burdens of the spoils system and reduced the amount of time they were required to spend with job seekers. It also reduced the influence that members of the Senate had come to expect, especially with regard to low-level positions in government. This led to the second major trend in appointment politics during this period—the reclaiming of the presidential right to nominate individuals of his or her choosing. Although most presidents during this era continued to consult with home state senators—and the Senate made life difficult for presidents who thwarted its will—deference to members of the Senate became less and less guaranteed, with some presidents openly opposing members of the Senate. Whereas the power of appointment had been primarily the president's during the early years of the American republic and primarily the Senate's during the second, during this third period of confirmation history, the president and the Senate shared the appointment power much more equally than they had before. Finally, toward the end of this period, the appointment process began to be institutionalized with President Truman's designation of a single staff member, whose job it was to review candidates for presidential appointment. In general, the years between 1883 and 1952 provide a crucial link between the inefficient, patronage-driven appointment process of much of the nineteenth century and the highly organized, pluralistic, and contentious process that characterizes contemporary appointments.

1952 to 1979: The Contemporary Process Emerges

When Dwight D. Eisenhower was elected president in 1952, Republicans were ecstatic—after all, they had been out of power for more than twenty years. This fact was instrumental in shaping appointment politics during

Eisenhower's administration—holdovers from the Roosevelt and Truman administration were quickly replaced by Republican partisans. Eisenhower also was very interested in creating a structured hierarchy for personnel decisions. He was not interested in being involved in low-level personnel decisions. This was a change from previous presidents, most of whom were integrally involved at all levels of the appointment process. Another important change to the appointment process was instituted under Eisenhower. That change was the requirement that all job seekers for appointive office undergo a Federal Bureau of Investigation (FBI) background check. Only after the background check had been satisfactorily completed would the offer of a nomination be made.[63] When John F. Kennedy was elected president in 1960, he desired the most qualified individuals to serve in his cabinet and across all levels of the federal government. During his presidency, White House aides further routinized selection procedures and centralized decisions about political appointments within the executive branch itself. In addition, aides were active in recruiting individuals to serve their government.[64] One important shift in the appointment process occurred during Kennedy's presidency; whereas previous presidents had relied heavily on the advice of members of the Senate (and ignored such advice at their peril), the Kennedy administration accepted advice from interest groups, agency leaders, and the White House personnel staff, as well as seeking advice from members of Congress.[65] Mackenzie (1981, 31) calls the new procedures implemented during the Kennedy administration "a turning point in the development of a modern and rational personnel function within the White House Office."

Overall, Lyndon Johnson followed many of the same procedures as his predecessor; however, he was much more actively involved on a personal level than Kennedy had been.[66] One important test for Johnson's appointees was whether they supported the president's position on the Vietnam War. Loyalty was an important consideration and was more important to Johnson than was party identification.[67] Johnson was especially interested in increasing the diversity of his appointments—women and minorities were recruited and appointed in greater numbers than ever before. By more fully participating in the appointment process himself, Johnson was able to ensure that his goals of loyalty and diversity were realized.

As the Watergate scandal heightened the distrust between the president and the Senate in the 1970s, the confirmation process began to change again. By the late 1970s, the Senate had started to formalize and tighten its confirmation requirements. In 1977, the Senate Commerce Committee developed new procedures for investigating presidential nominees that were independent of the investigations conducted by the White House and FBI.[68] Soon thereafter, other Senate committees began to enhance their screening processes for presidential nominees and adopted formal waiting periods between nomination and confirmation. Committees also began to use nominees' written responses to judge their professional, ideological, and political suitability for positions. In 1979, when Massachusetts Senator Edward M. Kennedy took control of the Senate Judiciary Committee, the committee began requiring detailed personal questionnaires and financial disclosure statements for all nominees to the federal courts.[69]

1980 to 1991: A Crucial Turning Point

If there is a single decade in which the appointment process most dramatically changed, it is the 1980s. President Ronald Reagan was in office and was appointing conservatives to all levels of the federal government. In 1984, Reagan announced that he would use the appointment process to remake the federal judiciary in a conservative image.[70] This one statement, more than any other in American history, helped to shape the dynamics of the contemporary appointment process. Interest groups, such as the Alliance for Justice, sprouted or retrenched in order to combat Reagan's "court-packing" plan. When Reagan nominated Robert Bork to the Supreme Court in 1987, interest groups mobilized an intense media campaign designed to discredit Reagan's nominee and force the Senate's rejection. Appointment process critic Stephen Carter writes: "[I]t was not the degree of media attention, not the heat of the rhetoric that carried the [Bork] contest along a road that would make it different from other equally or more bitter confirmation fights in American history. It was not the left-liberal culture war or the right-wing court-packing scheme that made the moment auspicious; it was the realization on the part of the Bork activists that the power of the media could be harnessed in the same manner as in an election campaign."[71]

Bork's nomination set the tone for the contemporary appointment process more so than any previous nomination. With regard to media coverage, interest group participation, partisanship, and intergovernmental conflict, never before had there been a nomination to match the spectacle of Bork's. Supreme Court appointment scholar John Maltese writes: "The Bork nomination was a watershed in terms of interest group involvement: more than 300 groups opposed Bork, and these groups 'used a wide variety of tactics, including advertising, grassroots events, focus groups, and polling.' The White House responded by using its Office of Public Liaison to mobilize group support for Bork. It targeted direct mailings at groups and helped outside groups place favorable editorials in states where there were crucial swing senators."[72]

Similarly, George Bush's nomination of Clarence Thomas in 1991 met with a barrage of media and interest group involvement following allegations by Anita Hill that Thomas had sexually harassed her. The Bork and Thomas hearings also marked the beginning of a reemergence of the role of the Senate in confirmation politics; this was due to the highly visible, televised confirmation hearings for these nominees. With increasing media exposure for the Senate's confirmation hearings between 1980 and 1991, the Senate gained greater and greater prominence in the appointment process. Indeed, many of the developments of the 1980s allowed the balance of power in the appointment process to tip toward the Senate.

1992 to the Present: The Senate Takes Control

As demonstrated in the previous section, the appointment process became more routinized after 1952. Presidents in the modern era rely heavily on staff input to select qualified nominees, and the implementation of FBI background checks means that presidents are assured that their nominees have met at least basic ethical standards. However, as we know, not all nominees are confirmed. In fact, as the Senate has reasserted its advice and consent authority in the wake of the Bork and Thomas nominations, the confirmation process has slowed and a greater number of civilian nominees to major positions are rejected. As figure 1.1 demonstrates, the percentage of major nominations rejected by the Senate peaked in the 100th Congress (the congress during which Robert Bork was rejected) and then peaked again during the 104th Congress, the congress in which the Republican party regained control of the Senate.[73]

In addition to the greater percentages of nominees rejected by the Senate, the confirmation process, measured as time elapsed from senatorial receipt of a nomination to the Senate's final confirmation vote, has grown increasingly longer throughout the second half of the twentieth century. What once took George Washington only two days to accomplish may now take nearly two years. Indeed, as recently as the mid-1980s, presidential nominees could expect swift action on their nominations. According to a report sponsored by the Pew Charitable Trust, "a nomination and confirmation process lasting more than six months was nearly unheard of between 1964 and 1984."[74]

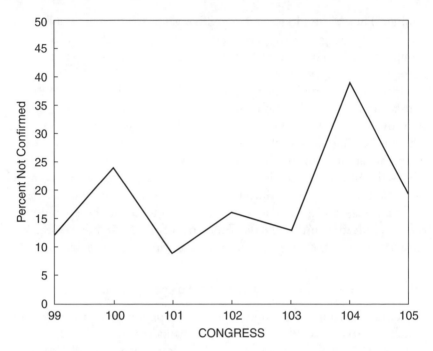

Figure 1.1.   Percentage of Nominees to Major Positions Rejected by the Senate, 99th–105th Congress.
Sources: Resumes of Congressional Activity, congresses indicated.

Today, 30 percent of presidential nominees can expect to wait more than six months, with nominees to lower-ranking federal offices waiting longer than those individuals nominated to higher-level offices.[75] The exceptions to this maxim are judicial nominees. Whereas in 1789 it took George Washington only two days to gain Senate confirmation for his initial judicial appointments, in 1997 it took the Senate an average of 212 days to confirm Bill Clinton's judicial nominees.[76]

Conclusion

Throughout American history, presidents typically have been able to count on the Senate to confirm their nominees. While levels of presidential and senatorial power waxed and waned between 1789 and the middle of the twentieth century, prior to the mid-1980s, there were few significant contests over non–Supreme Court presidential nominees. The Senate's confirmation process was swift and predictable. However, presidential nominees can no longer assume that they will be confirmed quickly or without controversy. While some nominees are confirmed quickly, others languish for months or even years before the Senate reaches a decision. Today, a nominee's success in the confirmation process is often constrained by the peculiar conditions of the political environment, which determines who gets nominated, who gets confirmed, and the tone and tenor of the process. In recent years, the political environment has reshaped the once-predictable process of securing Senate confirmation into one characterized by delays, uncertainty, and partisan foot-dragging.

By all measures, the confirmation process for major appointments is more contentious than ever before. Beginning in 1987, and especially since 1995, many nominees have been subjected to lengthy waits for confirmation. While a handful of every president's nominees has always been subjected to delay and heightened scrutiny, nominees to federal office now routinely face confirmation delays and partisan bickering.

Nearly all recent assessments of the current appointment process are dismal. In the late 1990s, academics, politicians, and journalists alike noted the crisis in confirming judges to vacant seats on the federal bench, while nominations to fill other positions, such as David Satcher's to be the Surgeon General and James Hormel's to be the ambassador to Luxembourg faced lengthy delays and bitter, partisan fights. In the last few years, nominees to relatively obscure positions have become household names, not because of their credentials or the importance of the jobs they have been nominated to fill, but because the Senate has refused to act on their nominations.

While the "advice and consent" clause of the Constitution is the foundation of the Senate's important confirmation authority, the confirmation process is no longer the simple one set out by its framers. Once thought to be above the fray of politics, the confirmation process now is now influenced by a plethora of external political factors and is especially susceptible to conflict between the president and the Senate. Political conflicts between the two institutions now constrain the process of confirming presidential nominees. The next chapter considers the changed nature of the Senate confirmation process in greater detail and offers some additional explanations for the changes to the process that have already been discussed. As we will see, it is no accident that the contemporary confirmation process is vastly different from the one that the nation's forefathers envisioned; the framers could not have anticipated such sweeping internal and external changes to the Senate, three interest group explosions, and a Supreme Court decision equating campaign contributions with free speech. Today's confirmation process is the result of all these factors.

2

How and Why the Confirmation Process Changed

> For almost thirty years the presidential appointment process has been evolving away from its constitutional roots. In the 1990s, this evolution has accelerated out of control.
>
> G. Calvin Mackenzie, *Starting Over*, 1998

It is clear that the confirmation process has changed dramatically in 213 years of American history and that conditions worsened during the 1990s. But while the evolution of the process over time provides some explanation—more nominees, more bureaucracy, centralized decision making within the White House and less deference to members of the Senate—it remains unclear why the process that once permitted nominees to be confirmed within forty-eight hours now routinely requires months, and sometimes years, to be completed. History does not explain why an increasing number of nominees are now being subjected to long delays or are being denied confirmation altogether.

At the same time, the modern confirmation process is a product of its history, a history that is not well understood. A closer look reveals the significance of several important phenomena that have occurred in the last half-century and that have contributed to the confirmation process that exists today.

Like most other political processes, the confirmation process has fluctuated over time. The contemporary confirmation process described in the previous chapter is the product of more than two hundred years of political struggle over the staffing of the federal government. As the United States has become more diverse, the number of actors participating in the confirmation process has grown. In addition, the contemporary appointment process also has been democratized; today, interest groups representing a broad range of diverse perspectives play an active role in the selection and confirmation of appointees to high-ranking federal offices.

As the previous chapter demonstrated, the shift from nominees as the president's teammates to nominees as political targets is a striking one. Today, nominees are bartering tools—chits to be traded among senators—and are often targeted for reasons having little or nothing to do with their nominations.

The Constitution has never been amended on the subject of the appointment process or on the role of the U.S. Senate within it. Nonetheless, many aspects of today's confirmation process are very different from the one established by its framers. The Senate no longer acquiesces to the president's choices. Nominees no longer can expect swift and certain confirmation to federal office. The contemporary confirmation process is very different from the amicable procedure envisioned by the framers and used by President Washington and nearly all other U.S. presidents. This chapter chronicles several of the changes to the process and attempts to put those changes into the broader context of change in Congress more generally.

Before proceeding to a detailed look at institutionally and politically driven differences in the confirmation process, it must first be noted that one major reason for these changes over time is that the burden of confirming presidential subordinates and federal judges has increased dramatically over time. In 1789, there were fewer than two thousand people employed in the federal bureaucracy. That number had grown to three million by 1988.[1] Likewise, the federal judiciary has grown exponentially since it was established in 1789. Whereas in 1789 there were six members of the United States Supreme Court and the total number of lower federal court judges was thirteen, today there are 824 lower federal court judgeships, whose work is reviewed by nine sitting Supreme Court justices.[2] And whereas in 1789, there were just two countries—Britain and France—to which the United States sent ambassadors, in 1991 the United States sent ambassadors to 138 countries and to several multinational organizations, including the North Atlantic Treaty Organization (NATO) and the United Nations.[3]

In a 1998 report, the Twentieth Century Fund summed up all these statistics: "There are forty-three times more appointees in the federal government today than there were in 1935, five times as many as in 1960."[4] Political scientist Paul Light has referred to this tremendous growth in the number of federal jobs and layers of management as "thickening government," a phenomenon that has dramatically affected the confirmation process. New positions mean that the Senate has more nominees to confirm. But new positions may also increase the tension between the Senate and the president as the latter attempts to use the appointment process to ensure the success of his agenda. According to political scientist Hugh Heclo: "More layers of technocratic political appointees may well reduce rather than increase bureaucratic responsiveness to broader political leadership by the president and department heads: this in turn increases incentives for the White House to politicize the civil service by trying to build an executive team of loyalists throughout the political and higher career levels."[5]

The additional number of positions on which the Senate is required to pass has dramatically altered confirmation dynamics. Consequently, the confirmation process takes longer as a result, and presidents have greater difficulty installing their own teams in a timely way. According to an April 2000 report by the Presidential Appointee Initiative (PAI), a joint task force of the Brookings Institution and the Heritage Foundation, it will likely take the next president nine months or more to see his initial cabinet and subcabinet appointees sworn in.[6]

While more nominees means a greater workload for the Senate, the dramatic increase in the number of federal employees and judges did not occur overnight, and as recently as 1960, the Senate still was able to process nominations quickly and with little controversy. Although increases in the number of positions that require Senate action are important, many modifications to the confirmation process are the result of structural and procedural changes in the U.S. Congress and, specifically, in the U.S. Senate.

Congressional Change

Scholars of the U.S. Congress have produced a rich body of literature to chronicle and explain institutional change to the House and Senate. Most existing studies agree that a combination of determinants have worked to convert the U.S. Congress from an ad hoc collection of amateur politicians to an institution with clearly defined boundaries, professional legislators and staff, and a highly regimented legislative process. These determinants include internal factors (changes to chamber rules and, more gradually, norms and increases in the congressional workload) and external factors (increases in population, changes to the two-party system, increasingly demanding constituents, and the rise of twenty-four-hour news organizations). Working in concert, these changes have transformed the U.S. Congress. As Allen Hertzke and Ronald Peters write in the introduction to *The*

Atomistic Congress: An Interpretation of Congressional Change: "The stodgy, clubby, conservative, and geriatric institution that was so well captured in the work of Ralph K. Huitt, Charles O. Jones, Nelson Polsby, Charles Goodwin, Randall Ripley, Donald Matthews and Richard Fenno was put to rest as soon as its political enemies were strong enough to kill it."[7]

The enemies of what might be called the "traditional" Congress (that is, the institution that existed in the first half of the twentieth century) began to gather strength in the late 1950s. Congressional scholar Burdett Loomis explains: "The congressional equilibrium began to change with the Democratic landslide in the 1958 congressional elections, which greatly increased the size of the party's majority in both chambers. More important, many of the newly elected legislators were relatively liberal and committed to policy changes."[8] Rather than respecting the Senate's norms, the freshmen senators who were elected in 1958 entered the institution determined to change it. Loomis continues: "Beginning in 1958, continuing through the 1960s, and culminating in the 1974 and 1976 elections for Democrats and the 1978 and 1980 elections for Republicans, we get different kinds of new members. . . . In general, the newly elected members were impatient, eager to use their expertise, and unconcerned if they ruffled some senior members' feathers."[9]

In the Senate, the cumulative result of these changes in membership was the breakdown of long-standing Senate norms. During the nineteenth and much of the twentieth centuries, the U.S. Senate was an inner-directed, hierarchical chamber that was resistant to outside influences and pressures. Even as late as the 1960s, examinations of the Senate captured a body deeply wedded to internal norms and folkways. Power flowed from the top down, with senior members of the majority party in the Senate coalescing at the top and junior members being left at the bottom. But the Senate election of 1958 brought a sea change of sorts to the chamber. No longer would "freshmen" senators be seen and not heard.

Of course, the young, liberal class of senators who entered the institution in 1959 might have been quickly assimilated into the Senate's traditions had it not been for two external conditions that converged at approximately the same time. First, there was a rapid expansion of the media that began at about the same time that the new senators were sworn in. Advances in communications technologies—especially television—coincided with the freshman term of the "Class of 1958," and senators began to realize that they could use the media as a tool to help them in their reelection campaigns. Many senators—including senior members—embraced instantaneous communications technologies, which catalyzed the decline of Senate norms. Once expected to serve an appropriate "apprenticeship" (one need only to have seen Hollywood's *Mr. Smith Goes to Washington* to understand the low levels of esteem in which junior senators were held), today's junior senators expect to be full members of the chamber.

Not only did the Senate's apprenticeship norm decline during the 1960s, but the chamber's age-old traditions of deference to fellow senators and a spirit of collegiality also began to disappear. Once television became a permanent fixture in the Congress (C-SPAN began operating in the House in 1979 and in the Senate in 1986), members recognized that they had a direct, uncensored, and unedited connection to their constituents. As one edited volume on the U.S. Congress notes: "[T]he decision to televise House and Senate proceedings led to members of Congress being able to address the nation directly from the floor. The debate became more polarized, with the comity norm being one of the first casualties."[10] Further, senators began to oppose their colleagues more frequently and more publicly. Instead of continuing to defer to their colleagues, in the 1960s and 1970s senators refined an already powerful arsenal of tools and techniques to delay consideration of legislation or to prevent enactment altogether.

The second external condition that coincided nearly perfectly with the important Senate elections of 1958 was a dramatic increase in the number of political interest groups, an increase that continued into the 1960s and 1970s. This expansion fortuitously coincided with expanded points of entry in the Senate, as younger senators refused to stand in the shadows of their senior colleagues. Moreover, in the aftermath of the United States Supreme Court's decision in *Buckley v. Valeo* (1976), political action committees (PACs) emerged. Some PACs were offshoots of existing interest groups, while others were independent fund-raising organizations. Regardless, senators were eager to support interest groups' causes for both the financial and constituency rewards they could accrue. As senators began to court the television networks and the interest group leaders (and vice versa), they grew increasingly independent of the Senate as a collection of members. Congressional scholar Donald C. Baumer writes: "The evolution of the Senate from the 1950s to the 1980s can be described rather succinctly: a tradition-laden institution run by a self-selected group of 'Senate types' was transformed into a body in which self-promoting individualism and collective disorder became predominant characteristics."[11]

How did these changes manifest themselves? There is ample evidence that the rise of the media and the exponential growth in political interest groups during the 1960s and 1970s, coupled with successive influxes of new members who were eager to change, significantly affected legislative work in the Senate. One manifestation was an increase in the use of delaying tactics. As Barbara Sinclair notes in *Unorthodox Lawmaking: New Legislative Processes in the U.S. Congress,* between 1951 and 1960 (the 82nd through 86th Congresses), there was an average of one filibuster per congress; between 1961 and 1970 (87th through 92nd Congresses), the number increased to 4.6 filibusters per congress. Recent congresses (103rd through 105th) have averaged nearly 30 filibusters per congress.[12]

There are as many reasons to filibuster as there are senators, but it seems clear that the breakdown in Senate norms, coupled with increased incentives for individual senators to seek media exposure can account for at least some of the dramatic increase in the number of filibusters per congress. As Congressional Research Service researcher Stanley Bach (1997, 2) notes: "The single most powerful weapon available to individuals and minorities in the Senate is the ability to delay." He adds that filibustering is used "not only to prevent action but also to extract substantive policy concessions from the majority, whether it is partisan or bipartisan."[13] According to Sarah Binder and Steven Smith, writing in *Politics or Principle? Filibustering in the United States Senate:* "The filibuster has been responsible for killing or delaying enactment of a considerable body of legislation otherwise headed for enactment into law. The filibuster also has political consequences for legislative outcomes and strategies."[14]

In addition to filibustering legislation, senators also began to use "holds" to delay or prevent altogether the Senate's consideration of an item of legislation or a nomination until such time as their demands were satisfied. Holds—requests of the majority leader to delay or deny floor debate on a bill or nomination—are now commonplace in the Senate; senators have traditionally requested holds to provide additional time to conduct research, prepare for debate, or accommodate busy schedules. Beginning in the late 1960s, the number of requests for holds began to increase, and today senators use hold requests to hold legislation hostage, seek revenge, or embarrass political enemies.[15]

Congressional Change and the Confirmation Process

Not surprisingly, the changes to the Senate that began with the election of 1958 led to alterations not only in the Senate's legislative processes, but also in its confirmation processes, to change during the 1960s and 1970s. Prior to 1960, presidential struggles over the appointment process were infrequent. On most confirmations, presidents needed to persuade only a handful of senior senators to approve their nominee, because the expectation was that the junior senators would fall in line behind their elders. According to Mark Silverstein, author of *Judicious Choices:* "In [President Lyndon B. Johnson's] view, the Senate consisted of a few 'whales' and many 'minnows.' The conventional wisdom held that in any battle in the Senate (particularly in securing its advice and consent on appointments) the president only had to negotiate with the appropriate whales. Once the consent of the powerful had been secured, the remainder of the Senate would fall in line."[16]

Throughout most of the Senate's history, any single vote on a nominee was unlikely to garner much attention from senators' constituents. As the costs of opposing a president's nominees were great and the costs of supporting the president's choice relatively low, senators typically acquiesced to the president. By the late 1960s, however, changes to the norms of the Senate made securing confirmation for presidential nominees much more difficult.[17] By 1968, and Johnson's nomination of Justice Abe Fortas to be Chief Justice of the United States Supreme Court, the distinction between whales and minnows had largely disappeared, primarily because of increased media scrutiny, an increasing number of very active pressure groups, and changes to the norms of the Senate. Although Johnson had the support of the "whales," the young, reform-minded senators refused to acquiesce to the more senior members of the body. When the Senate Judiciary Committee voted eleven to six to send Fortas's name to the full Senate for consideration, young reformers in the Senate began a filibuster that failed the Fortas's nomination.[18] The Fortas defeat signaled the end of nearly two centuries of Senate norms of courtesy and reciprocity. No longer would presidential nominees be carried to confirmation on the backs of just a handful of senior senators.

The shift from a system of whales and minnows to one where all senators enjoy approximately equal stature has had enormous consequences for the confirmation process, just as it did for the legislative process. For example, senators more often use delaying tactics in the confirmation process. Filibusters have been used to "kill" presidential nominations since 1881, and in recent decades the Senate has developed and refined additional delaying tactics—most notably the use of such tactics as the blue slip and the hold—each of which is designed to prevent presidential nominees from being confirmed. Eliot Mincberg, legal director for the organization People for the American Way, claims that the tactic of delaying Senate confirmation has never been so pronounced.[19] Today, delays are used not only to provide senators more time to consider nominees but to force nominees to withdraw before being confirmed.

Senators today are actually more likely to use blue slips and holds to delay or kill nominations rather than to use filibusters, which are more common in the legislative process. In the context of presidential nominations, the purpose of a hold request is to ask the majority leader not to bring a nominee's name up for consideration until such time as the requesting senator is ready to consider the nomination. Originally designed to give senators additional time to review the background and qualifications of nominees, the Senate hold has evolved through practice to become one of the most significant tools of delay in a senator's arsenal. Senators find holds more attractive than filibusters, because holds require only a brief communication to the majority leader, whereas a filibuster requires hours and sometimes days of planning and executing by a senator or a group of senators. In the 104th, 105th, and 106th Congresses, holds were used to delay consideration of several nominees to the lower federal courts, even as filibustering on confirmations was a rare event.[20]

Regardless of the tactic used, delay in considering a president's nominees is as much a part of the contemporary confirmation process as the threat of a filibuster is to the legislative process more generally. As Mark Silverstein writes, "delay is a particularly effective strategy in contesting a presidential nomination. Drawing the proceedings out over time permits the opposition to organize, new information to be discovered, the public to be aroused."[21] Senators who utilize the available processes to delay confirmation do so for the same reasons that they use filibusters and holds in the legislative process: to extract concessions from the majority, to extract concessions from the president, or to defeat a nomination that would otherwise be approved by a majority of the Senate. For example, in October 1999, Senate Foreign Relations Committee Chairman Jesse Helms (R-NC) agreed to hold a hearing on the nomination of former Senator Carol Moseley Braun (D-IL) to be ambassador to New Zealand only if the Clinton administration agreed to hand over internal documents related to an investigation of Senator Moseley Braun's alleged use of campaign funds for non-campaign purposes. In 1998, Senator Slade Gorton (R-WA), who was a swing vote during the confirmation process for law professor William Fletcher's nomination to the Ninth Circuit Court of Appeals, agreed to vote in favor of Fletcher on the condition that President Clinton nominate a judge of his choosing to fill the next vacancy on that court.[22] As one Senate Foreign Relations Committee staffer put it: "[Nominees] are currency, in a way. Currency to get things done."[23]

Across the board, nominations to positions in the highest levels of the federal government are waiting long periods of time to be confirmed. Figure 2.1 demonstrates that the time span between nomination and confirmation

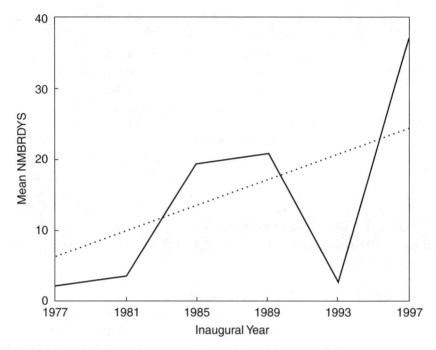

Figure 2.1. Average Number of Days between Nomination and Confirmation for Presidents' Initial Cabinet Choices, by inaugural year.

Source: Cabinet Nominees Data Set, compiled by author. The number of days is counted from the date the president actually submits the nomination to the Senate (not the date the president announces his intent to nominate a particular individual).

for presidents' initial choices for their cabinets has increased dramatically in recent years. Although the average number of days the Senate takes to confirm nominees increases during periods of divided government (a phenomenon that will be discussed shortly), it is also clear that cabinet nominees named in 1997 waited nearly twice as long as those named in 1989, when control of the presidency and the Senate also was shared between the two parties.

In addition to increasingly drawn-out cabinet confirmations, judicial nominees now wait longer than ever before for confirmation. Figure 2.2 demonstrates that the mean number of days that judicial nominees waited for confirmation between the 96th and 105th Congresses has also increased over time.

Of course, just as in the legislative process, senators' incentives to use delaying tactics in the confirmation process grew as a result of the media

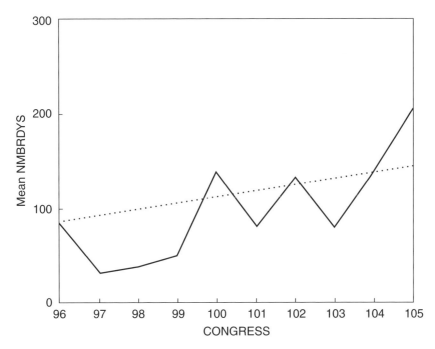

Figure 2.2.   Increases in Confirmation Process Delays for Judicial Nominees, 1979–1998.

Sources: Legislative and Executive Calendar, United States Senate Committee on Judiciary, congresses indicated.

and interest groups. As senators became more individualistic, they also became less likely to "go along to get along." To the extent that a president nominates someone whose agenda is contrary to that of any individual senator, that senator now has ample opportunities to oppose the nominee—often publicly—through the media and interest groups.

An increase in media coverage of the Senate provided a generalized incentive to senators to carefully scrutinize presidential nominees during the 1960s and 1970s. However, the 1980s saw important new linkages between the media and confirmation politics. Robert Bork's 1987 confirmation hearings were televised, which gave senators a new forum for expressing their views and influencing public opinion. With increasing media exposure for the Senate's confirmation hearings, the Senate gained greater and greater prominence in the appointment process. Beginning with Supreme Court nominees, "contesting the nomination . . . [became] a highly visible—and often necessary—event in a senator's life."[24] In the contemporary Senate, "[i]ncreased media coverage and the constant search for campaign funds invite independent action and encourage senators to become visible players in matters of national interest."[25]

Televised confirmation hearings for Robert Bork led segments of the population who had never before paid attention to confirmation politics to begin to call upon their senators to oppose some presidential nominees. Senators realized that through the media they could appear to be the champions of causes that were important to constituents and powerful interests within their home states, or they could appear to be detached from the people who elected them. When it came time to confirm nominees, senators could no longer be sure who was watching and what effect their confirmation vote might have on their approval ratings back home. As a result, constituency pressures became much more central to senators' confirmation decisions. This, in turn, expanded senators' incentives to oppose presidential nominees. Senators began to use the confirmation process to gain electoral and legislative advantages.

Courting interest groups became an important part of seeking electoral advantages for many senators between 1960 and 1980. Once reserving their participation for only the most important of presidential nominations, interest groups today are active players in the confirmation process across a wide range of nominations. Only a few studies of interest group participation in the political process include interest groups among the players in the appointment process.[26] In *The Advice and Consent of the Senate*, one of the first comprehensive treatments of the Senate's advice and consent power, Joseph Harris (1953) does not even mention interest groups. But there can be no doubt that interest groups, as the most recent addition to confirmation politics, also have contributed to its changed nature.

While interest groups had periodically mobilized against nominees to the Supreme Court since 1881, their regular participation in confirmation politics did not begin until the late 1970s, when they began to more closely monitor nominations to the federal courts. The timing is not a coincidence. On the heels of the Watergate scandal, groups took a more active role in "watching" the activities of the president. Mark Silverstein explains: "With the coming of the Carter Administration, both the degree of scrutiny and the number and political influence of groups engaged in the endeavor [of monitoring judicial nominations] increased materially. Groups with a professional, upper-middle-class focus such as the Women's Legal Defense Fund, the Center for Law and Social Policy, Common Cause, and the NOW Legal Defense Fund began regularly to set aside funds and staff for the express purpose of keeping watch on nominees to the federal bench."[27]

In the mid-1980s, interest groups stepped up their participation in the confirmation process for judicial nominees. President Reagan's 1984 announcement that he would use the appointment process to remake the federal judiciary in a conservative image sparked liberal interest groups to mobilize against Reagan's nominees. This was especially true following the midterm election of 1986, when Democrats regained control of the Senate after six years of a Republican majority.[28]

When Ronald Reagan nominated Robert Bork to the Supreme Court in 1987, interest groups responded by trying to discredit him in order to cause the Senate to reject him. In the aftermath of the Bork rejection, a report in the *Congressional Quarterly Weekly Report* summed up the impact of the Bork nomination: "Since 1987, when President Ronald Reagan nominated Robert H. Bork to the U.S. Supreme Court, outside groups such as the Free Congress Research and Education Foundation and People for the American Way have gained prominence on Capitol Hill, making their voices heard both on particular nominations to the federal bench and on the broader issue of the judicial confirmation process."[29]

Bork himself blamed the interest groups for his defeat. As Silverstein explains: "In the months following the failed appointment, Bork toured the country. Speaking before various conservative and business groups, he asserted that his defeat was the result of the first all-out political campaign directed at a nominee to the Supreme Court."[30]

Since Bork, interest groups have become even more active in the confirmation process. For one thing, they no longer focus exclusively on judicial confirmations. Once respectful of the president's choices to fill executive-branch vacancies, today nominations to nearly every position are cause for interest groups to participate in confirmation hearings and to lobby senators on behalf of or in opposition to the nominee. According to Robert Shogan, writing in *Obstacle Course:* "[T]he judicial-executive line of demarcation has been losing much of its meaning as contentiousness increases across the board of the appointment process."[31] During the 1990s, interest groups have actively participated in confirmation politics for nominees to every cabinet-level agency, as well as in the confirmation process for subcabinet and ambassadorial nominees. Even regulatory agencies and government commissions have seen their nominees become the targets of interest groups. In 1995, Supreme Court scholar Lawrence Baum noted: "In general, the role of interest groups in the confirmation process is higher than ever."[32]

Interest groups exacerbate existing tensions in the confirmation process. These groups, and the PACs with which they are associated, contribute to the growing number of incentives that senators have to delay or oppose nominees deemed unacceptable by the groups. These incentives are both electoral and financial; with their ability to educate and mobilize the grass roots, interest groups make senators' constituents aware of impending confirmation decisions. PACs frequently use their campaign-financing role to provide incentives to senators who act on the confirmation in the way desired.

Without interest groups to placate, senators would likely be less willing to confront the White House over confirmation of its nominees. Discussing the 105th Congress, People for the American Way's Eliot Mincberg noted: "It is very important to the Republicans' far-right constituency that [Republican senators] be responsive in some way. [Opposing Clinton's nominees is] a way that they can make their far-right allies happy without doing anything."[33] Shogan adds: "The interest groups that have proliferated across the spectrum, both as cause and effect of the erosion of parties, increasingly have become a force in the appointment process, second only in importance to the president."[34] In actuality, however, the president has become second in importance to interest groups, at least during the confirmation process.

Abe Fortas's 1968 defeat brought about another change to the confirmation process: a diminution of the power of the president vis-à-vis the Senate in the confirmation process. Once the dominant player in appointment politics, presidents today are often only peripherally involved in nominating individuals, and, thus have little credibility in pushing for Senate confirmation.

In the 1950s, changes in the White House's nomination system reduced the need for presidents to pay attention to most personnel decisions. Under President Dwight D. Eisenhower, "steps were taken to ensure that personnel decisions for all but the most important positions could be finalized without active presidential involvement."[35] Eisenhower, the former general, wanted a highly routinized process that could be run by subordinates on all but the most important of personnel decisions. White House staffers took on the primary task of selecting nearly all of Eisenhower's nominees to appointed positions.

The bureaucracy associated with selecting presidential nominees continued to grow during the 1960s and 1970s. In 1977, President Carter further reduced the role of the president in selecting judicial nominees by issuing Executive Order 11972, which created nominating commissions designed to select United States Circuit Court judges. The commissions were charged with narrowing the list of possible candidates for Circuit Court judgeships to five, from which the president or a member of his staff would make a choice.[36] Since the late 1970s, presidents have relied on staffers and nominating commissions to assist them with the task of selecting nominees. Many senior staffers on the Senate Judiciary Committee believe that Ronald Reagan allowed the White House staff to choose many of his high-level nominees and that Reagan relied on Attorney General Edwin Meese to suggest nearly all of his judicial nominees.[37]

Many of today's nominees, selected by nominating commissions or other nonpartisan groups, are forced to endure a lengthy vetting process, or background check, prior to being nominated, and may even be unknown to the president or to senators even at the moment of nomination. Increases in the number of positions requiring Senate confirmation made it difficult for presidents to handle the job of selecting nominees themselves—for that reason, they have delegated that task to members of their staffs, to home state senators, or to nonpartisan nominating commissions.

Far fewer nominees are known to the president who appoints them today than would have been known to him just a few decades ago. That presidents removed themselves from the process at the same time that the Senate was splintering into a loose collection of individual self-promoters might properly be blamed on the greater social and political fragmentation of the 1960s and the 1970s. Nonetheless, to navigate the confirmation process that emerged during that period, presidents needed to be able to persuade one hundred senators, not just a handful of powerful members. With little connection to their nominees, presidents found themselves in a weak bargaining position. Where once they could be reasonably certain that with a little pressure from the White House the Senate would confirm their nominees, pressure from the White House began to mean less and less in the polarized Senate that emerged between 1960 and 1980.

Rather than reassert their role in the appointment process, in the last several years, presidents have continued to reduce the amount of time and effort they are willing to spend to make the confirmation process run smoothly for their nominees. In many cases, nominees to high-ranking federal offices never meet with the president nominating them. And once the nomination is made, presidents virtually disappear from the process, instead delegating the responsibility of preparing nominees for the confirmation process to the legislative liaisons of the various federal agencies and departments. For example, when describing her confirmation to the

Environmental Protection Agency (EPA), Anne Burford recalls that President Reagan was noticeably absent from the process. She writes: "As I waited nervously [at the confirmation hearing] to begin my testimony with a statement, to be followed by the Senators' questions, it flashed through my mind that the White House had given me absolutely no help in my confirmation process. Zero. Zip."[38] Former ambassador to Liberia and Australia under President Clinton and former ambassador to the United Nations under President Bush, Edward Perkins concurs: "The White House is not involved [in the confirmation process]. Once my nomination went to the Senate, I never heard a word from the White House."[39]

Like his predecessors, President Bill Clinton was underinvolved in the confirmation process for his nominees. In *Starting Over*, G. Calvin Mackenzie writes:

> One of the great mysteries of the appointment process in 1997 was the whereabouts of the president of the United States. From time to time, the president would pop up to express his frustration at the slow pace of the confirmation process, but for most of the year he was a peripheral figure in nearly every appointment struggle. In the two most prominent appointment controversies of the year, over Anthony Lake and William Weld, presidential efforts to win confirmation were little in evidence. It was an uncommonly—and uncannily—passive performance.[40]

Eliot Mincberg, legal director for the liberal group People for the American Way, notes that Clinton's lack of public support for his nominees resulted from his unwillingness to expend political capital on Senate confirmations. According to Mincberg: "[Clinton's unwillingness to stand by his nominees] goes all the way back to Lani Guinier. Clinton sent a clear signal to Republicans that it doesn't take much push to get Clinton to abandon a nominee."[41] According to reporter Ken Bode: "In the Lani Guinier nomination, there was no fight. Bill Clinton collapsed before the fight."[42]

Presidential scandals also have weakened the influence the president has in the Senate confirmation process. The impact of scandal can be traced back to Watergate. By 1972, public distrust for President Richard M. Nixon led the Senate to view presidential nominees more skeptically. The Senate began to pay much more attention to the qualifications of nominees and began rejecting more and more presidential nominations as a result.[43] Beginning with Watergate, continuing with the Iran-Contra scandal, and most recently with the campaign finance investigations of the late 1990s, the Senate has scrutinized all presidential activities carefully. The confirmation process is the latest casualty of exacting Senate scrutiny. In their excellent treatment of the U.S. Congress, Roger Davidson and Walter Oleszek describe how the campaign finance scandal of 1997 affected the appointment process for President Clinton's diplomatic nominees: "After allegations in the press that foreign national and governments contributed money to his 1996 presidential campaign as a way to win favors, President Clinton was wary of naming foreign envoys. At the beginning of his second term, the selection of diplomatic personnel 'bogged down, a victim of White House indecision caused in part by the furor over campaign financing.'"[44]

Domestic nominations also suffered. Nominated to head the Central Intelligence Agency (CIA), Anthony Lake's nomination stalled while the Senate tried to sort out fact from fiction in the campaign finance scandal. Reporter Eric Engberg noted on *CBS This Morning* in March 1997: "[I]t's clear the expanding investigations into the Democrats' raising of funds from questionable and maybe illegal foreign sources have [made the administration vulnerable]; said Republican Senator John McCain, 'If it weren't for that, [Anthony] Lake would have slid through.' The fight was not about Lake. He was just a convenient target."[45]

While not all modern presidents have taken as much of a hands-off approach as President Clinton, the bottom line is that contemporary presidents are further removed from the confirmation process than ever before. Their staffs are handling most of the staffing decisions. The Senate has become less willing to accord the president latitude in choosing his own subordinates, which further reduces presidential influence over confirmation politics. The Senate knows that modern presidents rarely will intervene personally to expedite the confirmation process. Because it takes only one senator to put a hold on a nomination, presidents now have to please everyone, not just a handful of powerful senior members of the Senate.

The combined impact of changes to internal Senate norms and a reduced role of the president has been a dramatic change in the role of the Senate in the appointment process. If the president enjoyed the upper hand in the appointment process in the early years of the American republic, it is the Senate that is the dominant player today. Even the president's power to nominate a person of his or her choosing has been circumscribed as members of the Senate have sought to use the confirmation process for political gain. No longer is the Senate a "rubber stamp machine." Today, no president dares to nominate someone to fill a high-level vacancy without consulting with home state senators and key members of the Senate leadership. During the 105th Congress, for example, Senate Judiciary Committee Chairman Orrin Hatch worked closely with the White House to prevent the naming of individuals to the federal courts and other judicial positions who would have had no chance of being confirmed. An article in the *New York Times* reported: "[Hatch] has no doubt been a factor in Clinton's favoring centrists for his judicial choices."[46] In today's confirmation process, the president cannot afford to act without first consulting members of the Senate. And even then, the Senate may refuse to approve the president's choices, especially when partisan or ideological differences between the White House and the Senate exist.

Such differences began to be significant in the 1980s. Following the 1980 election of Ronald Reagan, the confirmation process changed more rapidly and more profoundly than it ever had before. Ideology became a litmus test for many nominees, and some were rejected outright because they held issue positions that senators considered to be extreme. Many observers agree that Ronald Reagan's election began the trend toward ideology as the primary consideration for both the nomination and the confirmation of presidential nominees. Robert Shogan (1996, 121) declares: "With the election of Ronald Reagan, ... polarized politics ... would return with a vengeance."[47] Rhett DeHart, formerly counsel to Senator Jeff Sessions and currently counsel to Senate Judiciary Committee Chairman Orrin Hatch agrees: "Reagan did make [the appointment process] more ideological."[48] From the beginning, Reagan expressed his intent to appoint only conservatives to high-ranking positions in the federal government. Reagan was especially anxious to appoint conservatives to the federal bench. As Supreme Court scholars Jeffrey Segal and Harold J. Spaeth (1993, 125) write: "The chief legacy of the Reagan Administration, when the twenty-first century rolls around, will likely be the Reaganizing of the judiciary."[49]

In 1987, Reagan nominated Robert Bork, a conservative judge on the District of Columbia Court of Appeals, to a seat on the U.S. Supreme Court. Bork was considered to be extremely conservative, but he held the respect of many members of the Senate. Doomed from the start, this single nomination ultimately did more to increase partisanship in the confirmation process than any other before or since. As soon as Reagan announced that he would nominate Bork to fill the vacancy on the Supreme Court, liberals in the United States Senate sprang into attack mode, with Massachusetts Senator Edward M. Kennedy leading the charge. Upon hearing of Bork's nomination, Kennedy declared: "Robert Bork's America is a land in which women would be forced into back-alley abortions, blacks would sit at segregated lunch counters, rogue police would break down citizens' doors."[50] This single statement, perhaps more than any other, galvanized the opposition to Bork, even as it distorted his political views. Liberal senators worked together with liberal interest groups to wage Capitol Hill, grassroots, and media campaigns against Bork that were unprecedented in their scope. In the end, Bork was defeated by a vote of fifty-two to forty-eight. The confirmation process would never again be the same.

Although nearly all of President Reagan's and, later, President Bush's nominees were confirmed by the Democratically controlled Senate, Republican senators never forgot the way in which Democratic senators had used the confirmation process to discredit and embarrass one of their party's most revered icons. The axiom "turnabout is fair play" perhaps best describes Republican senators' approach to the confirmation process when they recaptured the Senate in 1994. But the Republicans, engaging in a sort of senatorial one-upmanship, were not content to focus on discrediting just one or two of President Clinton's nominees. Instead, they waged an all-out attack on a number of nominees, even some who had been nominated to subcabinet and regulatory agency positions.

The Republican-controlled Senate increased its scrutiny of the president's nominees because of its fears that former President Bill Clinton, a Democrat, would be able to undo the twelve years of a Republican-dominated federal judiciary and bureaucracy. One popular press account noted that with regard to the federal judiciary: "Republicans are resisting Clinton nominees aggressively in part because they had to fight so long to get the judiciary to their liking."[51] People for the American Way's Eliot Mincberg notes: "Every Clinton judge you don't put on the bench is that much longer Reagan and Bush can continue to dominate the courts. Even if it's just a temporary advantage, that just means less Clinton judges and more Reagan and Bush Judges."[52] Senate Judiciary Committee Chairman Orrin Hatch himself acknowledged this point in a November 1996 speech to the Federalist Society: "[W]e are at a critical crossroad in the history of our federal judiciary. While the legacy of 12 years of Republican appointees to the federal bench has just begun to bear some fruit, and we have begun to see a handful of significant, albeit initial, steps toward returning the courts to their proper sphere, we are now faced with the prospect of four more years of Clinton appointees."[53]

Not only did the switch from Democratic to Republican control of the Senate increase partisanship in the confirmation process, but the particular combination of Republicans in the Senate specifically, and in the

Congress more generally, affected the conduct of Senate confirmations. Mincberg states: "I think it's the combination of having the Republicans in the majority, and which Republicans are in the majority." The interplay between Republicans in the House and in the Senate also contributed to the changed process. One Congressional Research Service researcher, who spoke on the condition of anonymity, believes that the strongly partisan Republican majority in the House of Representatives did not want the less strongly partisan Senate to undo the work it had done following the Republican takeover of the House after the 1994 midterm election. According to the researcher: "The House Republicans . . . don't want their counterparts in the Senate to screw up the 'revolution' that they're trying to start."[54] So, claims the researcher, the House Republicans began to put pressure on their Senate counterparts to prevent the appointment of liberal nominees to fill vacancies in government. These pressure tactics have ranged from one-on-one meetings with members of the Republican leadership to threats to withhold funding for key government functions unless the president agreed to nominate moderate appointees of their choosing. Victoria Bassetti, formerly Chief Counsel to Illinois Senator Richard Durbin (D-IL) and currently Legislative Director for Senator John Edwards (D-NC), explained: "[Republicans] are trying to make the process so long and drawn out and awful that the nominees drop out."[55]

The confirmation process of the late 1990s was plagued by partisanship at levels never before thought possible. As Walter Shapiro, a columnist for *USA Today*, noted in December 1997:

> The prime offender, it must be stressed, is the Republican Senate. The results were the same whether the titans of the Senate were pandering to right wing constituencies (Lee); settling old scores (Foreign Relations Committee Chairman Jesse Helms vetoing moderate Republican [William] Weld); or simply making mischief (Senate Intelligence Committee Chairman Richard Shelby by tormenting [CIA nominee Anthony] Lake). These debilitating games of "gotcha" have their roots in the scorched-earth tactics perfected by Senate Democrats in blocking the 1987 nomination of Robert Bork to the Supreme Court. But ancient enmities don't justify the conduct of the GOP Senate.[56]

Unfortunately, high levels of partisanship in the process are likely to get worse before they get better. Accounts in the popular press have been replete with negative appraisals. For example, Helen Dewar writes: "As Democrats and Republicans alternate in control of the White House and Congress, each party . . . pushes against the outer limits of established conduct in an ever-escalating cycle that keeps ratcheting up the partisan contentiousness of the process."[57] McCarty and Razaghian (1988) note: "Political conflict induced by divided government and party polarization clearly leads to a more drawn out confirmation process."[58] (1998, 24). Unlike most of the history of the confirmation process, partisanship is every bit as much a part of confirmation politics as it is on a broad range of legislative initiatives.

Some Illustrations

The changes discussed above make Senate confirmation less certain than ever before. These changes also have contributed to the confirmation process becoming much more like the legislative process, more generally, even as the legislative process itself has evolved from its original "textbook" model. Just as every piece of legislation now has its own unique process (Sinclair 1996), every presidential nominee is treated differently by the Senate. It is no longer accurate to talk about the confirmation process as a highly routinized mechanism for the approval of presidential nominees. Today, there are a multitude of steps involved in the confirmation process, some more easily navigated than others. As one Senate staffer put it, the confirmation process "depends on the nominee."

Some examples are illustrative. The first two case studies describe the process of confirming Dale Kimball and Margaret Morrow, both of whom were nominated by President Clinton to replace retiring federal district court judges. The third case study describes how Bill Lann Lee, Clinton's selection to head the Department of Justice's Civil Rights Division, fared when the Senate considered his nomination. Kimball's nomination might properly be viewed as representative of the "textbook" model of the confirmation process, while the other nominees represent the extent to which the confirmation process has evolved away from this model.

Dale Kimball

Although he is a contemporary nominee, Dale Kimball's nomination represents the traditional path that nominations take through the appointment process. He was both nominated and confirmed quickly and with little fanfare or controversy. President Clinton nominated Kimball on September 5, 1997, to fill a vacancy that had occurred less than ninety days earlier on the Federal District Court for the District of Utah. The Senate Judiciary Committee held a hearing on his nomination on September

30, 1997, and reported his nomination to the Senate by unanimous consent on October 9. On October 21, the Senate confirmed Kimball by unanimous consent. From start to finish, it took just forty-six days to confirm Kimball's nomination. Not a single group appeared before the Senate Judiciary Committee to address Kimball's nomination. There were no holds placed on his nomination, and no senator threatened to filibuster his confirmation.

Kimball's confirmation looks much like the textbook model of Senate confirmation. However, Kimball's appointment stands out as dramatically different from the appointments of other individuals. As the next three examples demonstrate, Kimball's swift, conflict-free, confirmation does not represent the norm for the last two congresses.

Margaret Morrow

Margaret Morrow's nomination stands in stark contrast to Dale Kimball's and highlights the ease with which he was confirmed. Morrow was nominated to the central district court in California in May 1996, to replace Judge Richard Gadbois, who had retired three-and-a-half months earlier. The Judiciary Committee held a hearing on her nomination on June 25, 1996, and two days later reported her nomination to the full Senate by unanimous consent. But the Senate took no action on her nomination, and it was returned to the Senate when the 104th Congress adjourned. Election-year politics were most likely to blame, as Republicans confirmed only seventeen judges in 1996, hoping that Republican presidential candidate Robert Dole would win the 1996 presidential election. If that occurred, Republicans could choose more conservative judges to fill the vacancies that existed in 1996.

Of course, Dole did not win the presidential election, and President Clinton renominated Margaret Morrow in January 1997 immediately upon the opening of the 105th Congress. She was given another hearing in March 1997, but the committee did not send her nomination to the Senate floor until June 12, 1997. Morrow waited an additional seven months, until February 11, 1998, to be confirmed by the full Senate. She was confirmed by a vote of sixty-seven to twenty-eight.

From start to finish, Morrow waited nearly two full years from the time she was nominated to the time she was confirmed. Two factors made Morrow's confirmation more difficult than Kimball's. First, the heightened partisanship of a presidential election year gave Republicans an incentive to prevent Morrow from being confirmed. Second, conservative interest groups mounted a campaign against Morrow, claiming that she was a judicial "activist" who would legislate from the bench. Several Republican senators, at the request of the conservative group The Judicial Selection Monitoring Project, agreed to vote against any nominee that was or had the potential to be a judicial activist.

Debating her confirmation, former Missouri senator John Ashcroft, who had previously appeared in a fund-raising videotape for the Judicial Selection Monitoring Project's campaign against judicial activism, stated: "I think judges who believe that the Constitution is written in pencil and who think that the Bill of Rights is written in disappearing ink are judges that are out of control. We have to be careful we don't put more individuals on the bench who have a disregard for the separation of powers and who do not understand that what the people do under the authority of the Constitution is valid and must be respected.[59]

Ashcroft also entered into the *Congressional Record* a letter from the Judicial Selection Monitoring Project, which was signed by 180 organizations, and which charged that Morrow was a judicial activist. Although she was confirmed, it was only over the objections of several conservative senators and interest groups, and only after Senate Judiciary Committee Chairman Orrin Hatch broke with his party to urge that she be confirmed, saying that her opponents had distorted her record.

Bill Lann Lee

In recent congresses, the Senate has not limited its increased scrutiny of nominees to judicial nominees. In fact, almost every appointment is fair game for heightened investigation. Bill Lann Lee found this out after Clinton nominated him to fill the position of Assistant Attorney General for Civil Rights on July 21, 1997. The politics of Lee's confirmation process illustrate the extent to which the president's ability to select his own subordinates has been circumscribed by the Senate in the last two decades.

Lee was a well-respected civil rights attorney in Los Angeles at the time of his nomination in 1997. His caseload included a number of situations involving employment discrimination and other controversial issues. The son of poor immigrants, Lee's rise to a respected position as a prominent attorney was truly an American success story. On top of his solid professional credentials, Lee was supportive of the Clinton administration's "mend it, don't end it" position on affirmative action. To the Clinton White House, Lee seemed like the perfect candidate to head the Justice Department's Civil Rights Division.

But Republicans lashed out at Lee for his position on affirmative action. Ironically, Senate Judiciary Committee Chairman Orrin Hatch, who typically restrained himself from opposing Clinton's executive branch nominees, led the charge against Lee's confirmation. According to political commentator Jacob Weisberg: "In Lee's case, Hatch says he's opposing a qualified nominee simply to draw the line on an administration policy he disagrees with—support for affirmative action."[60]

Republicans seized on the affirmative action issue and attempted to defeat Lee's nomination. Even Speaker of the House Newt Gingrich got involved, urging Senate Majority Leader Trent Lott to oppose Lee's nomination. On November 13, 1997, Democratic members of the Senate Judiciary Committee blocked a vote on Lee's nomination, "after determining they would lose if [a vote] were taken."[61] This tactic would have prevented Lee from being rejected by the Republican majority on the Judiciary Committee. On December 15, 1997, Clinton named Bill Lann Lee the Acting Assistant Attorney General for Civil Rights, a move that prompted one political commentator to declare: "Acting is now all the confirmation process can muster."[62]

Lee's nomination demonstrates the problems that increased partisanship and ideological litmus testing have created for the confirmation process. Today, nominees are rejected by the Senate because of their policy positions on particular issues. Lee's failed confirmation also illustrates how far afield the appointment of low-level cabinet positions has come. For most of American history, presidents were deemed entitled to the people they wanted to staff the executive branch. In this case, however, Lee failed to be confirmed for no other reason than that he supported the president's position on affirmative action.

Conclusion

The confirmation process in the last several congresses has defied classification, in large part because the expectation of a routinized, highly professionalized confirmation process has not been met. Today, no nominee can take for granted that his or her confirmation will be swift or easy. As the examples above have demonstrated, the confirmation process for major appointments is now more unpredictable than ever. Since the mid-1990s, many nominees have been subjected to lengthy waits for confirmation, usually because one or more senators has worked in concert with conservative interest groups to delay or prevent confirmation. While a handful of every president's nominees has always been subjected to delay and heightened scrutiny, nominees to federal office—even offices once viewed as requiring only a senatorial rubber stamp—now routinely face interest group opposition and confirmation delay.

The confirmation process at the beginning of the twenty-first century is vastly different from the process put into place by the framers of the Constitution at the end of the eighteenth century. The president is now only a peripheral actor in choosing nominees and securing their confirmation. Where the framers once intended the Senate to act as a "silent" check on the president's ability to nominate individuals to fill government jobs, today's Senate is far from silent. Senators use confirmation decisions as just another opportunity to gain name recognition, address supporters, and allay the concerns of critics. This is a result of changes to internal Senate norms, including the abandonment of the principles of comity and apprenticeship, as well as changes to the broader political environment. Today, senators see every vote—including votes on nominations—as having electoral implications because of an active media and interest group community that has developed since 1960. As a result, they are more willing to challenge their colleagues, and the White House, than they would have been at mid-century. As Barbara Sinclair has written: "An activist style based on participation in a broader range of issues and on the floor as well as in committee became attractive to more and more senators as the political environment and the Washington political community changed radically in the 1960s and 1970s."[63]

Most importantly, however, today's process is pluralistic, allowing interest groups to play an active part. The presence of interest groups in the confirmation process combines with already existing tensions to increase incentives for senators to delay or oppose presidential nominations. As Mark Silverstein explains with regard to judicial nominees: "The fact that politically powerful groups are willing to invest substantial time and resources to control the judiciary coupled with the erosion of the old Senate norms and the appearance of a new Senate style, has altered the political calculus for every senator confronting a vote on a nominee to the federal bench."[64] Senators' decisions on nonjudicial nominees likewise are now complicated by the presence of interest groups.

The next chapter considers the strategies interest groups use to influence confirmation politics. It demonstrates that interest groups are strategic actors, focusing on certain nominations rather than others and certain senators rather than others, all the while hoping to influence the Senate's confirmation decisions. Chapter 3 also demonstrates the powerful hold that interest groups have on some senators, with regard to their confirmation decisions.

Appendix to Chapter 2:
A Note on Divided Government

The careful reader will notice that I have not included divided government as an explanation for change to the confirmation process.[1] This is because I believe that divided government has exacerbated the effects of the changes I discuss, but that it has not in and of itself been primarily responsible for those changes. Nonetheless, I include some of the existing arguments for and against divided government as an explanatory variable below.

Since the mid-1950s, Republicans and Democrats have had to share control of the legislative and executive branches, and several previous studies have found that divided government makes consensus on legislative initiatives more difficult. For example, V. O. Key (1964) has written: "Common partisan control of executive and legislature does not assure energetic government, but division of party control precludes it."[1] Ripley concurs, noting that in periods of divided control "not much legislation is produced … particularly on domestic matters."[2] The presence of divided government also helps to explain the increasingly partisan and ideological nature of the sparring over presidential nominations. According to *Washington Post* staff writer David Broder: "We have had a number of spirited battles that simply resulted from divided government."[3]

Just as divided government may make it more difficult to reach consensus on legislative proposals, the president and the Senate cannot be counted on to work together to staff the government through the appointment process. According to the CRS researcher Rogelio Garcia: "Divided government creates problems for nominees. [Senate] parties won't be as docile about accepting the president's choices."[4] In 1993, Segal and Spaeth found evidence that the presence of divided government has a significant impact on the likelihood of confirmation for nominees to the Supreme Court.

When presidents have greater difficulty achieving success on domestic policy initiatives, their ability to appoint individuals to carry out such initiatives will usually be thwarted as well. The Senate is not generally anxious to confirm individuals who would support the president's initiatives at the expense of those favored by the Senate. Split party control of the federal government has even altered the dynamics of senatorial courtesy. If there is no home state senator of the president's party with whom to consult, the president may select a nominee who is unacceptable to the home state senators. The result is that the nominee is "orphaned," with no one to push for confirmation. In eras of divided government, presidents may seek out noncontroversial nominees for appointment rather than expend political capital attempting to shepherd a controversial nominee through a hostile Senate controlled by members of the opposing party.

It should be noted, however, that recent studies have found that divided government is an insufficient explanation for changes to the confirmation process.[5] For example, Robert A. Katzmann (1997) writes: "Divided government no doubt contributed to the rise in the length and intensity of the hearings; but today, even when the president and the Senate are of the same party, confirmation hearings consume far more time than they did a generation ago."[6] While divided government may increase the intensity of the confirmation process, it is unlikely that divided government alone can account for changes to the confirmation process. What is more likely is that pressure points in the confirmation process are weakened even further by the presence of split party control.

Interest Groups, American Politics, and the Executive Calendar

[I]nterest groups have injected themselves into the process . . . As we study the politics of judicial confirmations, we need to integrate this new phenomenon into our models and analysis.

Gregory Caldeira, *Kentucky Law Journal,* 1989

When President Clinton announced his nomination of Lani Guinier to head the Department of Justice's Civil Rights Division in 1993, conservative interest groups immediately mobilized against her confirmation. The conservative groups faulted Guinier for being too liberal and for taking controversial positions on racial issues. They labeled her the "quota queen" and claimed that she wanted to dismantle the principle of "one man, one vote."[1] The Institute for Justice and several other vocal opponents of Guinier's nomination ultimately were able to force President Clinton to withdraw her name. When he did, liberal organizations and civil rights groups decried his action. The Guinier controversy demonstrates that in the contemporary confirmation process, interest groups on all sides of the ideological spectrum are ready and willing to pounce on a president and his nominees. It also illustrates the extent to which interest groups are capable of influencing confirmation outcomes.

Of the factors identified in the previous chapter as contributing to the changed nature of the confirmation process, only interest group participation has not already been carefully explored by political scientists. Therefore, I turn to a discussion of interest group participation in this chapter.

There is no doubt that interest groups are active, influential participants in confirmation politics. But just as the confirmation process itself has been overlooked as an area of study, the motivations and influence of interest groups in the process also remain a mystery. This chapter aims to illuminate the motivations, strategies, and levels of influence of interest groups in the confirmation process. It explores the incorporation of interest groups into the confirmation process and considers the techniques and strategies they use as they attempt to influence its outcomes. Finally, the chapter develops the thesis that interest groups, and the money they have interjected in the confirmation process, have inexorably changed confirmation politics in the United States.

Background

In the United States, public policy is often made as a result of the aggregation of competing interests within society. As Robert Dahl explained in 1956: "A central guiding thread of American constitutional development has been the evolution of a political system in which all the active and legitimate groups in the population can make themselves heard at some crucial stage in the process of decision."[2] In 1961, Dahl added: "[M]ost of the actions of government can be explained . . . simply as the result of struggles among groups of individuals with differing interests and varying sources of influence."[3] The contemporary confirmation process, no less than any process of government, is a struggle among groups in society. Just as every interest group wants to see its favored candidate elected to high-ranking office in order to promote policies that are congruent with the group's interests, it also wants people who share its views appointed to serve at the highest levels of the executive and judicial branches.

In the last three decades, interest groups have become extremely prolific players in confirmation politics.[4] In 1994's *The Confirmation Mess*, Stephen L. Carter writes: "[I]n the past twenty years there has been a consistently high degree of involvement [in the confirmation process] by interest groups."[5] Since the late 1970s, such groups have become more frequent participants in the confirmation process across a broad range of nominations. Existing interest groups have retrenched to monitor the confirmation process, and new groups have organized for the sole purpose of influencing presidential appointments.

Although groups have long been interested in who serves in government's highest positions, several factors precluded their regular participation in confirmation politics until well into the twentieth century. First, senators were not popularly elected until passage of the Seventeenth Amendment in 1913. Prior to that time, senators were chosen by state legislatures. The lack of an electoral connection meant that interest groups could exercise little control over senators, and senators had little incentive to pay attention to the preferences of interest groups, not only with regard to confirmations, but also in the legislative process more generally. In addition, until 1929 the Senate considered nominations in executive session and did not permit floor debate. Maltese (1995) has documented the importance of these two turning points for the confirmation process for nominees to the Supreme Court:

> At least two structural factors stalled the institutionalization of routine [interest group] involvement in Senate consideration of Supreme Court nominees in the 1800s. First, senators were not popularly elected, but chosen by state legislatures. This undermined the potent threat of electoral retaliation against senators that interest groups now enjoy. Second, Senate consideration of Supreme Court nominees took place in almost absolute secrecy. . . . Both committee action and floor debate often took place with little discussion and no roll-call votes. Thus, interest groups seldom had either the time or the opportunity to influence the Senate confirmation process.[6]

Through the mid-twentieth century and beyond, the confirmation process usually was closed to interest group participation. Senators, following the age-old norms of the Senate, typically acquiesced to the president or to the Senate leadership. The confirmation process was not yet a political process, and there was no room for interest group participation. Further, the Senate's confirmation process for most nominees was ad hoc, with few committees requiring confirmation hearings and none requiring detailed personal or financial disclosures. The lack of standardized procedures combined with internal Senate norms to make interest group participation a rare event. As Flemming, MacLeod, and Talbert note: "Before Nixon's election, groups testified infrequently."[7]

The routinization of Senate confirmation, which began in the 1970s, changed the nature of the process by creating new levels of Senate bureaucracy that nominees had to navigate in order to be confirmed. Newly enhanced screening procedures created a greater number of "veto" points on nominations within the Senate. The greater number of veto points in turn enhanced opportunities for interest groups to participate in confirmation politics. Committee chairs began to seek out information from interest groups and even encouraged groups to participate in the confirmation politics. Senator Edward M. Kennedy, for example, was especially open to the participation of interest groups in the Judiciary Committee during his tenure as chairman in the late 1970s. Since the late 1970s, interest groups have been active participants in the confirmation process.

Today, interest groups approach the contemporary confirmation process in much the same way that they approach other legislative initiatives. Robert Shogan notes: "[P]residential appointments increasingly are viewed as just another political trophy and the confirmation process just another political battleground."[8] According to former United States Senator David L. Boren (D-OK): "[Interest groups] have turned the confirmation process into something that's not very different than passing a bill."[9] Like Barbara Sinclair found to be true for the legislative process in *Unorthodox Lawmaking*, the presence of interest groups in the confirmation process also has fundamentally altered confirmation dynamics.

Interest Groups and Confirmations

Interest groups are active in confirmation politics for two main reasons. First, they want to influence public policy outcomes. This, of course, is the reason that they spend time and money in the legislative process more generally. Second, groups participate in confirmation politics as part of a process of organizational maintenance. That is, interest groups know that in order to retain current members and attract new ones, they must appear to be doing something. Targeting a presidential nominee is a low-cost, low-sophistication activity that is easily understood by a lay observer of the political process.

Interest groups have learned that they can accomplish both of these goals through calculated participation in confirmation politics. As Mark Silverstein writes: in *Judicious Choices*: "It makes equally good sense for groups engaged in the [confirmation] process to court influence with senators. . . . The Senate has become the most accessible institution for those seeking to influence the national political agenda, with a membership acutely sensitive to the concerns of outside groups that champion causes with a national appeal. Increasingly this means that the proponents and opponents of any nomination will have willing advocates in the Senate."[10]

The primary reason that interest groups get involved in the confirmation process is that they want to influence public policy outcomes. Over the years, interest groups have recognized that the person who serves in appointive office can have a tremendous impact on the kinds of policies that government creates, as well as on policy implementation. By participating in the confirmation process, interest groups hope to ensure that the policies and issues that they care about will be championed by those who serve in appointed positions within the federal government.

Interest groups recognize that because of the networks of policy sub-governments that exist in Washington, D.C., a good relationship with the political appointees who oversee the federal agencies is essential in order to ensure that their group will not be marginalized from legislative and bureaucratic decisions.[11] As James Q. Wilson writes: "[Interest] groups recognize that political decisions are increasingly made in the executive branch rather than in the legislative branch and want not only a share of bureaucratic authority, but also permanent recognition of their claim to bureaucratic authority."[12] Because interest groups know that executive appointees have tremendous influence on public policy, they want to be sure that the individuals serving in the highest positions are not hostile to the group's objectives. Typically, interest groups work against those executive branch nominees whom they feel will be unwilling to consider their points of view.

Similarly, interest groups consider the impact that a judicial nominee will have on legislation and governmental actions that are supported by the group. Beginning in the 1970s, interest groups turned to the federal judiciary as a last-ditch attempt to secure favorable public policy for their group members. Recognizing that the Burger Court was more open to claims of injury by minorities and other disadvantaged groups in society than was the Congress, interest groups increasingly focused their attention on the federal judiciary and the judges and justices nominated to serve it. As Mark Silverstein explains: in *Judicious Choices:* "With the coming of the Burger Court in the early 1970s, an assortment of . . . interests—for example, environmentalists, feminists, consumer groups, political reformers—found in the judiciary an attractive alternative to the other branches. . . . [I]n the modern era . . . increased access to the courts has combined with the new tools of judicial power to make the judiciary an attractive ally for a host of powerful constituent groups."[13]

Interest groups actively monitor and attempt to influence the public policy-making process. To that end, many groups participate in the confirmation process because they want to promote certain types of nominees and bury others. But interest groups also participate in the confirmation process because they want to be certain that their issue positions are on the record. They want to be certain that nominees learn of and understand the issues that are important to their members, and they want to show their members that they are proactive and effective advocates. In their attempts to do this, interest groups also use the confirmation process to practice organizational maintenance. Many interest groups participate in the confirmation process in order to send a signal to their members that they are working hard, or to send a signal to members of the Senate that they are interested in confirmation outcomes. According to one member of the Congressional Research Service, who asked that her name be kept anonymous, interest groups use the confirmation process to assist them in maintaining and enhancing the prestige of the organization. "Interest groups use nominations to gain visibility, and thus, members," she said.[14] Former U.S. Senator David Boren notes, "Some groups even [get involved in confirmation politics] to make money."[15] Interest groups have discovered that participation in the confirmation process is another avenue for fund-raising and for generating additional interest in their causes. According to one newspaper account: "Groups on both sides . . . have often used the nomination fights as fodder in their membership and fund-raising drives."[16]

An example of organizational maintenance activity is the American Jewish Congress's January 1998 press release that decried the slow pace of Senate confirmation for President Clinton's judicial nominees. The press release took no position on any pending nominee and, in fact, made no mention of the impact of the confirmation slowdown on the members of the American Jewish Congress. It served to establish the American Jewish Congress as an interested party to the judicial confirmation slowdown and to send a signal to members of the American Jewish Congress the group's leaders were working on the members' behalf. Similarly, in 1997, the Judicial Selection Monitoring Project produced a fund-raising videotape that stressed the need to "judge the judges" and urged viewers to send in "generous" contributions to aid in the fight against activist judicial nominees. Both of these activities were designed to improve the organization itself, not to urge the confirmation or rejection of any specific individual.

Interest Groups as Strategic Actors

Despite the benefits that accrue to interest groups when they participate in the confirmation process, interest groups do not participate in all confirmations, and not all interest groups join their cohorts in supporting or opposing controversial nominees. Interest groups are just as strategic in their participation in the confirmation process no less as they are in the legislative process more generally. With the hundreds of major appointments that the president is called upon to make every year, interest groups cannot possibly have influence on them all. In addition, groups do not want to waste time and other scarce resources on confirmations that they have no hope of influencing or that are unimportant to their members. For these reasons, interest groups concentrate on affecting those appointments that are most directly related to the implementation of their policy goals. They strategically attempt to weed out nominees who are hostile to their group's goals, while promoting those nominees who they believe will work with them to alter the course of public policy in ways favorable to the group's members.

Because interest groups are most interested in influencing public policy outcomes to conform to the expectations of their members, they closely monitor nominees' policy positions. Those nominees with policy goals or positions that a group deems to be in direct conflict with the goals of its members are often fair game for interest group opposition. For example, in opposing the nomination of James Hormel to be the ambassador to Luxembourg, the Family Research Council (FRC) cited its concern that Hormel lacked respect for the basic family values—values that the FRC's mission directs it to uphold.[17] On the other hand, interest groups may refrain from participating in the confirmation process when they feel that the goals of their members are being adequately met. For example, the National Organization for Women (NOW) was an active participant in confirmation politics for federal judges during the Reagan and Bush administrations but rarely participated during the Clinton administration. According to Linda Berg, who works on confirmation politics in NOW's Washington headquarters, this lack of participation occurred because President Clinton nominated pro-choice judges to the federal bench. But, says Berg: "If an anti-choice president of either party got elected, then we would definitely increase our participation at the lower court level. We would oppose people who are hostile to women."[18] Interest groups are also strategic in that they direct most of their efforts at affecting confirmation outcomes for high-level appointments to the cabinet or to the circuit and Supreme courts. By targeting their scarce resources at influencing nominees to top positions, interest groups hope to influence lower-level appointees such as subcabinet subordinates and district court judges.

Interest groups also pay more attention to the confirmation process for high-level appointees than they do for lower-level appointments. For example, interest groups generally pay more attention to cabinet nominations and Circuit Court of Appeals nominees than they do to subcabinet nominations or nominees to the federal district courts. In this way, interest groups hope to influence a wider range of policymakers by focusing on the most important positions in the federal government.

The Tools and Techniques
of Interest Group Participation

In his 1996 book, *Participation in Congress,* Richard L. Hall notes that legislative decisions are made in two ways—through the *formal* participation of members in committee hearings and markups and on the chamber floor, or through the *informal* conversations members have with one another. The formal/informal distinction also applies to many aspects of the confirmation process and is especially relevant to the dynamics of interest group participation.

Interest group participation in the confirmation process is composed of these same dynamics. Interest groups participate *formally* in the process by appearing at committee hearings or making their position a part of the public record by submitting materials to the committee to be included as part of the formal hearing record. Groups also participate *informally* through engaging in behind-the-scenes contact with members of the Senate. Interest groups borrow extensively from their legislative strategies in attempting to influence confirmation outcomes through the informal mechanisms that are available to them. When lobbying senators on behalf of, or in opposition to, a nominee, interest groups write letters, make phone calls, lobby senators face-to-face, hold press conferences, stage demonstrations, organize petition drives, gather information, or try to mobilize the grassroots membership of their organizations to pressure senators. They also deliver large sums of money to senators who do as they wish.

Formal Interest Group Participation

Until the mid-1980s, the vast majority of interest group participation in the confirmation process was formal. Formal participation is that set of activities taking place within the regular governmental procedures of the confirmation process. It includes such activities as testifying at confirmation hearings or submitting testimony to the hearing record. For example, Anne Burford, President Ronald Reagan's pick to head the Environmental Protection Agency, describes her confirmation hearing: "At the end of the Senators' question period, the chairman thanked me . . . and then he turned the microphone over to a panel of environmentalists who'd filed statements in response to my nomination (most, though not all of them, in opposition), and had asked for the opportunity to question me."[19]

Interest group testimony, such as that which took place at the end of Burford's confirmation hearing, is an excellent example of formal participation in the confirmation process. Formal participation may also include submitting materials to the committee with the intent to make them part of the permanent hearing record.

Informal Interest Group Participation

The use of formal techniques by interest groups began to wane in 1987, following Robert Bork's failed attempt at confirmation. Katzmann (1997) notes that the Bork nomination took interest group participation in a different direction—toward more informal techniques. He writes: "With the Bork confirmation proceedings came a new dimension to interest group activity. In addition to trying to influence senators directly, several groups sought to reach public opinion."[20] To do so, many groups stepped up the use of techniques geared at indirectly influencing senators' confirmation decisions. Worried that interest groups would again create a spectacle out of the confirmation process, Senate committees simultaneously began to restrict the opportunities for them to participate formally. Beginning just a decade after Senate committees had first opened their doors to the widespread participation of interest groups, committees began to close off avenues of formal participation to the interest groups who had once been welcome to participate in hearings.

In the contemporary confirmation process, formal interest group participation is viewed with skepticism, and efforts have been made to reduce the amount of formal influence groups have on the confirmation process. For example, in one of his first official acts of the 105th Congress, Senate Judiciary Committee Chairman Orrin Hatch severed ties with the American Bar Association (ABA) in February 1997. According to the ABA's report on the activities of its the Standing Committee on Judiciary, the Senate had requested the ABA's input on every judicial nomination since 1948.[21] However, on February 18, 1997, Hatch's office issued a press release stating: "Sen. Hatch . . . has concluded that, while individual senators are free to weigh the input of any group how they see fit, the ABA should not play an official role."[22] Hatch's move to eliminate the ABA came after the House Republican Policy Committee had issued a policy statement that read: "The ABA consistently prefers liberal nominees to equally well-qualified conservatives. . . . The ABA . . . has no right to a formal role in the process of judicial selection or confirmation."[23] With Hatch's February 1997 statement, forty years of good relations between the Judiciary Committee and the ABA officially ended.[24] Further, Hatch's actions with regard to the ABA sent a clear message that interest groups were not welcome to participate formally in judicial confirmations, the largest group of nominees the Senate considers in any given year. According to one Republican senator, who agreed to be interviewed on the condition of anonymity: "Senator Hatch says, and I agree, that interest groups shouldn't have a formal role in a confirmation hearing. What's the use of hauling a bunch of them in to testify, when you can meet with them outside the hearing room?"

Yet, this Republican senator continued: "Just because [interest groups] don't testify, doesn't mean they don't have influence. Most of the time, it's below the surface. It's like a duck or a swan, most of the activity is underwater, where you can't see it." As the avenues of formal participation have become less and less available in the 1990s, interest groups' tactics have shifted. The vast majority of interest group participation in the contemporary confirmation process is informal. Organizations increasingly have turned to informal methods of participation as the chairs of many Senate committees have sought to prevent interest groups from testifying at confirmation hearings. Cut off from other, more formal avenues, interest groups now work primarily behind closed doors to persuade senators to act in ways supported by the interest groups. And as they have developed effective informal strategies, many groups have found they no longer have a need to participate formally in the confirmation process. As one study explains: "Informal consultation behind closed doors makes public testimony less critical to the groups' effectiveness."[25] Not insignificantly, interest groups can engage in tactics behind closed doors, such as promising campaign funds or threatening retaliation, that they cannot do in public.

Informal interest group participation includes activities that are designed to influence confirmation outcomes but that take place outside of the formal stages of the confirmation process. These activities are the private lobbying efforts that occur out of the public's line of sight. The most important, and most often used, method of informal participation is the direct lobbying of a senator on a particular nomination (either in person or by letter or telephone). But interest groups use direct lobbying in concert with other techniques. Interest groups disseminate information, try to set the Senate's agenda, promote or block a nominee's confirmation, and provide incentives to senators. They do all of these things without ever setting foot in a committee hearing room.

When the White House announces a nomination, interest groups on both sides of the ideological spectrum spring into action. Their first priority is to gather as much information as possible on the nominee. Interest groups will look at any records available to them to try to determine whether to support or oppose a nominee. According to Ronald Weich, former Chief Counsel to Senator Edward M. Kennedy, the advent of on-line databases makes it especially easy for interest groups to quickly determine a nominee's profile. "I can type in a name, punch a button, and see everything a nominee has ever written or see every time their name has appeared in the newspaper," says Weich.[26]

All interest groups who participate in the confirmation process share information with senators and their staffs. These groups recognize that just like other legislative decisions, information is at a premium in the confirmation process. Senators and staffers will gratefully accept any information that interest groups provide, often without any independent effort to check its accuracy or veracity. According to a Republican senator, speaking on the condition of anonymity:

> The good side [of interest group participation] is that many times they dig up information that we didn't know. The down side is that some members of the Senate will not look beyond what the group says. I've caught [the groups] a couple of times when they said one thing, but when you looked, yeah, the facts are there, sorta, but they didn't tell the whole thing, or put it in context. The danger is that the interest group puts its own spin on it. So what happens . . . do members look beyond? The problem is a question of resources and time. If it didn't come out of their committee, they look for a member of their party on the committee and they ask him. And, there are members on both sides who just take what the groups tell them, and don't do any independent checking, especially when it's a group they identify with.

Interest groups recognize that their work often goes unchecked. While some work diligently to provide senators with the information they need to make informed decisions about presidential nominees, other groups will distort nominees' records as they attempt to persuade senators to vote the way that the group prefers.

For most groups, information dissemination is a way to get a foot in the door with members of the Senate. It provides senators with important facts about a nominee to which they might not otherwise have access. Alex Acosta, director of the conservative Project on the Judiciary, sees the gathering and dissemination of information about nominees to federal judgeships as his most important job. "My goal is to educate people inside the beltway," says Acosta. To that end, he engages in a variety of information-gathering techniques: "I get the information that's available in paper form, like past opinions, speeches, and law review pieces. Then I call people and ask them 'What do you know of "X" individual?' Then I give out the information. I might cull out the controversial information, but I'm not all that proactive. I usually let the information speak for itself. I do not do blast faxes. I don't send around newsletters. I don't send weekly e-mails. I'm more of a clearinghouse."

Interest groups can, and do, fulfill an important role in the confirmation process by providing members of the Senate information that neither they nor their staffers have the time or resources to collect on their own. By disseminating information to senators, interest groups can help senators to make educated and informed decisions about whether to confirm a presidential nominee. At the same time, however, when interest groups distribute information that is false, misleading, or biased, such groups may ruin a nominee's chances at confirmation. Further, when senators and their staffs take and use information that was gathered by interest groups, they establish a relationship with the groups that the groups' leaders often attempt to exploit.

With regard to agenda setting, interest groups try to promote nominees that they care about while preventing the nominees that they oppose from coming to a vote in the Senate. They do this by influencing the Senate's agenda. As Shogan writes: "The interest groups cannot always decide who gets confirmed and who gets rejected, but they can determine who gets contested—and that is sufficient to give them plenty of weight with both the executive and legislative branches."[27]

Agenda setting actually begins with the president's selection process. Many interest groups use their contacts in the executive branch to tip them off as to whom the current administration is considering. When they find out that the president is considering nominating someone that they find to be objectionable, many interest groups try to persuade the White House not to risk a confirmation fight in the Senate by making the nomination. For example, Eliot Mincberg the legal director for People For the American Way explains that when the Republicans controlled the White House: "We'd go to the Administration and try to talk them out of nominating people."[28] Conversely, interest groups try to promote candidates to the White House personnel selection staff with the hope that their preferred candidate will get the nomination.

Interest groups use their allies in the Senate to convince the White House to nominate certain types of nominees and not to nominate others. For example, when Washington Senator Slade Gorton brokered a deal with the White House to nominate Barbara Durham, the Chief Justice of the Washington Supreme Court, for a circuit court judgeship, the Alliance for Justice circulated a draft of a lengthy report that was highly critical of Durham's record.[29] It was an attempt to persuade senators to pressure the

White House not to honor the deal with Gorton. The report concluded: "In sum, Chief Justice Durham's record and rulings suggest that she will be at odds with President Clinton's vision for the federal judiciary."[30] The Alliance was also hoping to persuade some senators to vote against Durham if she received a nomination. When Clinton officially nominated Durham in January 1999, the Alliance report was publicly released to widespread coverage in newspapers across the country.

Interest groups are not always successful at persuading the White House to kill a potential nomination. This is because frequently the groups are unable to determine whom the administration is considering for the nomination. Mary DeOreo, minority staff investigator for the Senate Judiciary Committee, explains that often, "The groups don't know [who the president is considering]. They're not that far ahead of the curve."[31] Thus, the groups typically focus on nominees already pending in the Senate.

Interest groups usually begin their campaigns in favor or against a nominee at the committee level by trying to push a nominee onto, or keep a nominee off of, the confirmation hearing agenda. According to Michael Carrasco, a former nominations clerk for the Senate Judiciary Committee, this is because most aspects of the confirmation process—especially who gets a hearing and when—"generally are worked out at the [committee] staff level."[32] Further, according to one senator: "The action is not on the Senate floor. It's at the committee level. If a nominee gets to the Senate floor, he or she will probably be confirmed—it's almost always 80–20 or 70–30. It's a rare case when the vote on the floor matters. The question is, do they get to the Senate floor?" By working at the committee level, where they only have to influence a few senators, interest groups recognize that they can affect confirmation outcomes to the same extent that they could if they focused on the entire Senate, but for a lot less time and resources.

Once an organization has determined whether to oppose or support a nomination, it typically will begin to exercise a strategy of informing the senators and staffers of the committee or jurisdiction by issuing a letter or report stating its views. For groups who oppose a nominee, this is also an attempt to set the committee's agenda and prevent consideration of a nominee. If communications from interest groups raise concerns in the minds of staff investigators, a nomination may be delayed or may simply be killed by the committee. According to Carrasco, "if there is too much opposition, the [committee] chairman might not want to move a nominee. You don't want to embarrass someone, you want to save face for the nominee."[33]

Often, committee staff investigators cannot corroborate information brought to them by an interest group or do not feel that the information is credible. So a nomination may move forward regardless of interest group opposition. If the groups cannot convince committee staffers that a nominee should not be granted a hearing or confirmed, they may refocus their efforts on individual senators. As Richard Hall (1996, 10) notes in *Participation in Congress,* in the U.S. Congress, "not all members are involved in each legislative decision."[34] Like the Senate's deliberative process, more generally, the design of the Senate's confirmation process permits a single senator to influence confirmation outcomes. As was discussed in the previous chapter, a single senator may prevent an individual from gaining confirmation by placing a hold on his or her nomination. Any senator can personally contact the committee chair to oppose scheduling the nominee for a hearing or can place a hold on a nomination should the nominee be voted out of committee. According to Carrasco and Melody Barnes, Chief Counsel to Senator Edward M. Kennedy, interest group pressure may persuade a senator to work against the nomination.[35] And a single senator may be enough to thwart confirmation for some nominees. Thus, for groups who support a nomination, it is important to shore up as much support as possible and to reduce the risk of opposition.

The reverse scenario is also true. Both Carrasco and Barnes point out that a single senator's work on behalf of a nomination can be sufficient to move a nominee forward, and Barnes notes that pressure from an interest group or set of groups with whom a senator has worked closely may encourage a senator to go to bat for a nominee.[36] Carrasco notes: "The most important tool a senator has is his vote. . . . I wouldn't be surprised if at any time a nominee were confirmed because one senator traded his vote."[37] Interest groups know that at any time, a single senator's efforts may convince the chair of the committee to schedule a hearing. Despite a nominee's controversial record, a committee chair generally will not deny a nominee a hearing when pushed by another member of the Senate, according to Carrasco. Thus, groups who support a nomination typically will try to persuade individual members of the Senate to champion their nominee, even as the opposition is working to persuade individual senators to put a hold on the nomination.

Interest groups are not always successful at setting the Senate's confirmation agenda, nor are their reports and analyses always enough to persuade senators to vote in the direction they prefer. So groups pursue additional means of persuading senators to vote the way the groups would like by pulling. The groups pull out their two "big guns"—the senators' constituents and campaign contributions. The impact of the former is without compare; there is disagreement about the impact of the latter.

To reach senators' constituents, interest groups turn to outside, grassroots means of trying to influence the confirmation process. Often, their strategies are borrowed from legislative and electoral activities in which they already engage. Groups engage in "astroturfing"—the instigating of grassroots campaigns—and use their state and local affiliates to mobilize support for or opposition to pending nominees. For example, in 1998, several Hispanic organizations organized a petition drive in New York State to urge former Senator Alfonse D'Amato (R-NY) to push the nomination of Sonia Sotomayor to the Second Circuit Court of Appeals to a vote. The drive yielded the signatures of hundreds of New Yorkers who demanded that Sotomayor be brought to a vote. The Hispanic groups hoped that the petitions, coupled with D'Amato's impending senatorial election, would convince him to push the Senate leadership for a vote on Sotomayor's nomination. The overriding goal was to link Sotomayor's confirmation vote with the electoral process.

Interest groups know that senators will not often vote against the wishes of a large number of their constituents. In fact, in the contemporary confirmation process, senators will often seek out constituent opinions before casting confirmation votes. According to Ronald Weich: "Too few senators have a sense of history and our constitutional scheme. They want to see what their constituents think."[38] Indeed, there is evidence that senators are paying attention to constituents' and grassroots organizations' views on nominations. When Susan Oki Mollway was confirmed by only a six-vote majority to a seat on the Hawaii District Court, the director of the Judicial Selection Monitoring Project praised conservative senators who had voted against the nomination, saying: "The 34 No votes show that the Senate heard the cry of Grassroots America to stop this nominee."[39]

The most important incentive that interest groups can offer is the ability to affect a senator's electoral chances. Interest groups have learned that all senators respond to constituency pressures and that many respond to financial incentives, and the groups act accordingly. In the contemporary confirmation process, some interest groups devote substantial resources to educating the public about issues or about public officials' voting behaviors on presidential nominations. Many also provide resources directly to candidates through financial and "in-kind" contributions. These groups then turn around and threaten to make the senators' votes an issue in the upcoming election.

More than one hundred organizations routinely publish "vote scorecards," which are designed to give the public a quick reference tool for determining how their representatives or their senators voted on legislation that is important to the group. In recent years, some interest groups, including the Christian Coalition, have begun to include senators' confirmation votes among the votes the groups select. For example, in April 1998, the Christian Coalition released its 1998 U.S. Senate Scorecard. Compiled every election year, the scorecard charts senators' votes on legislation or issues on which the Christian Coalition has taken a position. In 1998, two of the twelve votes that the Coalition used to rate senators were confirmation decisions—the confirmation of David Satcher to be U.S. Surgeon General and the confirmation of Margaret Morrow to be a federal judge for the district of central California. Two years earlier, the scorecard had included no confirmation votes.[40]

Liberal groups also employ the threat of voter scorecards to attempt to influence the Senate's confirmation decisions. Unlike their conservative counterparts, however, liberal organizations have threatened to punish senators for delaying votes on several nominees. For example, after their nominations to the circuit courts stalled in the Senate, federal district court judges Richard Paez and Sonia Sotomayor received overwhelming support from interest groups representing the Hispanic community. In June 1998, two dozen members of the National Hispanic Leadership Agenda (NHLA) marched from the front of the U.S. Supreme Court to the offices of Senate Majority Leader Trent Lott inside the U.S. Capitol to protest what they believed were inordinate delays in confirming President Clinton's Hispanic judicial nominees. In a press release, the NHLA declared: "In October, the NHLA will publish a scorecard rating the voting record of each member of Congress and the Senate on legislation that affects Hispanics."[41]

Rhett DeHart, formerly counsel to Senator Jeff Sessions (R-AL) and currently counsel to Senator Orrin Hatch (R-UT), asserts that voter scorecards are an effective way to provide senators an electoral context to their confirmation decisions. He says: "I've noticed for certain controversial nominees [some interest groups] send out letters saying 'We're gonna score your vote on this person's nomination.' That's kind of a new angle and I think that absolutely has an effect [on senators' voting behaviors]."[42] Michael Carrasco, minority nominations clerk for the Senate Judiciary Committee adds: "The reason a bunch of judges received 'no' votes [from some senators] is because the Christian Coalition and other groups came out and said 'we're scoring.' To some senators, having a 100 percent record with some groups helps define their [legislative] record."[43]

The Republican senator who spoke on the condition of anonymity, added: "This is a very complex issue. [A senator] may not want an interest group beating them up. If an interest group says this is a key vote, we're watching this vote, then the easy thing to do is to vote the way the group wants." A Senate Democrat adds: "My colleagues who have announced their intention to seek reelection are often more sensitive to these interest groups and pay close attention to the messages of these groups."

Senators pay attention to the interest groups because they know that they cannot afford to ignore the electoral consequences of confirmation decisions. As former Senator David Boren (D-OK) states: "Senators let it happen because they're under so much pressure by their constituents."[44] In the contemporary confirmation process, interest groups put pressure on senators to consider the ramifications of their confirmation votes. "Their power is their mailing list," says the anonymous Republican senator. "They can send out letters and make phone calls to everyone in your state. Within 48 hours you have a couple hundred people calling your office bitching about your vote." According to Project on the Judiciary's Alex Acosta: "Groups play an important role because groups remind the Senate about its responsibility to do the right thing." "And," he adds, "groups can reward Senators when they do the right thing."[45] Interest groups also try to punish senators for failing to act in the way the groups prefer.

Punishing and rewarding senators may also have a financial component. For many senators, campaign contributions may make the best incentives. At the outset of this section it must be mentioned that campaign contributions, lobbying costs, and soft money are exceedingly difficult to track. Even when it is possible to determine the amount of money spent by an organization for lobbying or campaigning, it is difficult to determine how much money was spent lobbying on any particular piece of legislation or nomination. Nonetheless, money is a crucial weapon for interest groups and Political Action Committees, and it has found its way into the confirmation process.

Evidence suggests that money is important in the confirmation process, both with regard to campaign contributions and in terms of the amount of money spent to lobby in Washington, D.C., and at the grass roots. Congress itself addressed the role of money in the confirmation process when, in 1995, it included a provision in the Lobbying Disclosure Act. Section 3 (8)(iv) of the Lobbying Disclosure Act of 1995 requires organizations to report their activities with regard to lobbying that concerns "(iv) the nomination or confirmation of a person for a position subject to confirmation by the Senate."

Of the more than four hundred organizations who were active in the confirmation process during the 105th Congress, 25 percent also made financial contributions or spent significant amounts of money lobbying. During the 105th Congress, more than $103 million was spent by organizations who participated in the confirmation process to lobby the Congress.[46] This figure, which is based on reports filed under the Lobbying Disclosure Act of 1995, does not include money spent by interest groups to influence the grass roots, nor does it include money spent by organizations to "educate" members of the Senate about nominees. Many of the groups who have been most active in the confirmation process are what are known by federal tax law as 501 C(3) organizations, which are organizations that are educative in function. These groups, while claiming not to engage in lobbying (which would cause them to lose their tax-exempt status) engage in activities designed solely to "inform" senators about nominees. These activities do not, under federal law, have to be reported as lobbying. So, for example, costs associated with the activities of the Judicial Selection Monitoring Project, which included the organization of grassroots and organizational campaigns against President Bill Clinton's judicial nominees, are not documented because they are not considered to be lobbying expenses. The Judicial Selection Monitoring Project is registered with the Internal Revenue Service (IRS) as a 501 C(3) organization.

While it is impossible to know for certain precisely how many lobbying dollars were spent on lobbying activities related to the confirmation process, one senator acknowledges that his staff spends "some time" meeting and talking with interest groups concerned about the confirmation process. If even a fraction of the $103 million dollars spent during the 105th Congress by groups who were active in the confirmation process were used to lobby senators regarding their confirmation decisions, it would result in a substantial sum of money spent to influence confirmation outcomes.

In addition to lobbying, interest groups and PACs who are active in the confirmation process also have contributed to senatorial campaigns. Many Senate staffers believe that the senators who participated in the Judicial Selection Monitoring Project's fund-raising videotape were offered access to the Heritage Foundation's mailing list. While not a direct contribution, the list itself would have been valuable for the access it would provide to wealthy, conservative contributors.[47] It should be noted, however, that there is not universal agreement that campaign contributions influence confirmation outcomes. Speaking on the condition of anonymity, a Republican senator stated: "Campaign contributions, money doesn't have much to do with this. Interest groups' power has never been their money. . . . They give you $5,000 or $10,000, but so what? My reelection campaign is going to cost $8 million. Money in nominations just doesn't matter much, it's what [the groups] can do. So that's where you get your power in this, as a group." A Democratic senator, who also agreed to discuss these issues on the condition of anonymity, agrees: "I am certain that interest groups engage in lobbying activities, and I have been told that in some cases these activities include campaign contributions. As to their level of influence, I do not believe campaign contributions play any significant role in the confirmation process." Former Senator Warren Rudman (R-NH) categorically denies that campaign contributions have any substantial impact on senators' confirmation votes, although he acknowledges that groups give large sums of money hoping that senators will be responsive on a wide range of issues and that "eventually you would get to a confirmation."[48]

Despite these senators' protests, anecdotal evidence suggests that money has become an important motivator in the confirmation process. Michael Schattman, whose nomination was derailed in part by conservative interest groups, explains: "There's certainly a symbiotic relationship between some members of the Senate with regard to fund-raising and defeating nominees that has been underestimated."[49] Tom Jipping, Director of the Judicial Selection Monitoring Project, agrees that money has begun to influence the confirmation process in negative ways: "The [confirmation] process operates in a patronage, exclusionary environment. Senators are more interested in getting a former law partner or contributor a judgeship than they are in getting qualified judges."[50] In a conversation, Scott Olson of Common Cause agreed: "There has been a history of ambassadorships going to big campaign contributors,"[51] and a staff member from the Senate Foreign Relations Committee notes: "Take for example the recess appointments that were just made. If you look at the three foreign policy nominees that [Bill] Clinton just recess appointed, they're all big campaign donors. That's why you had the DNC [Democratic National Committee] and several of the candidates pushing for them to be recess appointed."[52] Jipping believes that it takes the work of organizations like his, and others, to counteract instances of patronage in the confirmation process. The irony, of course, is that money is also used by outside groups, including Jipping's, to influence who gets confirmed.

Money now structures many facets of the Senate confirmation process, from grassroots lobbying of senators, to campaign contributions when senators "do the right thing." While rewarding senators with campaign contributions may not affect all senators, some clearly are affected. Further, interest groups are now spending vast sums of money to lobby at the grassroots levels and behind the scenes of Senate confirmation hearings.

Conclusion

In a pluralist system, public policy results from the struggle between and among groups in society. To the extent that governmental institutions are involved, they are merely the arenas within which groups struggle for supremacy. Institutions provide boundaries and bear the ultimate responsibility for enactment and enforcement of public policies. But interest groups constrain the policy options available to lawmakers. Earl Latham (1965) articulated this situation well, noting that the products of the legislative process tend to reflect the preferences of successful groups in society. In his view: "The legislature referees the group struggle, ratifies the victories of the successful coalitions, and records the terms of the surrenders. . . . The legislative vote on any issue tends to represent the composition of strength, i.e. the balance of power, among the contending groups at the moment of voting. What may be called public policy is the equilibrium reached in this struggle at any given moment."[53]

Robert Katzmann adds: "Legislators, eager to be reelected, avoid choices on critical issues that could antagonize energized groups. They do not work to develop coherent policy, but instead seek to accommodate the preferences of interest groups through *ad hoc* bargaining."[54] In the contemporary confirmation process, senators now respond to interest groups in much the same way as they do in other legislative decisions. The result is that interest groups are able to exercise some control over confirmation outcomes as senators strive for a middle ground in a process that provides only two alternate choices.

Interest groups' techniques vary depending on whether they support or oppose a presidential nominee. Interest groups who support nominees appear to engage in more public techniques, while interest groups who oppose nominees seem more likely to try to influence senators in more circumspect ways. For example, in 1998, several interest groups held rallies outside the Supreme Court to demonstrate their support for Hispanic nominees whose nominations were not moving forward in the Senate. In contrast, the Judicial Selection Monitoring Project produced a fund-raising videotape that was sent to individuals on a conservative mailing list, asking for help to prevent President Clinton's judicial nominees from being confirmed.[55] Similarly, evidence suggests that interest groups opposing presidential nominees approached senators in private to seek promises of holds or filibusters on the nominees they deemed unacceptable, while groups who supported nominees seemed to seek public assurances that the nominees would be brought to a vote. It is likely that this difference in strategy results from the fact that it takes only one senator to delay or prevent confirmation, through the use of a hold or similar delaying tactic, while it takes at least fifty-one senators to confirm a nominee. Interest groups recognize this distinction and tailor their strategies to the goals they wish to achieve. This chapter has explored the roles and functions of interest groups in the confirmation process. From this exploration it is clear that interest groups use the confirmation process in much the same way that they use other legislative processes. Interest groups try to influence public policy outcomes by weeding out nominees who are hostile to their groups' goals. But interest groups are strategic actors. They typically target only those nominees and those positions that are likely to have the most impact on the groups' abilities to achieve their objectives. In this way, groups can conserve scarce resources while still influencing public policy outcomes.

The dynamics of interest group participation in the confirmation process have changed from what they were even just two decades ago. In the 1970s, interest groups used the formal procedures of the confirmation process by testifying at hearings and submitting materials to the hearing record. Beginning in the late 1980s, the Senate began to close off opportunities for interest groups to participate formally in the confirmation process. Today, interest groups take full advantage of the wide range of informal techniques that are available to them, including setting the agenda, disseminating information, creating incentives for senators, and punishing and rewarding senators for their confirmation decisions. In the contemporary confirmation process, interest groups use a wider range of techniques to influence senators than they once did. But their goals remain the same: to influence public policy and to maintain their organization's membership roster and prestige.

The next two chapters provide practical measures of interest group participation in the confirmation process. Chapter 4 explores the dynamics of interest group participation in the confirmation process for federal judges. It is clear that interest groups' formal participation has markedly declined with regard to judicial confirmations as the Senate Judiciary Committee has reduced opportunities for groups to give testimony and submit materials. But the following chapter illustrates that groups have become extremely innovative in the techniques that they use. Chapter 5 examines interest group participation in the confirmation process for cabinet secretaries-designate and ambassadors. While formal interest group participation in confirmations for these nominees appears not to have been as drastically curtailed, it is clear that interest groups are now borrowing extensively from the techniques they refined in the judicial confirmations to attempt to influence confirmation outcomes for cabinet and ambassadorial nominees. Together, the next two chapters provide important evidence of the extent to which interest groups shape the contemporary confirmation process.

Appendix to Chapter 3:
Interest Groups in the Confirmation
Process, 105th Congress

The following is a list of those organizations that expressed an opinion about one or more nominees, or about the confirmation process in general, during the 105th Congress. Some organizations listed below were active participants in the process, compiling information and communicating it to senators. Other organizations merely signed on to materials produced by another organization.

This list was compiled by a search of the Congressional Record and by an examination of available committee transcripts of confirmation hearings. Every effort has been made to provide a complete listing of interest groups that participated in the process during the 105th Congress.

60 Plus Association
Accuracy in Media
Adirondack Solidarity Alliance
AIDS Action Council
Alabama Citizens for Truth
Alabama Family Alliance
Alliance for America
Alliance Defense Fund
Alliance for Justice
American Academy of Child and Adolescent Psychiatry
American Academy of Family Physicians
American Academy of Pediatrics
American Association of Christian Schools
American Association of Clinical Endocrinologists
American Association of Health Plans

American Association of Neurological Surgeons
American Association of Nurse Anesthetists
American Association of Public Health Physicians
American Association of Small Property Ownership
American Association of University Women
American Bar Association
American Cancer Society
American Center for Law and Justice
American Center for Legislative Reform
American Citizens and Lawmen Association
American Coalition of Life Activists
American College of Chest Physicians
American College of Emergency Physicians
American College of Gastroenterology
American College of Nuclear Physicians
American College of Obstetricians and Gynecologists
American College of Physicians
American College of Preventative Medicine
American Conservative Union
American Correctional Association
American Council on Economic Security
American Council for Immigration Reform
American Dental Association
American Diabetes Association
American Dietetic Association
American Family Association
American Family Association of Alabama
American Family Association of Kentucky
American Family Association of Michigan
American Family Association of New Jersey
American Family Association of New York
American Family Association of Oregon
American Family Association of Virginia, Inc.
American Family Defense Coalition
American Focus
American Foundation (OH)
American Freedom Crusade
American Gastroenterological Association
American GI Forum
American Hospital Association

American Immigration Control
American Jewish Congress
American Loggers Solidarity
American Lung Association
American Medical Association
American Medical Group Association
American Medical Women's Association
American Nurses Association
American Policy Center
American Pro-Constitutional Association
American Psychiatric Association
American Public Health Association
American Public Philosophy Institute
American Rights Coalition
American Society of Cataract and Refractive Surgery
American Society of Clinical Pathologists
American Society of Pediatric Nephrology
American Society of Reproductive Medicine
American Society for Transplant Physicians
American Sovereignty Action Project
Americanism Foundation
Americans for Democratic Action
Americans for Tax Reform
Americans for Voluntary School Prayer
Arizona Eagle Forum
Arizona Policy Union
Arkansas Policy Foundation
Armstrong Foundation
Asian American Bar Association of the Delaware Valley
Asian American Legal Defense and Education Fund
Association of American Medical Colleges
Association of Attorney-Mediators
Association of the Bar of the City of New York
Association of Maternal and Child Health Programs
Association of New Jersey Rifle and Pistol Clubs
Association of Schools of Public Health
Association of State and Territorial Health Officials
Barrister Association of Philadelphia
Bazelon Center for Mental Health Law
Black Women Lawyers Association of Los Angeles

Boston Bar Association
Business and Professional People for the Public Interest
California Correctional Peace Officers Association
California Medical Association
California Narcotics Officers Association
California Women Lawyers
Californians for America
Campaign for Working Families
Capital Research Center
Catholic League for Religious and Civil Rights
Center for Arizona Policy
Center for Equal Opportunity
Center for Faith and Freedom, Inc.
Center for Individual Rights
Center for Law in the Public Interest
Center for Law and Social Policy
Center for New Black Leadership
Center for the New West
Center for Public Representation
Center for Reclaiming America
Center for Reproductive Law and Policy
Center for Science in the Public Interest
Chicago Committee for Civil Rights Under Law
Children's Defense Fund
Children's Health Fund
Christian Action Network
Christian Civic League of Maine
Christian Coalition
Christian Coalition of California
Christian Coalition of Georgia
Christian Coalition of Hawaii
Christian Coalition of Kansas
Christian Coalition of Kentucky
Christian Coalition of Louisiana
Christian Coalition of Montana
Christian Coalition of New York
Christian Coalition of North Carolina
Christian Coalition of Pennsylvania
Christian Coalition of Rhode Island
Christian Committees of Correspondence

Christian Exchange, Inc.
Christian Home Educators of Kentucky
Christian Home Educators of New Hampshire
Christian Values in Action Coalition, Inc.
Citizens Against Repressive Zoning
Citizens Against Violent Crime
Citizens for Action Now
Citizens for Better Government
Citizens for Budget Reform
Citizens for Community Values
Citizens for Excellence in Education
Citizens for Independent Courts
Citizens for Judicial Reform
Citizens' Justice Programs
Citizens for Law and Order
Citizens for Responsible Government
Citizens United
Coalition Against Pornography
Coalition for America
Coalition for Constitutional Liberties
Coalition for Health Funding
Coalition on Urban Renewal and Education
College of American Pathologists
Colorado for Family Values
Colorado Term Limits Coalition
Commercial Law Affiliates
Community Law Center
Concerned Women for America
Concerned Women for America of Virginia
Congress of Neurological Surgeons
Consumer's Union
Coral Ridge Ministries
Council of State and Territorial Epidemiologists
Crooked Lake North Shore Association
Defenders of Property Rights
Delaware Home Education Association
Dialogue on Diversity
Direct Legislation League
Disability Rights Education and Defense Fund
Eagle Forum

Eagle Forum of Alabama
Eagle Forum of Arkansas
Eagle Forum of California
Eagle Forum of Delaware
Eagle Forum of Florida
Eagle Forum of Hawaii
Eagle Forum of Idaho
Eagle Forum—Illinois
Eagle Forum of Louisiana
Eagle Forum of Minnesota
Eagle Forum of Mississippi
Eagle Forum of Ohio
Eagle Forum of Washington
Eagle Forum of Washington, DC
Eagle Forum of Wisconsin
Education Law Center
Emergency Nurses Association
Employment Law Center
English First
Equal Rights Advocates
Eugene (OR) Police Employees' Association
Fairness to Land Owners Committee
Families USA
Family of the Americas Foundation
Family First
Family Foundation (VA)
Family Friendly Libraries
Family Policy Network
Family Protection Lobby of Maryland
Family Research Council
Family Research Institute of Wisconsin
Family Taxpayers Network
Family Violence Prevention Fund
First Principles, Inc.
Focus on the Family
Food Research and Action Center
Fraternal Order of Police
Fraternal Order of Police—Philadelphia Lodge
Freedom Foundation
Freedom in Medicine Association

Frontiers of Freedom
Georgia Family Council
Georgia Public Policy Foundation
Georgia Sport Shooting Association
Greenfield Movement to Impeach Federal Judge John T. Nixon
Gun Owners Action League Help America First
Gun Owners of South Carolina
Hispanic Association of Colleges and Universities
Hispanic Association on Corporate Responsibility
Hispanic National Bar Association
Hispanic United of Maryland
Home School Legal Defense Association
Hospital and Health System Association of Pennsylvania
Human Life Alliance of MN
Human Rights Council
Illinois Citizens for Life
Illinois Family Institute
Illinois Right to Life Committee
Independence Institute
Independent American Party of Nevada
Independent Women's Forum
Indiana Conservative Union
Indiana Family Institute
Institute for Justice
Institute for Media Education
Institute for Public Representation
Interamerican College of Physicians and Surgeons
Intercultural Cancer Council
International Union of Police Associations, AFL-CIO
Iowa Family Policy Center
Joint Action Committee for Political Affairs
Judicial Selection Monitoring Project
Judicial Watch, Inc.
Justice for Homicide Victims
Justice for Murder Victims
Juvenile Law Center
Kansas Conservative Union
Kansas Family Research Institute
Kansas Taxpayers Network
Labor Council for Latin American Advancement

Land Rights Foundation
Landmark Legal Foundation
Lane County (OR) Peace Officers Association
Latino Civil Rights Center
Law Enforcement Alliance of America
Lawyers Club of San Diego
Leadership Conference on Civil Rights
League of American Families
League of United Latin American Citizens
Libertarian Party of Utah
Liberty Foundation
Liberty Matters
Life Advocacy Alliance
Life Coalition International
Life Decisions International
Local Government Council
Los Angeles County Bar Association
Los Angeles County Professional Peace Officers Association
Madison Project
Maine Grassroots Coalition
Maine State Bar Association
March of Dimes Birth Defects Foundation
Maryland Conservative Caucus
Massachusetts Family Institute
Medina County Christian Coalition
Memory of Victims Everywhere (M.O.V.E.)
Memphis (TN) Bar Association
Mexican American Legal Defense and Education Fund
Michigan Decency Action Council
Michigan Family Forum
Milwaukee Police Association
Mississippi American Family Association
Mississippi Family Council
Mississippi State Medical Association
Missouri Association of Teaching Christian Homes
Missouri Christian Coalition
Morality Action Committee
National Abortion Rights Action League
National Abstinence Clearinghouse
National Asian-Pacific American Bar Association

National Asian Women's Health Organization
National Association for the Advancement of Colored People (NAACP)
National Association for Bilingual Education
National Association of Blacks in Criminal Justice
National Association of Children's Hospitals
National Association of County and City Health Officials
National Association of Evangelicals
National Association of Hispanic Publications
National Association of Latino Elected and Appointed Officials
National Association for Neighborhood Schools
National Association of People With AIDS
National Association of Police Organizations
National Association for Public Health Policy
National Association of Public Hospitals and Health Systems
National Association of Social Workers
National Association of Women Judges
National Black Child Development Institute
National Black Nurses Association
National Black Women's Health Project
National Breast Cancer Coalition
National Center for Constitutional Studies
National Center for Public Policy Research
National Center for Youth Law
National Citizens Legal Network
National Clearinghouse for Legal Services
National Coalition for the Protection of Children and Families
National Conference of Puerto Rican Women
National Conference of Women's Bar Associations
National Council of La Raza
National District Attorneys Association
National Education Association
National Employment Lawyers Association
National Family Legal Foundation
National Family Planning and Reproductive Health Association
National Hispanic Caucus of State Legislators
National Hispanic Council on Aging
National Hispanic Leadership Agenda
National Hispanic Medical Association
National Immigration Law Center
National Institute of Family and Life Advocates

National Latina/o Lesbian and Gay Organization
National Law Center on Homelessness and Poverty
National Legal Aid and Defender Association
National Legal Foundation
National Legal and Policy Center
National Medical Association
National Mental Health Association
National Multiple Sclerosis Society
National Organization of Black Law Enforcement Executives
National Organization for Women
National Organization for Women Legal Defense and Education Fund
National Osteoporosis Foundation
National Parents' Commission
National Pharmaceutical Association
National Puerto Rican Coalition
National Task Force on AIDS Prevention
National Tax Limitation Committee
National Urban Coalition
National Veterans Legal Services Program
National Wildlife Federation
National Women's Law Center
Native American Rights Fund
Natural Resources Defense Council
New Hampshire Christian Coalition
New Jersey Family Policy Council
New Mexico Shooting Sports Association
New York Eagle Forum
New York Lawyers for the Public Interest
New Yorkers for Constitutional Freedoms
North Carolina Family Policy Council
North Dakota Christian Coalition
NW Council of Governments and Associates
Oklahoma Christian Coalition
Oklahoma Conservative Committee
Oklahoma Council of Public Affairs
Oklahoma Family Policy Council
Oklahomans for Children and Families
Oregon Bar Association
Oregon State Police Officers Association
Organized Victims of Violent Crime

Palmetto Family Council
Parents Rights Coalition
Partnership for Prevention
Pennsylvania District Attorneys Association
Pennsylvania Landowners Association
Pennsylvania National Organization for Women
Pennsylvania Rifle and Pistol Association
People for the American Way
Philadelphia Bar Association
Philadelphians Against Crime
Planned Parenthood Federation of America
Plymouth Rock Foundation
Professional Fire Fighters of Wisconsin, Inc.
Project 21
Project on the Judiciary
Providence Foundation
Public Advocates, Inc.
Public Interest Institute
Public Justice Center
Puerto Rican Bar Association
Puerto Rico Federal Affairs Administration
Religious Freedom Coalition
Religious Roundtable
Right to Life of Greater Cincinnati
Santa Clara County (CA) Bar Association
Save America's Youth
Seniors Coalition
Society of Nuclear Medicine
Society for Public Health Education
Society of Thoracic Surgeons
South Dakota Family Policy Council
Southeastern Legal Foundation
Southwest Voter Registration and Education Project
Stop Promoting Homosexuality America
Strategic Policies Institute
Students for America
Sutherland Institute
Take Back Arkansas, Inc.
TEACH Michigan Foundation
Tennessee Eagle Forum

Tennessee Family Institute
Tennessee Medical Association
Tennessee Public Policy Foundation
Texas Right to Life Committee, Inc.
Tides Center
Toward Tradition
Traditional Values Coalition
United Seniors Association
U.S. Business and Industrial Council
U.S. Taxpayers Alliance
United States Department of Health and Human Services Hispanic
    Employee Organization
Utah Coalition of Taxpayers
Virginia Eagle Forum
Wall Builders
Washington Women Lawyers
Watchdogs Against U.S. Government
We the People of West Virginia
Welfare Law Center
West Virginia Family Foundation
Western Growers Association (Newport Beach, CA)
Wilderness Society
Wisconsin Christians United
Wisconsin Coalition Against Domestic Violence
Wisconsin Information Network
Wisconsin Professional Police Association
Wisconsin State Sovereignty Coalition
Wisconsin Troopers Association
Women Lawyers Association of Los Angeles
Women for Responsible Legislation
Women's Law Project
Women's Legal Defense Fund
Yankee Institute for Public Policy
Young America's Foundation

4

Group Dynamics and the Senate Confirmation Process: The Case of the Federal Judiciary

> We strongly oppose the nomination of Frederica Massiah-Jackson to the U.S. District Court because of her record of bias and outrageous behavior. . . .The Senate has hardly been careless in opposing President Clinton's judicial nominees. Indeed, neither the Judiciary Committee nor the full Senate has defeated a single one. We join the Pennsylvania and national Fraternal Order of Police and National Association of Police Organizations in strongly urging that this should be the first.
>
> Letter signed by the Judicial Selection Monitoring Project and 225 additional organizations, March 11, 1998.

While interest groups care about a wide range of federal appointments, there is perhaps no group of nominees they consider more important than nominees to the federal courts. Federal judges serve lifetime terms, are impervious to electoral challenge, and rule on cases that affect nearly every aspect of social, political, and economic policy. These judges may strike down state or federal laws that interest groups' members care deeply about. They may even strike down legislation on which interest groups have spent a lot of time, money, and effort to get enacted through the legislative process. For these reasons, interest groups pay close attention to judicial nominations and to the Senate confirmation process for federal judges. Groups care deeply about who is appointed to the federal bench and often work hard in support of nominees that they favor and equally as hard against nominees they oppose.

Many previous studies of the Supreme Court confirmation process have found an important role for interest groups.[1] These studies of Supreme Court confirmations have also found that the activities of such groups can significantly influence confirmation outcomes. While the previous studies are useful, their primary focus has been on the failed confirmation of Robert Bork, asserting that as a result of the Bork controversy, interest groups became more prominent actors in the appointment process across all types of nominations. The aftermath of the interest group campaign against Robert Bork even produced a new verb: "to Bork; which means to unleash a lobbying and public relations campaign of the kind employed against Robert Bork."[2] Even former U.S. Senator David L. Boren (D-OK) equated the Bork confirmation process with the rise of interest groups, noting: "The Bork nomination became the prototype of interest groups using the confirmation process."[3]

Despite evidence from scores of case studies of the Bork hearings suggesting that interest groups are important actors in the confirmation process, there has been little scholarly attention to whether interest groups influence lower court confirmations in the same way they do Supreme Court confirmations. There is a lack of comprehensive studies that consider the extent to which interest groups affect the confirmation process for judicial nominees more generally. As scholars Gregory Caldeira and John Wright point out: "Despite the power many people have attributed to organized interests, research on judicial nominations affords little insight into the role and impact of interest groups."[4] Although one recent study has made steps in the direction of considering interest group activity in the confirmation process for lower federal court judges, much remains unknown about the dynamics of interest group overall participation in the confirmation process.[5]

This chapter aims to put interest group participation and the role of money in the confirmation process into some context by exploring the ways in which these two factors have become fixtures in the judicial confirmation process. To explore the formal mechanisms that interest groups use in participating in judicial confirmations, data were gathered from 1,242 nominations to positions in the federal judiciary made between 1979 and 1998.[6] The quantitative data were then used to analyze the formal mechanisms of interest group participation, and the effects of such participation on confirmation outcomes for judicial nominees.

In addition, this chapter focuses on the informal mechanisms that interest groups use to influence confirmation outcomes. These data are drawn from interviews with key interest group leaders and Senate staffers, and they explore the behind-the-scenes work that interest groups conduct in their attempt to affect confirmation results. In all of these interviews, respondents were asked to discuss their perceptions of interest groups and money politics as they related to the confirmation process. Additional evidence was gathered through participant observation between November 1997 and August 1998. A full description of the qualitative methodology employed also appears in appendix 2 at the end of this book.

Background

Lower federal court confirmations typically are the largest group of nominees that the Senate must approve in any given congress. Since 1990, when the Congress approved 72 new federal judgeships, there have been 829 Article III judgeships requiring presidential nomination and Senate confirmation. This compares with fewer than 200 ambassadorships and just 14 cabinet secretary positions that must be filled. Presidents routinely fill more federal judgeships than any other office. For example, during the 104th Congress, President Clinton submitted 141 judicial nominations to the Senate for consideration. In comparison, he nominated 88 individuals to ambassadorships, 33 individuals to positions in independent government agencies and 22 individuals to positions on regulatory boards and commissions.[7]

Throughout U.S. history, most judicial nominees have been confirmed easily. David O'Brien notes: "Although the Senate has the power to reject nominees to the federal bench put forward by the president, the overwhelming majority of nominees are routinely approved by the Senate Judiciary Committee and confirmed by the Senate after only perfunctory investigation and according to no fixed standards."[8] Further, because senatorial courtesy has tended to govern the selection of lower court judges, lower federal court confirmations often were viewed by scholars as an example of the quid pro quo politics that is typical of the Senate and, as such, not worthy of detailed study.[9]

Despite conventional wisdom suggesting otherwise, recent developments in the confirmation process generally, and in judicial confirmations specifically, indicate that it is no longer appropriate to exclude lower federal court confirmations from study. The conventional wisdom of an amicable process free from much Senate scrutiny no longer holds true. The confirmation process for federal judges has become increasingly contentious over the last few years. According to United States Court of Appeals Judge Alex Kozinski: "[H]ighly alarming are the recent battles in the Senate over the appointment of the Chief Justice, Judge Bork, Justice Thomas, and some of the judges of the lower courts. Judicial appointment and tenure has suddenly become a political football in a way that has serious implications for our way of life. It will not stop there."[10]

Numerous accounts in the popular press have documented the extent to which nominees to the federal courts faced a contentious and uncertain confirmation process during the 104th and 105th Congresses. Nominees waited longer periods of time from nomination to confirmation, were subjected to heightened scrutiny, and faced uncertain confirmation outcomes. More than any other group of nominees, lower federal court judicial nominees highlight the changed nature of the contemporary confirmation process and demonstrate the new, nearly omnipresent power of interest groups and role of money in the process.

Indeed, both the 104th and the 105th Congresses provide the backdrop for a number of unusual occurrences that make the study of the role of such factors in judicial confirmations extremely timely and important. Beginning with the Republican takeover of the Senate in 1995 and intensifying after the 1996 congressional elections, the confirmation process has become a flash point of conflict among many of the key actors in the confirmation process. Whereas prior to 1995, most lower-court judicial confirmations were nonevents, recently the confirmation process for federal judges has become much more contentious. With the Republican takeover of the Senate, conservative senators made judicial activism an issue, forced increases in roll-call votes for judicial nominees, fought among themselves, and ultimately increased the length of time and the uncertainty involved in navigating the confirmation process. The contemporary confirmation process for judicial nominees looked very different in 1999 than it did just five years earlier.

The first inkling that the judicial confirmation process would change under the new Republican leadership came immediately following the Republican takeover of the Senate in the 1994 congressional midterm elections. Conservative interest group leaders were ecstatic with the Republican victory and vowed that the confirmation process would change. One week after the 1994 congressional midterm election, the legal publication *The Legal Times* quoted Clint Bolick, leader of the conservative Institute for Justice as saying: "It's definitely the dawn of a new day. . . . I think the Republicans have chafed under Democratic control of the Judiciary Committee, and that the tables will very much be turned."[11]

Despite Bolick's prediction, during the first session of the 104th Congress, the judicial confirmation process proceeded with very little controversy. In 1995, President Clinton's nominees were confirmed at a rate and pace similar to the rate and pace with which they were confirmed during the 103rd Congress, when Democrats controlled the Senate. But the second session of the 104th Congress was an election year—and Republican candidate Bob Dole focused some of his campaign energy on the federal courts, suggesting that during his first term in office President Clinton had appointed judges who were soft on crime.

The presidential campaign, coupled with Dole's accusations about Clinton's nominees resulted in an abysmal year for judicial confirmations in 1996. During the second session of the 104th Congress, the Senate confirmed just seventeen judicial nominations of the forty-nine nominations that were pending, for a confirmation rate of approximately 35 percent. The 1996 presidential election also set the stage for the 105th Congress, in which the pace of judicial confirmations again slowed, this time even without the specter of a presidential election looming over the process.

Following the 1996 presidential election, the Republicans in Congress picked up on Dole's campaign theme of opposing Clinton's judicial nominees. The first order of business was attacking President Clinton's nominees as judicial activists, despite evidence from University of Massachusetts public law professor Sheldon Goldman and other judicial appointment experts that Clinton was nominating primarily centrist judges. On November 15, 1996, less than two weeks after the 1996 presidential election, Judiciary Committee Chairman Orrin Hatch declared at a meeting of the Federalist Society: "A judicial nominee must appreciate the inherent limits on judicial authority under the Constitution, must demonstrate the self-discipline and professional humility to be faithful to these limits, and must interpret the law, not legislate from the bench. A judicial activist, on the left or right, is not in my view qualified to sit on the federal bench."[12]

By the end of the 104th Congress, the conservative revolution that had swept through the Congress and affected legislative initiatives had also begun to affect the confirmation process. Unlike the aftermath of the 1994 election, major changes to the confirmation process were underway at the beginning of the 105th Congress.

The dawn of the 105th Congress brought changes almost immediately. In March 1997, the Republican-controlled Senate began a new policy of taking roll-call votes on all judicial nominees. Beginning in January 1997, conservative North Carolina Senator Lauch Faircloth launched a campaign to persuade members of the Republican Conference that it was inappropriate to confirm individuals to lifetime appointments by voice vote. On March 19, 1997, he told the full Senate:

> [O]ur vote today is an important precedent since it marks the beginning of the Senate's new commitment to hold roll call votes on all judicial

nominees. This is a policy change which I had urged on my Republican colleagues by a letter of January 8, 1997, to the Republican Conference. Voting on federal judges, who serve for life and who exert dramatic—mostly unchecked—influence over society, should be one of the most important aspects of serving as a U.S. Senator. Roll call votes will, I believe, impress upon the individual judge, the individual senator, and the public the importance of just what we are voting on. I hope my colleagues will regard this vote, and every vote they take on a Federal judge, as being among the most important votes they will ever take.[13]

As a result of this policy change, during the 105th Congress, nominees to federal judgeships were more likely than at any other point in history to be subjected to a roll-call vote for confirmation. In 1997, eleven district court judgeship nominees—nearly 38 percent—were confirmed by roll-call vote; between 1979 and 1996, only one district court nominee total had ever been put to a roll-call vote for confirmation. Clearly, not every nominee was subjected to this type of vote. But many judicial nominees faced lengthy floor debates and close roll-call votes on their confirmations, which represented a striking departure from the way in which the Senate had always handled district court confirmations. The increased use of roll-call voting also provided another potential "veto point" in the confirmation process.

In April 1997, more controversy surrounded the Senate confirmation process. In an unusual move, conservative members of the Republican caucus attempted to strip Senate Judiciary Committee Chairman Orrin Hatch of much of his committee's authority to advise and consent to judicial nominations. Upset that Hatch had made deals with liberal members of the Senate, some members of the Republican leadership attempted to give increased veto power over judges to Republicans from the home states or regions where a nominee would serve. According to a report in the *New York Times*, a small group of Republican senators wanted to "have the power to block any Clinton Administration nominees they thought were not conservative enough or were unsuitable for any other reason."[14]

While Hatch was able to fend off the attacks on the Judiciary Committee, he was forced to do so without help from party leaders. According to a report in *The National Journal*: "[W]hen [Sen. Slade] Gorton [R-Wash] and Phil Gramm [R-Texas] launched an attack to divest the Judiciary Committee of a major chunk of its judicial-nominations turf, Lott didn't lift a finger to help."[15] *Roll Call* quoted a Republican aide, who stated: "Hatch should realize that half of his Conference is not happy with the way he is handling the Judiciary Committee. . . . Hatch is on notice . . . there's going to be continuing tension."[16] Never before had the majority party sought such influence in the confirmation process at the expense of one of its own members.

Perhaps in response to concerns about his party loyalty and ability to run the Judiciary Committee, Hatch began to slow Judiciary Committee consideration of President Clinton's judicial nominees. This was, of course, his prerogative, since as chairman of the Senate Judiciary Committee it is his responsibility to set the committee's agenda. During the 105th Congress, nominees to the lower federal courts waited dramatically longer periods of time between their initial nomination and their confirmation than did nominees in any other congress in the last two decades. Such a slowing had never happened before in a nonpresidential election year. Table 4.1 below clearly identifies the pace and rate of confirmation for federal judges between 1979 and 1998, and it is clear that confirmations slowed significanly during the 105th Congress. In addition, the 105th Congress stands out as unique in that the pace of judicial confirmations noticeably slack-

Table 4.1
Confirmation Rates for Judges Confirmed, 1979–1998

Congress	Average Number of Days, Nomination to Confirmation[1]	Number (and Percent) of Nominees Confirmed
105th	220.5	101 (83%)
104th	131	71 (66%)
103rd	72	125 (89%)
102nd	112.5	120 (66%)
101st	74	70 (93%)
100th	121	92 (80%)
99th	43	128 (95%)
98th	32.5	89 (91%)
97th	33	95 (100%)
96th	77	201 (92%)

Sources: Unpublished data from the Administrative Office of the United States Courts; statistics routinely compiled by the Senate Committee on the Judiciary (minority staff); Congressional Record for the years indicated; Democratic Policy Committee 1998, 1998b.

[1]This average is uncorrected for Senate recesses, per the method used y the Administrative Office of the United States Courts.

ened in a congress that did not precede a presidential election. In general, the percentage of confirmations was slightly lower than what might have been expected for nonpresidential election years.[17]

Lengthy delays during the 105th Congress even caused some nominees to withdraw their names from consideration. One such nominee, Lynne Lasry, withdrew her name from consideration for a judgeship in the Southern District of California federal district court in February 1998. She had waited nearly a year for the Senate to act on her nomination. In withdrawing, Lasry stated: "I am honored to have been considered for this important position, but I cannot leave my life and my practice on hold indefinitely."[18] In the year she had waited, the Senate Judiciary Committee had not even held a hearing on her nomination.

The slowing of the confirmation process came as the Senate attacked the federal judiciary on other fronts. Most notably, members of the Senate began to hint that they would use congressional authority to allocate judgeships and to impeach sitting judges to exercise control of the federal judiciary. During the 105th Congress, interest groups and members of Congress put forth several "court-curbing" proposals, including a proposed reduction of the current number of judgeships in the federal courts and the suggestion that an amendment to the Constitution be passed to limit judges' terms. Some conservative Republicans, including House Majority Whip Tom DeLay (R-TX) suggested that judges be impeached for rulings that the Congress disliked. Throughout 1997, the Congress drew clear battle lines with the federal judiciary, the president, and the president's nominees to the federal courts. Delay was their primary strategy. Senate Republicans held up many Clinton nominees for more than two years.[19] A report in *Congressional Quarterly* noted: "Republican senators who were elected in 1994 have not had a crack at a Clinton nominee to the Supreme Court yet. But in lower court positions, their main strategy in the past three years has been to hold up scores of nominees, preventing them from even coming up for a vote."[20]

By the middle of the second session of the 105th Congress, the confirmation process for lower court judges had reached a near stalemate. The situation was so bad that President Clinton was forced to, as one newspaper article put it, "negotiate for hostages," by making the deal with Republican Senator Slade Gorton that was discussed in chapter 3. Clinton agreed to nominate Washington State Chief Judge Barbara Durham in exchange for Gorton's support in confirming William Fletcher to the Ninth Circuit Court of Appeals. A report in the legal publication *The Recorder* declared:

"The deal reportedly struck by President Clinton with conservatives who have been blocking his choices to the federal judiciary constitutes nothing short of ransom paid to senatorial terrorists."[21]

Interest Groups and Judicial Confirmations

Changes to the Senate's confirmation process during the 104th and 105th Congresses demonstrate the new power of interest groups and money in the confirmation process. Case study and anecdotal evidence suggest that conservative interest groups—bolstered by the Republican takeover of the Senate in 1994—were greatly to blame for increased contentiousness in the judicial confirmation process. A 1998 *Congressional Quarterly* piece notes: "The Senate has turned the process of confirming federal judges into a political sideshow for the two parties to curry favor with their hard-core supporters."[22] Many observers of the confirmation process believe that an increase in activity by conservative interest groups attempting to keep Democratic President Bill Clinton's nominees off of the federal bench is responsible for the strange circumstances surrounding judicial confirmations in the 105th Congress.[23] And a number of observers of the process have suggested that the primary reason for being involved in the confirmation process is because of the financial incentives and rewards for that involvement.[24]

Of course interest groups have long been interested in judicial confirmations. As was noted in chapter 3, such groups began to take an interest in judicial confirmations in 1930, when President Herbert Hoover nominated John J. Parker to a vacancy on the United States Supreme Court. Concern over Parker's views on organized labor and racial equality led the American Federation of Labor (AFL) and the National Association for the Advancement of Colored People (NAACP) to testify against him at his confirmation hearing. It was the first time ever that interest groups appeared before a Senate Committee to urge the defeat of a president's nominee.

Between 1930 and 1978, interest groups were involved in only a handful of judicial confirmations, usually for nominees to the Supreme Court or to the Circuit Courts of Appeal. And group participation was almost always nominee specific. Only rarely did interest groups express concerns about more general issues relating to the Senate's confirmation process.[25] Between 1979 and 1993, interest group involvement in the confirmation process held relatively steady. Groups participated both publicly and behind closed doors, and although they began to refine their strategies and to target groups of nominees or issues related to nominations, the interest groups were not generally subversive of the confirmation process. In 1994, however, that trend came to an abrupt halt as conservatives took control of the Senate and its Judiciary Committee. At that time, confirmation scholar Robert Shogan predicted: "With the Senate in Republican hands, right-wing interest groups will be even more emboldened to challenge any attempt on [President Bill Clinton's] part which seems to them as an attempt to undo the gains conservatives made during the Reagan–Bush era.[26]

By 1996, conservative interest groups—incensed over Bill Clinton's victory in the 1996 presidential election—had developed and implemented strategies to prevent Clinton from securing a judicial legacy. Stunned that they had been unable to recapture the White House, these conservative groups, many of which had poured vast amounts of time and money into the election, set their sights on the federal judiciary. Conservative interest groups turned to conservative members of Congress and stepped up their opposition to Clinton's judicial nominees.[27] According to a 1997 *New York Newsday* editorial: "A coalition of right-wing groups has launched what it sees as a war to save the courts from Clinton. Enlisting grassroots activists and radio talk-show hosts, it is pressuring senators to drag out the nomination process."[28]

The campaign against the Clinton nominees was led by the Judicial Selection Monitoring Project's Tom Jipping. Just days after the 1994 midterm election, Jipping was quoted in a Utah newspaper, saying that his organization would closely monitor the Republicans and new Judiciary Committee Chairman Orrin Hatch, because "they're the majority now."[29] During the 105th Congress, interest groups such as the Judicial Selection Monitoring Project (JSMP), the Project on the Judiciary, and the Family Research Council actively lobbied the Republican Senate to reject Bill Clinton's judicial nominees. According to one report: "[S]ome conservatives, led by Tom Jipping, of the far-right Free Congress Foundation's Judicial Selection Monitoring Project, and their allies in the U.S. Senate have embarked on a new strategy: Block most Clinton appointees, regardless of ideology, so as to deny Clinton his appointments and save the slots for a Republican president to fill."[30] Jipping stated in December 1997: "Our goal is to blunt the worst excesses of nominations by a Democratic president."[31]

The presence of money and the pressure of interest groups in the Senate confirmation process can be linked to the changes to the judicial confirmation process that have been discussed in this chapter and in chapter 3. For example, with regard to the increasing focus of Republican senators on judicial activism, it was interest groups who seized on Hatch's statements to the Federalist Society in 1996 and turned judicial activism into a litmus test for President Clinton's judicial nominees. Conservative interest groups lauded Hatch's statements and stepped up their pressure to prevent Clinton nominees from assuming seats on the federal bench. The JSMP even asked senators to sign the "Hatch Pledge" and to vow to keep judicial activists off the bench. Hatch himself refused to sign the pledge, although eleven senators did agree to block Clinton's "activist" nominees.[32]

Interest groups were also involved in the "coup" attempt against Hatch's chairmanship. The unusual move to strip Hatch of much of his power came as conservative interest groups were expressing their concerns about Hatch's loyalty to conservative objectives. Tom Jipping was quoted in a March 1997 article in *The Weekly Standard* as stating: "'Senator Hatch has overseen a process geared toward confirming judges, not weeding out judicial activists.'"[33] Further upset that Hatch had cosponsored a children's health insurance bill "with liberal Sen. Ted Kennedy," conservatives both inside and outside the Senate questioned whether they could trust Hatch. Paul Weyrich, leader of the conservative Free Congress Foundation, summed up conservatives' view of Hatch this way: "What he does behind the scenes, in cooperation with the liberals renders his committee chairmanship useless."[34]

During the 104th and 105th Congresses, conservative interest groups also aggressively lobbied senators to put holds on nominees. According to Mary Ellen Schattman, who acted as her husband's personal assistant during his confirmation process, all the JSMP had to do was call one of the senators on its list of signatories to the Hatch pledge and tell them that a nominee was a judicial activist.[35] This appears to be what happened to Margaret Morrow. After nearly two years of aggressive lobbying against Morrow's confirmation on the grounds that she was a judicial activist, interest groups were forced to retreat when Orrin Hatch reported to the full Senate that her record had been distorted by her conservative detractors.

Finally, while there is no evidence to suggest that interest groups were behind the move to increase roll-call votes for judicial nominees, many benefited from the change in Senate procedure. Groups like the Christian Coalition could use senators' votes on individual nominees against them as they prepared their voter scorecards for their members. As chapter 3 indicated, assessments made by Senate staff members suggest that the scorecards were an effective way for interest groups to influence the confirmation process beginning with the 104th Congress.

Interest groups were an integral part of the partisan in-fighting, court-curbing proposals, and lengthy waits for confirmation that characterized the confirmation process during the late 1990s. Although some of the evidence linking interest groups to the Republicans' activities in the judicial confirmation process in these two congresses is circumstantial, it is clear is that a small cadre of conservative interest groups sought to undermine the efficiency of the Senate's confirmation process.

An Analysis of Interest Group Participation

It remains unclear why the interest groups participated in some judicial confirmations and not others. Using judicial nominees as case studies, it is possible to test some of the theoretical explanations for interest group participation in the process that were offered in chapter 3. This section considers both the formal and informal participation of interest groups in the confirmation process. It explores the causes of each type of participation and demonstrates how interest groups use both formal and informal techniques to influence confirmation outcomes.

A variety of factors encourage interest groups to participate formally in the confirmation process for lower federal court judges. Previous research has suggested that these factors include divided government, the position for which an individual is nominated, and the disposition of the Judiciary Committee chair to the participation of such groups in confirmation hearings. Each of these is considered briefly below, using the data gathered from confirmation hearings as well as nominations data.

Divided Government

As was mentioned in the appendix to chapter 2, divided government itself does not seem to explain changes to the confirmation process. And, evidence from confirmation hearings demonstrates that divided government does not increase interest group participation. As table 4.2 demonstrates, interest groups did not participate more frequently when government was divided than they did in periods of unified government. Interest groups appear to participate less often in confirmation hearings during periods of divided government than they do during periods of unified government. When control of the Congress and the White House was unified, interest groups participated in 56.5 percent of hearings, as compared with just 43.5 percent of interest group participation that took place during periods of divided government. This seemingly counterintuitive finding may be because presidents choose their nominees more carefully in periods of divided government, with the goal of avoiding costly political conflicts over

Table 4.2

Association of Interest Groups and Divided Government

			Groups		
			No	Yes	Total
Divided	No	Count	596	78	674
Gov.		% within INTRSTGR	54.0%	56.5%	54.3%
	Yes	Count	508	60	568
		% within INTRSTGR	46.0%	43.5%	45.7%
Total		Count	1104	138	1242
		% within INTRSTGR	100.0%	100.0%	100.0%

N=1,242

$X^2 = .318$ (1 df)

their federal court nominees. For example, several analyses of President Bill Clinton's nominations to the lower courts indicate that Clinton chose more moderate nominees than he might have if the Senate had been controlled by Democrats.[36] Whatever the reason, it is clear that interest groups do not more often participate formally in the confirmation process when control of the political branches is divided between the two major political parties.

Position for Which an Individual Is Nominated

Table 4.3 demonstrates another possible explanation for interest group participation in confirmation proceedings, namely, that the position for which an individual is nominated may influence whether interest groups participate. Table 4.3 summarizes the association between interest group participation and the position for which an individual was nominated. The table indicates that, as the theories suggest, the position to which an individual is nominated affects groups' decisions to participate in the confirmation process. As was noted in chapter 3, interest groups are strategic, recognizing that their resources are scarce. Therefore, they must make strategic decisions about which nominations to contest or support. According to the data, these groups are more likely to set their sights on nominees to higher-level judicial positions. Interest groups participated in 50 of 261 (19.0 percent) of confirmation hearings for Circuit Court of Appeals nominees, compared with 85 of 885 (9.0 percent) of confirmations for nominees to the other lower federal courts. This is consistent with previous studies, such

Table 4.3
Association of Interest Groups and Position

			Groups		
			0	1	Total
Position	Int'l Trade	Count	8	3	11
		% within Groups	.7%	2.2%	.9%
	District	Count	885	85	970
		% within Goups	80.2%	61.6%	78.1%
	Circuit	Count	211	50	261
		% within Groups	19.1%	36.2%	21.0%
Total		Count	1104	138	1242
		% within Groups	100.0%	10.0%	100.0%

N = 1,242
$X^2 = 25.432$**** (2 df)

as Katzmann (1997), that have found that circuit court confirmations are more likely to draw interest group attention than are district court or other lower court confirmations.

Disposition of the Committee Chair

A third factor that may contribute to interest group participation is the disposition of the chair of the Senate Judiciary toward the appearance of interest groups at confirmation hearings for federal judges. Interest group participation at the hearing stage is almost exclusively under the control of the chair of the Senate Judiciary Committee.

According to Michael Carrasco, nominations clerk for the Senate Judiciary Committee minority staff, "it's up to the chairman" whether interest groups are permitted to testify during confirmation hearings.[37] Table 4.4 demonstrates that there is a highly significant association between interest group participation and who the chair of the Senate Judiciary Committee is. These results indicate that interest groups participated in a greater percentage of hearings during Ted Kennedy's chairmanship than during any other period of time. This is consistent with previous studies. For example, judicial scholar David O'Brien explains that under Senator Kennedy's chairmanship of the Judiciary Committee, "interest groups were invited to give their views on nominees." But, O'Brien notes, when Strom Thurmond (R-SC) took over as chair of the committee in the 97th Congress, "Thurmond and his principle investigator . . . were less open to the concerns of outside groups."[38]

Table 4.4
Association of Interest Groups and Committee Chairmanship

| | | | Groups | | |
			No	Yes	Total
Chairman	Kennedy	Count	162	53	215
		% within Groups	14.7%	38.4%	17.3%
	Thurmond	Count	302	21	323
		% within Groups	27.4%	15.2%	26.0%
	Biden	Count	442	50	492
		% within Groups	40.0%	36.2%	39.6%
	Hatch	Count	198	14	212
		% within Groups	17.9%	10.1%	17.1%
Total		Count	1104	138	1242
		% within Groups	100.0%	100.0%	100.0%

N = 1,242
X^2 = 51.667**** (3 df)

In general, Democratic Committee chairs are more open to the formal participation of interest groups; Senator Biden was only slightly less open to it than Senator Kennedy had been. Further, Senator Hatch was less open to the formal participation of interest groups during confirmation hearings than had been any of the three previous chairmen. According to members of the Senate Judiciary Committee, Chairman Hatch did not believe that interest groups should be permitted to appear before the Judiciary Committee during confirmation hearings. This is consistent with the findings presented above, indicating that interest groups least often participated formally during Orrin Hatch's chairmanship during the 104th and 105th Congresses.

In light of the significant associations among these variables, it is now important to determine the extent to which divided government, the position for which an individual has been nominated, and the committee chair are useful for predicting interest group participation in confirmation hearings for lower federal court nominees. To do so, the data are submitted to a logistic regression analysis, where group participation is the dependent variable, and the position to which an individual is nominated (circuit/non-circuit) and committee chairmanship (Hatch/not Hatch; Thurmond/not Thurmond; and Kennedy/not Kennedy) are the independent variables.[39] The divided government variable is excluded from the logistic regression analysis because it was not found to be significant in the preceding bivariate chi-square analysis.

The data indicate that in 88.9 percent of cases, interest groups are not present in the confirmation process. Thus, the hope is that including these independent variables in a model of interest group participation would provide a greater ability to predict interest group participation. The results of the logistic regression analysis appear in table 4.5.

In general, the logistic regression model is highly significant (p < .001). All the variables in the analysis are significant at less than the p < 10 level, and both the position to which an individual is nominated and Senator Kennedy's chairmanship significantly (at the p < .001 level) affect the likelihood of interest group participation. Interest groups are more likely to participate in confirmation hearings for Circuit Court of Appeals nominees than for nominees to the Federal District Courts, Court of International Trade, or United States Court of Claims. Overall, the model predicts 88.89 percent of all cases, which does not improve the proportional reduction of error in the analysis.

Table 4.5 also includes an impact column, which indicates the relative impact of a one-point change in each of the independent variables on the dependent variable, above and beyond the probability of the dependent variable's probability of occurring in the absence of the independent variable. As Segal and Spaeth explain, the impact variable measures "the difference in the probability of [the dependent variable occurring] when [an independent variable] is present as opposed to its absence."[40] Kennedy's chairmanship results in a .42 increase in the probability that interest groups participated in confirmation hearings; the probability of interest group participation in confirmation hearings for lower federal court judges decreases during both Thurmond (−.13) and Hatch's chairmanships (−.17). It is clear that O'Brien's (1988) anecdotal discussion of the importance of the committee chair's disposition toward interest group participation is borne out

Table 4.5
Determinants of Interest Group Participation

Variable	B	Standard Error	Significance	Impact[3]
Kennedy	1.060	.220	.000****	.42
Thurmond	−.508	.272	.061*	−.23
Hatch	−.528	.318	.097*	−.27
Position	.794	.198	.000****	.36
Constant	−3.17	.301	.000****	—

Model Chi-Square (Improvement): 59.57 (4 df); p < .001****
[3]Assumes a starting odds ratio of .5.

through the analysis above. In addition, the likelihood of formal interest group participation in the confirmation process for federal judges is increased by a probability of .36 for each one-point increase in the position variable; this suggests that the probability of interest group participation in Circuit Court confirmation hearings is .72 higher than their probability of participating in confirmation hearings for Court of International Trade nominees.

The Consequences of Formal Interest Group Participation

It is clear that formal interest group participation in the confirmation is primarily a result of groups targeting nominees to the circuit courts coupled with the openness of the Senate Judiciary Committee chair's willingness to permit interest groups to testify at confirmation hearings. These findings do not, however, provide any indication of the impact that formal participation has on the confirmation process for judicial nominees. Additional evidence is needed to shed light on that issue.

First, it is important to measure the impact of interest group participation on confirmation outcomes. In addition, an important determinant of the effect of interest groups' formal participation on the confirmation process should be the direction of such participation in favor of or in opposition to a nominee. Segal and Spaeth's (1993) study of Supreme Court confirmations notes: "[S]trong interest-group mobilization against a nominee can hurt a candidate, whereas interest-group mobilization for a nominee only has substantively slight, but still statistically significant, positive effects."[41] Table 4.6 explores the association of direction of interest group participation and ultimate confirmation outcome. Interest groups participated in confirmation hearings for lower federal court judges a total of 144 times between 1979 and 1998. In 43 (29.9 percent) of these instances, the groups participated but took no position on the specific nominee under consideration. That is, the groups indicated that they neither supported nor opposed the nominee before the Judiciary Committee but instead wished to express their concerns about some aspect of the judicial process unrelated to the specific nomination under consideration. In 52 (36.1 percent) of the cases of interest group participation, interest groups participated unanimously in support of the pending judicial nominee. Unanimous group support of a pending nominee resulted in his or her confirmation over 94 percent of the time. In contrast, groups participated in unanimous opposition to nominees 33 times (22.9 percent). Nominees that were unan-

Table 4.6

Association of Confirmation Outcome and Direction of Interest Group Participation

			Direction of Formal Interest Group Participation						
			No Opinion	Unanimous Support	Mostly Support	Mixed	Mostly Oppose	Unanimous Opposition	Total
Confirm	No	N	2	3		1	3	4	13
		Percent	4.7%	5.8%		16.7%	50.0%	12.1%	9.0%
	Yes	N	41	49	4	5	3	29	131
		Percent	95.3%	94.2%	100.0%	83.3%	50.0%	87.9%	91.0%
Total		N	43	52	4	6	6	33	144
		Percent	100.0%	100.0%	100.0%	100.0%	100.0%	100.0%	100.0%

imously opposed by interest groups were confirmed 87.9 percent of the time. When interest group support was nonunamimous, or evenly mixed (the remaining 16, or 11.1 percent, of the cases), nominees were confirmed just 75.0 percent of the time.

Although a chi-square analysis is not feasible (since eight cells have an expected count of less than five), it is clear from the table 4.6 that the direction of interest group support for judicial nominees has at least a marginal effect on a nominee's confirmation success or failure. So, what of interest group participation and the direction of such participation? In order to test whether interest group participation in confirmation hearings has an effect on confirmation outcomes, a statistical model that posits that likelihood of confirmation is affected by the direction (pro or con) of the participation of the interest group(s) is needed.

The results of this test appear in table 4.7 and suggest that both the presence and direction of interest group participation have statistically significant effects on a nominee's likelihood of confirmation. As interest group participation becomes more negative, a nominee's chance of confirmation decreases.

In general, this model is also highly significant at the $p < .001$ level. With regard to the individual variables in the analysis, the presence of interest groups in the confirmation process reduces the likelihood that a nominee will be confirmed by .48. In addition, the direction of interest group participation also has a relatively strong negative impact on the probability of a *yes* vote for confirmation, reducing that probability by .18 for each one-unit change in the level of negative interest group participation.

Ted Kennedy's and Strom Thurmond's tenures as chair of the Senate Judiciary Committee favorably affected the probability that a nominee would be confirmed. Nominees' chances of being confirmed increased by .40 during Kennedy's chairmanship and increased by .39 under Thurmond, when compared with a nominee's chances of confirmation during Senator Joseph Biden's chairmanship. Under Chairman Orrin Hatch during the 104th and 105th Congresses, the probability that an individual nominee was confirmed decreased by .16. This last finding is consistent with the anecdotal evidence presented earlier in this chapter, indicating that since 1995 there has been a fundamental change in the confirmation process for federal judges.

In addition, the analysis demonstrates that the position for which an individual is nominated does not have a statistically significant effect on confirmation outcomes. However, the analyses have demonstrated that interest groups are more likely to testify during confirmation hearings for

Table 4.7
Effect of Interest Group Participation and Other Factors
on Confirmation Outcomes

Variable	B	Error Standard	Significance	Impact[4]
Kennedy	.956	.282	.0007****	.40
Thurmond	.916	.230	.0001****	.39
Hatch	−.286	.200	.153	−.16
Position	−.152	.192	.430	−.09
Interest Group Participation	−1.604	.956	.093*	−.48
Direction of Participation	−.317	.144	.028**	−.18
Constant	4.458	1.318	.0007****	—

Model Chi-Square (Improvement): 46.34 (6 df); p < .0000****
[4]Assumes a probability of .5.

Circuit Court of Appeals nominees and that those nominees are slightly less likely to be confirmed than their counterparts on the district courts and Court of International Trade.

This examination of formal interest group participation indicates that their presence in the confirmation process is most likely during Democratic Judiciary Committee chairmanships and when a nominee has been selected to fill a vacancy on the Circuit Courts of Appeal. When interest groups are opposed to nominees, their likelihood of being confirmed is again reduced.

The models of interest group participation presented above are useful, as they shed light on the determinants of such participation. However, across the board, interest groups are less formally involved today in judicial confirmations than they were during Senator Kennedy's chairmanship of the Judiciary Committee in 1979 and 1980. Moreover, the data indicate that interest groups are also are less formally involved than they were immediately preceding and following the Bork rejection in 1987. Table 4.8 demonstrates that while interest group participation spiked somewhat during the 100th Congress (the congress in which Robert Bork was defeated), participation had been increasing up until that point and quickly diminished immediately after.

The data presented in table 4.8 demonstrate that formal interest group participation has actually declined since 1987, despite the conclusions that have been drawn by a number studies of the failed Bork confirmation.

Table 4.8
Interest Group Participation in Judicial Confirmations,
1979–1998

Congress	Dates	Total Nominees	Number (and Percent) where Interest Groups Participated
96th	1979–1980	218	57 (26%)
97th	1981–1982	89	3 (3%)
98th	1983–1984	99	5 (5%)
99th	1985–1986	135	13 (11%)
100th	1987–1988	105	24 (24%)
101st	1989–1990	73	14 (20%)
102nd	1991–1992	178	10 (8%)
103rd	1993–1994	137	4 (3%)
104th	1995–1996	88	4 (6%)
105th	1997–1998	124	10 (8%)

Source: United States Senate Committee on the Judiciary. Confirmation Hearings on Federal Appointments. Congresses indicated.

Additional evidence corroborates this finding. Nan Aron, director of the Alliance for Justice, a Washington, D.C., organization that has monitored judicial appointments for more than fifteen years, says: "I don't know that more groups are involved or that groups are more involved."[42] According to People for the American Way's Eliot Mincberg, interest groups got involved in the confirmation process in response to Ronald Reagan's attempt to create a conservative judiciary, but once Reagan left office, interest groups paid less attention to the confirmation process. According to Mincberg, "[Interest group involvement] culminated in Bork."[43] In addition, the advent of new technologies made it less important for interest groups to present testimony about a nominee. Former Senator Warren Rudman (R-NH) believes that interest groups generally have actually become less important as information technologies have increased. "By the time I left the Senate, I could tell a staffer to run a name through a Lexis-Nexis search and get all the information I needed. I didn't need interest groups to bring me information I could get on my own," he said.[44] Indeed, the data in table 4.8 bear out this assessment.

It is clear that not only are there relatively few instances of group participation at confirmation hearings for lower federal court judges, but also that interest groups do not participate in confirmation hearings more frequently now than they did prior to Robert Bork's nomination. Although table 4.8 indicates that interest groups continued to be present in a small percentage of confirmation hearings during the 104th and 105th Congresses, it should be noted that no interest group actually testified before the Senate Judiciary Committee in either of these congresses.

This exploration of formal participation has captured only part of the dynamics of interest groups in the confirmation process for lower federal court nominees. To understand the whole picture of interest group participation it is necessary to turn to an examination of groups' informal participation.

While the quantitative data indicate that interest groups have become less formally involved in the confirmation process since the Bork confirmation, these findings are the opposite of what would be expected based upon interviews with Senate staff members. These interviews suggest that interest groups play an important and possibly increasing role in the confirmation process. According to Ronald Weich, former Chief Counsel to Senator Edward M. Kennedy (D-MA) states: "The interest groups have played a big role in judicial nominations since the Bork nomination died in the Senate. They are there now and they weren't before."[45] Mary De-Oreo, Investigator for the Senate Judiciary Committee's minority staff, notes: "There is no question that these groups are important."[46] Victoria Bassetti, formerly chief counsel to Senator Richard Durbin's (D-IL), says: "In my experience, the right-wing interest groups are really actively involved right now."[47] Both Melody Barnes, Chief Counsel to Senator Edward M. Kennedy (D-MA), and Michael Carrasco, former minority nominations clerk for the Judiciary Committee, point out that interest groups are important because they can encourage individual senators to push nominees forward or to hold up confirmations.[48] Rhett DeHart, formerly counsel to Senator Jeff Sessions (R-AL) and currently counsel to Senator Orrin Hatch (R-UT), adds that interest groups are important because they can provide an electoral connection to senators' confirmation decisions.[49]

Interviews with Senate staff members indicate that interest groups have become more involved in the process, not less, despite the findings presented above, indicating that formal participation in the confirmation process decreased substantially beginning in the 101st Congress. Informal interest group participation in the confirmation process—that is, interest group activity on behalf of or in opposition to a nominee that takes place out of the formal confirmation process—probably accounts for staffers' assessments that interest groups are now more involved in the confirmation process for lower federal court judges. As former nominee Michael Schattman says: "It's obvious that interest groups play a significant behind-the-scenes role in the confirmation process."[50]

While evidence presented in chapter 3 makes this point generally, the following example illustrates this point more fully. The nomination of

Frederica Massiah-Jackson, a Pennsylvania state trial court judge, to serve on Pennsylvania's Eastern District Court brought out interest groups in droves, both in favor of and in opposition to her confirmation. Yet not a single interest group testified before the Senate Judiciary Committee regarding her confirmation. As Judge Massiah-Jackson's nomination was pending on the Senate floor, the Pennsylvania District Attorney's Association and the Law Enforcement Alliance of America (LEAA) began to lobby senators behind closed doors to reject Massiah-Jackson. The groups claimed she possessed an unfit judicial temperament and that she was prone to leniency in her judicial decisions. In a March 1998 letter to all members of the Senate, the LEAA wrote: "LEAA stands vehemently opposed to this judge's appointment to the U.S. District Court. We believe that she is unqualified for a position so highly regarded and should not be presiding over death penalty and habeas corpus appeals. Her confirmation to the federal judiciary would be detrimental to the sanctity of the law and the dignity of the judicial system."[51]

Yet, the LEAA never testified before the Senate Judiciary Committee. The only public indication of opposition to her confirmation from organized interests came at Massiah-Jackson's second confirmation hearing in February 1998, at which Senate Judiciary Committee Chairman Orrin Hatch stated: "We've never had a situation where law enforcement has come out this strongly against a nominee."[52] On March 16, 1998, even as the Senate was scheduled to debate her nomination, Judge Massiah-Jackson withdrew her name from consideration, writing to President Bill Clinton: "I have recently been subject to an unrelenting campaign of vilification and distortion as I waited for a vote on my nomination by the full Senate."[53] This campaign took place entirely behind closed doors, however.

Many interest group leaders have turned toward informal means of influencing confirmation outcomes, such as letter writing, direct lobbying of senators, and grassroots lobbying. Part of the explanation for high rates of such participation may be the greater number of informal access points available at a time when the formal points of entry into the confirmation process were being closed off from interest groups. Although Senator Orrin Hatch did not permit interest groups to testify in confirmation hearings, since 1997, these groups have had the additional access point of floor debate, even on even district court nominees, with the Senate's decision to hold roll-call votes on these nominations.

Another possible explanation for significant informal participation in the confirmation process is that conservative groups have been engaging in these kinds of activities for decades, and liberal groups have come to realize that behind-the-scenes participation is their only option. Indeed, since the Republicans took control of the Senate in 1995, the ideological background of an interest group seems to be an important determinant of its participation in the confirmation process. Since 1995, the ideological incompatibility of liberal interest groups with the Senate majority party has forced some of the more liberal groups to rethink their means of participating in the confirmation process. While these groups now testify less often at hearings and submit fewer materials for the hearing record, they use other, more informal techniques to make their opposition to or support of a particular nominee known. Many liberal groups, which were very active participants in the confirmation process during the Reagan and Bush presidencies, now use behind-the-scenes techniques nearly exclusively. This is because conservative control of the Congress means that they are somewhat limited with regard to the strategies available to them. The liberal groups are forced to "play defense," as one group leader put it, by responding to allegations raised by conservative interest groups who oppose a nominee. However, the liberal groups could not be too proactive in expressing their support for President Clinton's judicial nominees. For groups like People for the American Way (PFAW), a liberal-leaning organization, testimony at confirmation hearings did not make much sense. According to Eliot Mincberg, the organization's legal director: "During the 105th Congress, we haven't made an effort to testify. We haven't felt it would be particularly useful. What good does it do for a liberal group to testify?" Instead, says Mincberg, People for the American Way has used television advertisements, newspaper advertisements, lobbying on Capitol Hill, and grassroots lobbying to attempt to influence confirmation outcomes. "In differing combinations, those tactics have been used to a differing degree on nominations we oppose," says Mincberg.[54] At the same time, says Tracy Hahn-Burkett, legislative representative at PFAW, PFAW will put out reports or visit members of the Senate to set the record straight or encourage confirmation of nominees it supports.[55] Other groups such as the JSMP, the Alliance for Justice, and the Project on the Judiciary also use similar behind-the-scenes tactics, according to the leaders of these organizations.[56]

Informal interest group participation may affect confirmation outcomes for specific nominees. For example, in a press release following Judge Frederica Massiah-Jackson's withdrawal from consideration for a federal district court judgeship, Missouri Senator John Ashcroft issued a statement saying: "The strong opposition from police and prosecutors in Pennsylvania made it possible for me and others to bring attention to the shortcomings of this nomination."[57] Not one interest group had testified before the Senate Judiciary Committee to oppose Massiah-Jackson's nomination.

While informal interest group participation in the confirmation process may provide cover for a senator to vote against a nominee, or may force nominees to withdraw from the process, such participation may have other effects on the confirmation process as well. For example, People for the American Way's Hahn-Burkett agrees that with more negative participation from interest groups comes a more negative view of the judiciary overall, which in turn prevents individuals from wanting to serve. She says: "You don't call for a judge's impeachment because you disagree with their decisions. That's entirely inappropriate and destructive to the process. Good candidates don't want to get involved. And you get judges listening to the political winds, not the merits of the case."[58]

Money and Judicial Confirmations

In the contemporary confirmation process, interest groups do not only participate in the judicial confirmation process because of their desire to ensure that particular kinds of judges sit on the federal bench. Today, the judicial confirmation process also represents a revenue-generating enterprise. During the 1990s, a number of interest groups touted their confirmation activities in their annual reports and fund-raising literature. One group, the Judicial Selection Monitoring Project, built an entire fund-raising campaign around the judicial confirmation process in 1997.

The most significant example of informal interest group participation in the confirmation process is also the most significant example of the way in which money now plays a role in the confirmation process. This example is the fund-raising videotape that the Free Congress Foundation—a conservative interest group headquartered in Washington D.C.—sponsored in 1997. The video urged recipients to contribute money to the Judicial Selection Monitoring Project, a subsidiary of the Free Congress Foundation, whose mission is to prevent the appointment of "judicial activists" to the federal bench.

On September 9, 1997, contributors to the Free Congress Foundation received a letter from Robert Bork that asked: "Can we afford to give President Clinton a free ride with his judicial appointments over the next three and a half years?" Indicating that the correct answer was *no*, Bork continued: "That is why I am taking the unusual step of sending you the enclosed video from the Free Congress Foundation's 'Judicial Selection Monitoring Project.'" The videotape featured testimony from prominent conservatives—including Republican Senators James Inhofe (R-OK), Jeff Sessions (R-AL), Phil Gramm (R-TX), and Bob Smith (R-NH)—touting the JSMP and the need to block President Bill Clinton's judicial nominations.

Three other Republican senators—Kay Bailey Hutchison (R-TX), John Ashcroft (R-MO), and Christopher (Kit) Bond (R-MO)—lent written testimonials to the videotape's producers. Among the comments from Republican senators were Senator Gramm's: "The Judicial Selection Monitoring Project has the resources to get the facts, to people like me who are willing to use it." And from Senator Sessions: "The Judicial Selection Monitoring Project is important because [it] shares information that senators may not have known and wouldn't have had time to consider."[59]

Included with the videotape was a fund-raising pledge sheet, which promised that in recognition of gifts of ten thousand dollars or more, donors would receive "invitations to attend periodic briefings and intimate dinners in Washington with Paul Weyrich [director of the Free Congress Foundation], JSMP Director Tom Jipping, and leading conservative elected and public figures closely involved with the judicial confirmation process."[60]

According to Paul Weyrich, the senators who appeared in the video knew that their likenesses were being used in a fund-raising appeal. Further, anecdotal evidence suggests that the senators who appeared in the video were given access to the Heritage Foundation's mailing list of contributors, which, if true, means that the video participants were given access to the names and addresses of donors to conservative causes. At the very least, the senators who lent their names and likenesses to the video were identified with supporting this conservative cause. For the four senators who would be standing for reelection in 1998 and 2000—Bond, Ashcroft, Inhofe, and Hutchinson—this publicity would have been invaluable.

The videotape, the letters from Robert Bork, and the promise of access to "elected and public figures closely involved with the judicial confirmation process," represents a convergence of confirmation politics, interest groups, money, and senators that is unprecedented in its scope. It also represents a danger of informal participation—many of the examples used by the JSMP in the videotape came from judges who actually had been appointed by President George Bush. Yet, because the video was part of a private fund-raising effort, the veracity of its message was beyond public scrutiny of the type that would have occurred had the group participated in a formal way in the confirmation process.

Conclusion

Just as in the confirmation process more generally, interest groups get involved in the judicial confirmation process because of concerns about a nominee's policy positions or to promote an individual's candidacy. Interest groups may also promote or oppose a nominee simply because they wish to draw attention to their message. This chapter has focused on the role of interest groups in the confirmation process for nominees to the lower federal courts by examining their formal and informal participation.

Several conclusions are warranted. First, interest groups have been integrally involved in the changes to the confirmation process that occurred during the 104th and 105th Congresses. They are robust, active players in that process. In the aggregate, they bring a full range of techniques to pushing for nominees that they support and to opposing nominees that they do not support. However, it appears that interest group involvement in the confirmation process for federal judicial nominees has changed in the last two decades.

The conventional wisdom that indicating that interest groups are now more involved in the confirmation process should be revised to reflect that their *formal* participation has actually declined.[61] Whereas previous studies of Supreme Court confirmations have concluded that interest groups are more involved in the confirmation process since the Senate's rejection of Robert Bork in 1987, the data analysis in the preceding pages indicates that this is not entirely true. Instead, the analyses above demonstrate that while interest groups have maintained or even increased their behind-the-scenes participation, they have become less formally involved than they once were, testifying less often at confirmation hearings and submitting fewer materials for the hearing record.

These findings suggest that the traditional thoughts regarding the formal role of interest groups in judicial confirmations must be revisited. First, in terms of formal participation, interest groups are actually less often present at the confirmation hearings of federal judges today than they were in the late 1970s and early 1980s. Yet, while interest groups are now less formally involved in the confirmation process, their participation still can have a powerful impact on confirmation outcomes. In November 1996, the *New Jersey Law Journal* pointed out: "These groups, which have played critical roles, especially in high-profile nominations, can trigger a firestorm of controversy and may force political showdowns."[62] The analysis above demonstrates that when interest groups do participate formally in confirmation hearings—especially when they oppose a nominee—the likelihood of confirmation is significantly reduced. However, group participation also has more generalized effects on the confirmation process, including delays in confirmation, difficulty recruiting people to serve as federal judges, increasingly lengthy judicial vacancies, and the inability of the president to craft a legacy through the federal courts. Informal interest group participation also leads to delays. For example, in 1997 and 1998, the JSMP aggressively lobbied signatories of the Hatch Pledge to put holds on so-called judicial activist nominees. As a result, a number of nominees were held up for extended periods. In his 1997 *Year-End Report on the Federal Judiciary,* United States Supreme Court Chief Justice William Rehnquist wrote: "Judicial vacancies can contribute to a backlog of cases, undue delays in civil cases, and stopgap measures to shift judicial personnel where they are most needed. Vacancies cannot remain at such high levels indefinitely without eroding the quality of justice that traditionally has been associated with the federal judiciary. . . . Some current nominees have been waiting a considerable time for a Senate Judiciary Committee vote or a final floor vote."[63] People for the American Way's Hahn-Burkett adds: "The positions that are not filled are not just empty vacancies. They mean something to the people whose cases are held up."[64]

In addition, the analyses above demonstrate that the political environment constrains the extent to which interest groups participate in the process. These groups participate in confirmation hearings more often for nominees to the Circuit Courts of Appeals than they do for other lower federal courts. But interest group participation at confirmation hearings appears to be largely determined by the Judiciary Committee chair's willingness to open up confirmation hearings to outside witnesses. Whereas Senator Kennedy welcomed interest group participation, according to Judiciary Committee staff, Senator Hatch was much less open to group participation during the hearings themselves.

In the end, the most striking conclusion to be drawn from the preceding analysis may be how prevalent—and potentially misleading—the *informal* participation of interest groups in the confirmation process can be. As the example of the JSMP fund-raising videotape demonstrates, informal participation in the confirmation process cannot be monitored for accuracy or fairness, even as it is being used to generate revenue for these organizations. Thus, senators who use the information provided by interest groups in closed-door meetings may be relying on information that is false or misleading. As interest groups have been forced out of public participation in the formal mechanisms of the confirmation process, they have continued their campaigns in favor or opposed to nominees behind the scenes. This gives these groups immeasurable influence over the confirmation process for judicial nominees. The next chapter considers the impact of interest groups on nominees to other positions.

5

From the Bench to the Cabinet, and Beyond

> Bill Clinton's nomination of James Hormel sends the message that radical homosexual activists are perfectly fine in the eyes of the government as our representative.
>
> Steve Schwalm, Family Research Council

Unlike federal judges, members of a president's cabinet do not serve lifetime terms. Nor do ambassadors serve in their positions longer than the length of a presidential administration. In fact, many nonjudicial nominees serve only through the first congressional midterm election.

Because of the high rates of turnover, it is important to understand the dynamics of interest group participation in confirmation hearings for these sets of nominees. Cabinet secretaries oversee the most important of federal agencies, supervising their regulatory and rule-making functions. Ambassadors represent the president of the United States abroad, working with leaders of other nations to craft important, bi- and multilateral trade, environmental, and defense agreements. Interest groups view the confirmation process for nominees to these positions as another point of entry for the interjection of their policy preferences.

As the previous chapter demonstrated, interest group participation in the confirmation process for federal judges slows down the pace of confirmations and reduces the likelihood that judicial nominees will be confirmed. As the Senate Judiciary Committee tightened control of confirmation hearings and closed off the formal avenues of participation to interest groups, their participation in confirmation hearings significantly declined. In the contemporary confirmation process, interest groups rely instead on informal techniques, including agenda setting, information dissemination, and punishing and rewarding senators to affect confirmation outcomes. Reports from Senate staff indicate that the use of these informal techniques has increased substantially in the last decade.

But what about nominees to other positions? While judicial nominees typically are the largest group of nominees sent to the Senate by the president in any given congress, the Senate must act on the nominations of literally hundreds of nominees to everything from independent regulatory boards to the Director of the U.S. Census. This chapter explores the dynamics of interest group participation for nominees to fill vacancies in the president's cabinet and nominees to serve as United States ambassadors. It considers whether the same factors that determine interest group participation in the confirmation process for federal judges also apply to their participation in the confirmation process for cabinet secretaries-designate and U.S. ambassadors. Each group is considered separately below.

Cabinet Secretaries-Designate

According to G. Calvin Mackenzie: "The first and most formidable of the tasks facing a new president is the problem of finding men and women to fill the most important positions in his administration."[1] Especially upon his election, but no matter when a vacancy arises during his presidency, the president must choose individuals to head the fourteen major government departments.[2] The heads of these departments are responsible for helping the president carry out his responsibility to enforce the laws through the rule-making and program-monitoring functions their agencies perform. Mackenzie adds: "These initial [cabinet] selections are important because they provide the President with a chance to lay the groundwork for political relationships that will directly affect the future success of his administration. Not only do they allow him to reward those who have supported him in the past, they also permit him to broaden his base of support within his own party, with organized interest groups, and with the Congress."[3]

Although the Constitution makes no mention of a presidential cabinet, every president since George Washington has had one. There is evidence that the framers even intended for the president to consult with the heads of the executive departments before making important decisions. Richard Fenno, in the first comprehensive treatment of the cabinet in the American political system, notes: "By 1787, the roots of the American

Cabinet were already sunk deep in American practice. Most of the colonial governments provided for a council of assistants to consult with the governor, though they were selected in a variety of ways."[4] Fenno notes that the first "cabinet" meeting was held in 1791, at President Washington's request.

Like nominees to the federal judiciary, cabinet secretaries-designate must appear before the U.S. Senate and receive its approval before taking office. Unlike judicial nominees, nominees to the president's cabinet appear before different committees, depending on which Senate committee has jurisdiction over the federal agency that a nominee has been selected to head. Also unlike judicial nominees, cabinet secretaries-designate enjoy a strong presumption of suitability for confirmation. Fenno writes: "As a matter of courtesy, the Senate has from the very outset (in all cases but two) consented to confirm [the president's] choice." He adds: "Though the president's appointment power is subject to 'the advice and consent of the Senate,' in practice that is hardly a limitation at all on the legitimacy of the presidential decision. The Senate ordinarily extends him the courtesy of approving his selections."[5]

The Senate has rejected only ten nominees to the president's cabinet in its two-hundred-plus-year history, and has only twice rejected a nomination made at the beginning of a presidential term: George Bush's nomination of John Tower to be Secretary of Defense, and Bill Clinton's nomination of Zoe Baird to be Attorney General. As Stephen Carter has written: "Cabinet nominations . . . have traditionally been handled with kid gloves by the Senate. . . . Until recently, the handling has been so gentle as to make nomination to a cabinet post tantamount to appointment."[6] Even conservative interest group leader Paul Weyrich notes: "One should more readily oppose a lifetime nominee to the Court than a presidential appointee to one of the departments. . . . [The president] is entitled to an appointment like that by virtue of having won the election."[7]

The Clerk of the Senate also has acknowledged that the president is given nearly free reign to select the cabinet secretaries of his choice. In a study published by the Government Printing Office in 1954, the Clerk wrote: "The president is accorded wide latitude in the selection of members of his cabinet."[8] The 1993 confirmation of Robert Reich to be President Bill Clinton's Secretary of Labor provides an illustration of the presumption of confirmability that surrounds cabinet nominees. In his 1997 memoir, *Locked in the Cabinet*, Reich recalls "cramming" for his Senate confirmation hearing. He recounts: "I'm cramming for my Senate confirmation hearing on Thursday, helped by several coaches including the lawyers who investigated me and several Democratic staffers from the Hill. I feel like a prizefighter getting ready for the big one."[9] But the bottom line, Reich is told, is that unless a scandal is revealed, the Senate will confirm him. Reich notes that one of the individuals helping to prepare him for his confirmation hearing tells him: "Look: The President has nominated you to be a cabinet secretary. They have to consent to your nomination. Barring an unforeseen scandal, they will."[10] A high-ranking staffer on the Senate Foreign Relations Committee agrees: "The hurdles are the Secretary of State's office and the White House. Once [the nominees] get to us, we're just confirming that they made a good choice."[11]

Interest groups care about who serves as the head of an executive-branch agency for the same reason that they care about who serves as a federal judge. Agency heads oversee the federal rule-making process that can determine how a law affects a group's constituents in the same way that federal judges' interpretations of laws can determine how particular statutes affect groups' members. Unlike federal judges, who can rule only on those cases brought to them, federal agencies are proactive in promulgating rules and regulations. Interest groups know that it matters who sits at the top of the federal agency hierarchy and they pay close attention to whom the president has nominated.

Interest groups also care about the confirmation process for cabinet nominees because cabinet appointments are additional opportunities for policy discussions. As Chapter 3 pointed out, the primary reason that interest groups participate in the confirmation process is because they desire to affect public policy outcomes. Executive branch nominations are a good opportunity for interest groups to engage in policy debates with nominees and to go on record with their policy preferences. For these reasons, interest groups participate in the vast majority of confirmation hearings for cabinet secretaries-designate. Table 5.1 demonstrates that interest groups were present at 64 of 88 hearings (72.7 percent) for cabinet secretaries-designate between 1977 and 1998. This compares with just 144 of 1,112 confirmation hearings (12.3 percent) on federal judicial nominees between 1979 and 1998.

In addition to the active participation of interest groups in confirmation hearings for cabinet secretaries-designate, it is possible to identify several trends from the data reported in table 5.1. First, nearly every nominee tapped by the president to fill a cabinet vacancy since 1977 has been given a hearing by the United States Senate. In addition, cabinet secretaries-designate have

Table 5.1

Interest Group Participation in Confirmations
for Cabinet Secretaries-Designate 1977–1998

Congress	Dates	Number of Nominees	Number (and Percent) Receiving Hearings	Number (and Percent) Confirmed	Number (and Percent) of Hearings where Interest Groups Were Present
95th	1977–78	11	11 (100%)	11 (100%)	10 (91%)
96th	1979–80	8	8 (100%)	8 (100%)	6 (75%)
97th	1981–82	12	12 (100%)	12 (100%)	11 (92%)
98th	1983–84	3	3 (100%)	3 (100%)	3 (100%)
99th	1985–86	9	9 (100%)	9 (100%)	8 (89%)
100th	1987–88	5	5 (100%)	5 (100%)	2 (40%)
101st	1989–90	13	13 (100%)	12 (92%)	9 (69.2%)
102nd	1991–92	4	4 (100%)	4 (100%)	3 (75%)
103rd	1993–94	17	17 (100%)	16 (94%)	10 (59%)
104th	1995–96	1	1 (100%)	1 (100%)	0 (0%)
105th	1997–98	5	5 (100%)	5 (100%)	2 (40%)
Totals		88	88 (100%)	86 (97.7%)	Average: 72.7%

been approved by the Senate in every case except for just two. Nearly 98 percent of presidential nominations to fill vacant cabinet positions have been confirmed since 1977.

Although interest groups are regular participants in confirmation hearings for cabinet nominees, most nominations garner just a handful of letters or requests to testify. Only a few nominees have sparked large amounts of interest group participation. Since 1977, the nominees that have received the most attention are nominees to be the Secretary of the Interior, mainly because of the mobilization of environmental organizations. For example, in January 1981, thirty-one interest groups testified in January 1981 at the Senate Committee on Energy and Natural Resources' confirmation hearings for President Reagan's nominee to be Secretary of the Interior, James Watt. An additional fifteen groups submitted materials to the committee. The direction of the testimony was mostly positive, but the amount of interest group attention was unprecedented for a cabinet nominee. Eighteen interest groups testified and four groups submitted materials to the Energy and Natural Resources Committee during William Clark's confirmation hearings in 1983. Thirteen interest groups testified and seventeen groups submitted materials when Reagan nominated Donald Hodel in 1985 to replace Clark. Again, the direction of the testimony and submitted materials was mostly positive. Only Edwin Meese, Reagan's nominee to be Attorney General was met with similarly high levels of interest group participation during his confirmation hearings in 1985.[12]

In the aggregate, interest group participation is less polarized with regard to cabinet nominees than it is for judicial nominees. The previous chapter noted that interest group participation in confirmation hearings for federal judgeships breaks down as follows: unanimous support for the nominee in 39.4 percent of cases, mixed participation in 11.8 percent of cases, unanimous opposition to the nominee in 27 percent of cases, and no position taken on the nominee in 21.8 percent of cases. The trend in direction of participation in confirmations for cabinet secretaries-designate is somewhat different. First, a lower percentage of groups unanimously supported the cabinet nominees. Participating interest groups unanimously supported a cabinet secretary-designate in only 35.9 percent of the cases. However, the percentage of cases in which interest group participation was unanimously in opposition to the pending nominee was also substantially lower than the corresponding figure for judicial confirmations. In just 7.8 percent of hearings for cabinet secretaries-designate was interest group participation unanimously in opposition to the pending nominee. No position was taken on 14.1 percent of nominees.

The biggest difference between participation for lower federal court nominees and cabinet secretaries-designate comes in the middle ground, where group participation is mixed. In 42.2 percent of the cases of interest group participation, interest group participation was not unanimous in either direction. This compares with just 11.8 percent of cases of nonunanimous participation in confirmation hearings for lower federal court judges. Table 5.2 gives the breakdown in the direction of interest group participation in confirmation hearings for cabinet secretaries-designate between 1977 and 1998.

Factors Affecting Interest Group Participation

There are a number of factors that may have an effect on interest group participation in cabinet confirmation hearings. First, interest groups consider the position to which an individual is nominated when making the calculation whether to participate in the confirmation hearing. In addition,

Table 5.2

Frequency Distribution of the Direction of Interest Group Participation in Confirmation Hearings for Cabinet Secretaries-Designate, 1977–1998

Direction	Frequency	Percent
Support	24	35.9
Mostly Support	21	32.8
Mixed	3	4.7
Mostly Oppose	3	4.7
Oppose	5	7.8
No Position	10	14.1

Source: Cabinet Nominees Data Set, compiled by author.

N=64

several aspects of the political environment have been identified in previous studies as having an effect on interest group participation in the confirmation process, including the position to which an individual is nominated, which party is in control of the Senate, and the president making the nomination.[13] Each of these is discussed separately below.

The position to which an individual is nominated seems to have an impact on the extent to which interest groups participate in cabinet confirmations. Not only do interest groups participate at varying levels of intensity in cabinet confirmations, they also participate at varying frequencies. That is, some cabinet positions appear to encourage more group participation than others. Table 5.3 shows that over the last two decades, every nominee to head the Departments of Energy, Interior, and Transportation was confronted with interest groups at his or her confirmation hearing. In contrast, only one of six nominees to head the Department of Defense faced interest groups during his confirmation hearings—and that was John Tower, one of only two cabinet nominess to be failed by the Senate during the period of study. Nominees to the Departments of Commerce, Labor, and Treasury also were among those nominees least likely to face interest groups during their confirmation hearings. As was the case with judicial nominees, the position for which an individual is nominated is positively associated with the presence or absence of interest groups during confirmation hearings. Table 5.3 provides the breakdown of interest group participation in confirmation hearings by cabinet position.

One reason for differences in interest group participation in confirmation hearings for cabinet secretaries-designate is suggested by Jeffrey

Table 5.3

Interest Group Participation by Cabinet Position, 1977–1998

Cabinet Position	Number of Hearings in Which Groups Participated	Total Number of Confirmations for This Position	Percentage of Hearings Where Groups Were Present
Agriculture	3	5	60%
Attorney General	6	8	75%
Commerce	4	7	57%
Defense	1	6	16.7%
Education	4	5	80%
Energy	7	7	100%
Health and Human Services	6	7	85.7%
Housing and Urban Development	5	6	83.3%
Interior	7	7	100%
Labor	4	8	50%
State	6	7	85.7%
Transportation	6	6	100%
Treasury	4	7	57%
Veterans' Affairs	2	2	100%

Source: Cabinet Nominees Data Set, created by author.

Cohen's 1988 study of the genesis of cabinet agencies. He notes that the way in which an agency is created may determine the extent to which interest groups seek to influence the agency's policy-making function. Cohen writes: "Some departments, such as agriculture, interior, labor, and education were created because of political interests."[14] Cohen finds that interest groups frequently attempt to affect these agencies' decision making. Although the data in table 5.3 do not indicate that interest groups are any more interested in the Departments of Agriculture or Labor, Cohen's theory may be useful for exploring which factors contribute to interest group participation. This question is addressed shortly.

In addition to the position for which an individual is nominated, two additional factors may affect whether interest groups participate in the confirmation process for cabinet nominees. The previous chapter found that interest groups are more often involved during periods of Democratic control of the Senate than they are when the body is controlled by the Republican party. Thus, one might expect that partisan control of the Senate also affects organized interests' participation in cabinet confirmations. Table 5.4

presents the results of the chi-square analysis of the association of interest group participation and partisan control of the Senate in confirmation hearings for cabinet secretaries-designate. It is clear from the results presented in the table below that interest group participation and party control are not statistically significantly associated with one another. With a chi-square value of .271 and a gamma value of .286, it is clear there is not a statistically significant relationship between the two variables. Nonetheless, the relationship indicated in table 5.4 is interesting. Interest groups participate more often when the Senate is controlled by Republicans than they do when it is controlled by Democrats. This is precisely the opposite of what was found in the previous chapter's examination of judicial nominees.

Finally, it is also possible that the nominating president may be associated with the participation of interest groups in the confirmation process for agency heads. For example, interest groups are widely perceived to have challenged Ronald Reagan's nominees to cabinet positions during the 1980s. Table 5.5 suggests that who the president is may have some marginal significance in determining whether interest groups participate in confirmation hearings for nominees. Because of data limitations it is impossible to run an accurate chi-square analysis. However, the data presented below demonstrate that while interest groups are active participants across all four of the presidents—Carter, Reagan, Bush, and Clinton—considered in this project, they have not participated in cabinet confirmations equally. In fact, interest group participation in confirmation hearings has steadily declined since the Carter administration. Between 1977 and 1980, interest groups participated in 84.2 percent of the confirmation hearings held on nominees to the president's cabinet. In contrast, interest groups

Table 5.4

Association of Interest Group Participation and Party Control of the Senate-Confirmation Hearings for Cabinet Secretaries-Designate, 1977–1998

		Party Control of the Senate		
		Republican	Democrat	Total
Groups	No	6 (20%)	18 (31.1%)	24 (27.3%)
	Yes	24 (80.0%)	40 (68.9%)	64 (72.7%)
	TOTAL	30 (34.1%)	58 (65.9%)	88 (100%)

Pearson Chi-Square: 1.214, 1 df, p < .271

Gamma: .286

Table 5.5
Association of Interest Groups and Nominating President

		President				
		Carter	Reagan	Bush	Clinton	Total
Groups	No	3	5	5	11	24
		(15.8%)	(17.3%)	(29.4%)	(47.8%)	(27.3%)
	Yes	16	24	12	12	64
		(84.2%)	(82.7%)	(70.6%)	(52.2%)	(72.7%)
	TOTAL	19	29	17	23	88
		(21.6%)	(33.0%)	(19.3%)	(26.1%)	(100%)

Source: Cabinet Nominees Data Set, compiled by author.

were present at only slightly more than half (52.2 percent) of the confirmation hearings for cabinet nominees during the first six years of Bill Clinton's presidency.

In order to determine the extent to which the variables described above contribute to the likelihood of interest group participation in the confirmation process, it is necessary to submit the cabinet-level confirmation data to a logistic regression analysis. The logistic regression analysis helps to determine the significance and impact of several factors on the likelihood of interest group participation. Partisan control of the Senate, the agency to which an individual was nominated,[15] and the nominating president are all are included in the model, the results of which appear in table 5.6.

Although the model itself is not statistically significant, several of the independent variables are suggestive. Partisan control of the Senate appears to have an impact on the likelihood that interest groups participate in the confirmation, although interest group participation is not substantially affected by the position for which an individual has been nominated.

The Effects of Interest Group Participation on Cabinet Confirmations

Although interest groups have (since the 1970s) been important actors in the confirmation process for cabinet secretaries-designate, their participation does not seem to have a quantifiable impact on the outcome for these positions. During the period of study, only two of eighty-eight cabinet nominees failed to be confirmed by the Senate, and each had substantial problems that had nothing to do with interest groups. Unlike judicial

Table 5.6

Influences on Interest Group Participation in Confirmation Hearings
for Cabinet Secretaries Designate, 1977–1998

Variable	B	Standard Error	Significance	Impact
Party in Control of Senate	.575	.752	.445	.14
Carter	1.732	.783	.023**	.35
Reagan	1.170	.763	.125	.26
Bush	.937	.705	.183	.22
Group-Dominated Agency	−.020	.563	.972	.00
Constant	−.055	.488	.910	−.01

N=88

Model Chi-Square (Improvement): 8.040 (df=5)

p < .15

nominees, interest groups appear to be unable to affect confirmation outcomes through their formal participation in confirmation hearings. Further, there is evidence that interest groups might not have as much need to influence confirmation outcomes with regard to cabinet secretaries as they would with judicial nominees, because they have other avenues of formal participation. According to a Senate Foreign Relations Committee staffer, who spoke on the condition of anonymity: "I think the opportunity to influence the confirmation process is in the Secretary of State's office. There's a committee over there that compiles a list and makes cuts. And I am pretty sure that there is representation from outside interest groups there."[16]

Evidence suggests, however, that interest groups are beginning to use the informal means available to them to influence confirmation outcomes. Though he offered no testimony at Alexis Herman's confirmation hearing to be Secretary of Labor in March 1997, NAACP Chairman Kwesi Mfume was present in the audience—in fact, Senator Paul Wellstone noted for the hearing record the presence of the NAACP chair.[17] In addition, interest groups have become active players in confirmation proceedings for sub-cabinet nominees such as Bill Lann Lee, whose nomination was discussed in chapter 2, and Dr. David Satcher, whose nomination to be Surgeon General garnered ninety-six separate endorsements from interest groups. While not even beginning to approach the informal role that groups play in judicial confirmations, interest groups are increasingly prominent actors in the confirmation process for cabinet nominees.

Ambassadors

Ambassadors are the president's official representatives abroad. They are part of the executive branch and often are called upon to represent the president and his policy initiatives overseas. Like cabinet secretaries, ambassadors are appointed to carry out the president's policies.

Ambassadorial nominees represent another large group of individuals whom the Senate must confirm. All told, there are approximately two hundred ambassadorships requiring Senate confirmation, and while this is a substantially smaller number than the number of federal judgeships, presidents often end up appointing almost as many ambassadors as judges during their presidencies as a result of high levels of turnover among ambassadors. Nonetheless, there is relatively little information available about ambassadors. As has been noted elsewhere: "The American public has little information about these men and women, who they are, where they come from, or how they become ambassadors. Except for the famous or near famous, the American ambassador remains an unknown quantity."[18] Just as there is little known about the men and women who serve as ambassadors, there has been little study on the influences on the confirmation process for ambassadorial nominees.

The history of ambassadorial appointments sheds some light on the confirmation process for ambassadors. During the first 150 years of American history, neither interest groups nor the Senate itself deemed ambassadorial confirmations worthy of much attention. Ambassadorships were seen as prizes that presidents could use almost unchecked to reward loyal partisans and campaign supporters. Today, many ambassadors work their way up through the foreign service to achieve the rank of ambassador. But this is a recent phenomenon. Throughout much of the nineteenth century, presidents simply named political friends to important ambassadorial posts. According to Mak and Kennedy (1992, 3): "From the presidency of Andrew Jackson on, the guiding principle to the selection of American chiefs of mission was 'to the victors belong the ambassadorial or ministerial appointments.' Both U.S. embassies and consulates were staffed by politically appointed Americans until the turn of the 20th century."[19]

The notion that ambassadors are appointed to repay electoral debts persists. According to a Congressional Research Service report, there is a "perceived tendency of [presidential administrations] ... to reward large campaign donors and other party loyalists."[20] In addition, ambassadorial nominees were considered to be part of the lower tier of appointments that presidents were called upon to make. Mak and Kennedy (1992, 3) explain: "The U.S. had no actual ambassadors abroad until 1893. While the major European countries exchanged ambassadors among themselves, the United States was considered to be a second-class power and rated only ministers."[21] The result was that no one paid particular attention to ambassadorial nominees.

Presidential nominees to fill vacant ambassadorships come from a wide variety of backgrounds and interests. Many have previous foreign policy experience, although some are appointed in reward for campaign contributions. While there are a number of ambassadors confirmed in each congress, ambassadorial nominees are among the most difficult of all of the president's major appointments to study. This is because with the exception of a handful of high-profile positions, confirmation hearings for ambassadorships are almost always strictly perfunctory. For example, according to a study by Washington Report, an organization that monitors activities relating to the U.S. Department of State, a September 18, 1997, confirmation hearing for four ambassadors and one nominee to be assistant secretary of state "lasted only two hours, with more than half of the session devoted to the [assistant secretary's nomination]."[22] Jonathan Sanford, a CRS research specialist, finds that between 1987 and 1996, seventeen ambassadorial nominees were confirmed without any hearings at all.[23]

Table 5.7 records confirmation outcomes for confirmation hearings for ambassadorships between 1977 and 1998. Between those years, 94.5 percent of all ambassadorial nominations were confirmed by the Senate. Nominees who were granted hearings by the Senate Foreign Relations Committee were confirmed 98.0 percent of the time. It is clear that like nominees to fill vacant cabinet positions, ambassadorial nominees are almost always confirmed. As a CRS researcher notes: "The vast majority of nominations referred to the Senate Foreign Relations Committee in the foreign affairs field are confirmed."[24]

The lack of variation in confirmation outcomes for ambassadorial nominees makes such outcomes difficult to analyze. Data analysis of ambassadorial confirmations suffers, as did the analysis of confirmation outcomes for cabinet secretaries-designate, because with so little variation in outcomes it is impossible to research quantitatively the factors contributing to confirmation or non-confirmation. Yet there is another, more fundamental difficulty in analyzing ambassadorial confirmations: not only are nearly all ambassadorial nominees confirmed, but records of ambassadorial confirmation hearings are not organized or kept in any readily available format. As a 1997 Congressional Research Service (CRS) Report on the disposition of ambassadorial nominations notes: "Unless specifically indicated, nomination hearings are not printed, and all votes are by voice," and within the CRS report, not a single ambassadorial confirmation hearing appears to have a printed hearing record.[25]

Table 5.7
Confirmation Outcomes for Ambassadorial Nominations, 1977–1998

Congress	Dates	Number of Nominees	Number (and Percent) Receiving Hearings	Number (and Percent) Confirmed
95th	1977–78	113	110 (97%)	110 (97%)
96th	1979–80	91	88 (97%)	84 (92%)
97th	1981–82	103	103 (100%)	103 (100%)
98th	1983–84	81	81 (100%)	81 (100%)
99th	1985–86	97	95 (98%)	92 (95%)
100th	1987–88	44	43 (98%)	37 (84%)
101st	1989–90	121	112 (93%)	109 (90%)
102nd	1991–92	105	89 (85%)	87 (83%)
103rd	1993–94	120	120 (100%)	119 (99%)
104th	1995–96	49	49 (100%)	49 (100%)
105th	1997–98	69	67 (97%)	67 (97%)
TOTALS		993	957	938 (94.5%)

Sources: Senate Foreign Relations Committee. Legislative and Executive Calendar. Congresses Indicated.

According to staff members of the Senate Foreign Relations Committee, the committee of jurisdiction for the consideration of ambassadorship nominations, any records of ambassadorial confirmation hearings are sent to the National Archives within a few weeks. Neither the Foreign Relations Committee library nor any of the government's federal depository libraries keep copies of the majority of confirmation hearings for these nominees. Further, most ambassadors are confirmed by voice vote, including nominees to important posts such as Israel and India. Thus, any study of the confirmation process for ambassadorships suffers from a lack of quantifiable data. Unlike the explorations of judicial confirmation hearings, and confirmation hearings for cabinet secretaries-designate that appear in previous sections of this project, there is no set of comprehensive data that will allow for a solid study of the role of interest groups in the confirmation process. However, that is not to say that interest groups are unimportant to the confirmation process for ambassadorial nominees. Rather, like their counterparts in the judiciary and in the cabinet, ambassadorial nominees may be confronted by interest groups during their confirmation process in the United States Senate.

Unlike cabinet and judicial confirmations, where interest groups have been major players for decades, and where certain interest groups are repeat participants, interest groups have not typically been active in the confirmation

process for ambassadors. Instead, their participation is a relatively recent phenomenon. According to Nan Aron of the Alliance for Justice, and
Steve Schwalm of the Family Research Council (whose organization was
active in opposing the nomination of James Hormel to be ambassa-dor to
Luxembourg), there is no organization that devotes a substantial amount
of time to the monitoring of ambassadorial nominations. Even Schwalm
notes: "[The Family Research Council does not] ordinarily get involved
in foreign policy and ambassadorial nominations. Nobody cares about
ambassadors."[26]

Schwalm overstates the apathy toward ambassadorial nominees. For
example, former Ambassador Edward Perkins recalls that interest groups
were very involved in participating in all four of his confirmations—to be
ambassador to Liberia, South America, the United Nations, and Australia.
Perkins notes that different groups were present at each of his confirmations, but that across the board, interest groups were involved.[27] A Foreign
Relations Committee staffer, speaking on the condition of anonymity,
noted: "Open letters, confidential information, you name it, I think it's happened, the groups have done it."[28]

Like the confirmation process for other groups of nominees, interest
groups can be important in the confirmation process for ambassadorships.
But despite their participation in Perkins's confirmation proceedings, interest group participation in confirmations for ambassadorial nominees is not
a universal phenomenon.

The lack of interest group participation is a function of the perception
that ambassadorships are the president's exclusive prerogative. Interest
groups typically have avoided involvement in the confirmation process for
nominees to fill vacant ambassadorships. During the 105th Congress, that
practice changed, as conservative interest groups mobilized to attempt to
defeat the nomination of James Hormel to be ambassador to Luxembourg.
The Family Research Council, the most outspoken group in opposition to
Hormel's confirmation, claims success; Hormel's nomination was returned
to the president at the expiration of the 105th Congress.

The Hormel Case

As was discussed in chapter 2, James Hormel, a philanthropist and former
Dean of Students at the University of Chicago, was nominated by President Bill Clinton in October 1997 to serve as the ambassador to Luxembourg. Prior to his nomination, Hormel had also served as a member of the

United States delegation to the United Nations Human Rights Commission and was an alternate representative to the United Nations; the latter required Senate confirmation, which was granted without problem.[29]

Yet despite his diplomatic credentials, Hormel is also a longtime Democratic Party activist who has contributed large sums of money to the party. He is also openly gay. For that reason, his nomination was opposed by a handful of Republican senators who expressed concerns that Hormel's open homosexuality would lead him to promote a homosexual agenda while stationed as ambassador to Luxembourg. An editorial in the *Washington Post* noted: "The Senators who object—Tim Hutchison of Arkansas, James Inhofe of Oklahoma, Robert Smith of New Hampshire, and a fourth who remains anonymous—say they fear he would use his ambassadorship to advance a gay rights agenda."[30] According to the Family Research Council's Steve Schwalm, conservative North Carolina Senator and Chairman of the Senate Foreign Relations Committee Jesse Helms was the fourth senator to place a hold on Hormel's nomination.[31]

Although the four conservative senators held up Hormel's confirmation, he also received broad support, for his confirmation, not only among Democrats but among a few prominent Republicans as well, including former Senator Alfonse D'Amato (R-NY) and Senator Orrin Hatch (R-UT).[32] Hatch stated: "My personal belief is that although I do not approve of the gay lifestyle, I'm still not going to discriminate against someone who is otherwise qualified."[33] On April 3, 1998, forty-two Democratic senators sent a letter to Senate Majority Leader Trent Lott requesting a vote on Hormel's nomination, which had been approved by the Foreign Relations Committee sixteen to two in November 1997. But Lott refused to move Hormel's nomination. A *Rocky Mountain News* editorial declared on April 21, 1998: "If Hormel's being gay is the only issue, the Senate should vote on and approve his nomination."[34] Early in the second week of June 1998, Democratic senators Robert Torricelli (NJ) and Dianne Feinstein (CA) sent an opinion piece to newspapers around the country, challenging their Republican colleagues to confirm Hormel. They wrote: "We urge our colleagues to part with the Republican Party's extreme faction and bring the nomination of this talented man to a vote of the full Senate."[35] James Hormel's nomination to serve as ambassador to Luxembourg was returned to the president when the 105th Congress adjourned in October 1997.

While Hormel's failure to be confirmed is interesting in and of itself, in light of the ease with which most ambassadorial nominees are confirmed, his experience is also important because it marks the first instance of interest group warfare over an ambassadorial nominee in recent memory.[36] According to one report: "Hormel's nomination has become a test case for the social conservatives, among them the Family Research Council, which has accused the Clinton administration of 'cultural imperialism' for promoting a nominee offensive to family values. At the same time, the nomination has been a rallying point for gay advocacy groups, who are using the stalemate to disparage Republicans."[37]

On the conservative side, the Family Research Council immediately mobilized to oppose Hormel's nomination. According to Steve Schwalm: "When Bill Clinton nominated Hormel in October [1997] right away red flags came up because we were aware of his funding of [gay] activist organizations."[38] The group immediately began gathering information on Hormel's past activities with regard to homosexual advocacy and support of the Democratic Party. According to Schwalm, in the assessment of the Family Research Council, Hormel "was all over the map doing everything that's contrary to Christian values. His activities are a direct attack on the family."[39]

Once the Family Research Council had gathered and analyzed information concerning Hormel's previous political activities, the group made it available at both the grassroots and Capitol Hill levels. According to Schwalm, the Family Research Council targeted Catholics, the Promise Keepers (Schwalm claims that the Human Rights Campaign has attacked the Promise Keepers), educators, the Boy Scouts (who were forced to defend their refusal to permit homosexuals to be members of their organization), and members of the military.[40]

On the liberal side, the Human Rights Campaign ("the nation's largest gay and lesbian organization," according to published reports) countered the conservative campaign against Hormel with articles in its *Human Rights Campaign Quarterly* as well as attempts to mobilize supporters of Hormel and nondiscrimination in federal appointments. In the spring 1998 issue of this publication, executive editor Kim Mills highlighted Hormel's plight. The article included endorsements from three sitting Democratic senators, Secretary of State Madeleine Albright, and President Clinton. The organization was even invited to participate in a strategy session at the White House in June 1998 to explore ways to end the Senate impasse and confirm James Hormel.[41]

As has been noted above, Hormel's nomination was returned to the president at the end of the 105th Congress. Although it is unclear to what extent interest group participation in Hormel's confirmation contributed to his inability to be confirmed, it is possible to conclude that with regard to ambassadorial nominees, the extensive nature of the Family Research

Council's campaign against Hormel was without parallel. It is possible, as well, that the Hormel nomination is a harbinger of things to come. Schwalm notes that the Family Research Council's measure of success was whether or not Hormel was confirmed by the Senate. He said: "If Hormel becomes the ambassador to Luxembourg, we've failed." When asked whether success in the campaign against Hormel would encourage the Family Research Council to get involved in future ambassadorial nominations, Schwalm replied that the Council would oppose any nominee whose views were hostile to Christian values.[42]

Cabinet and Ambassadorial Confirmations

Cabinet and ambassadorial nominations are, more than judicial nominations, considered to be spoils of the presidency. Nonetheless, interest groups frequently participate in the confirmation process for both these groups of nominees. For nominees to cabinet positions, interest groups expend sizeable amounts of time and money to influence both the nomination and the confirmation process.

Although there is no good way to measure the influence of money on the confirmation process for cabinet nominees, financial contributions appear to be a driving force in the appointment of many ambassadors. According to Scott Olson of Common Cause, a prospective nominee's donation history to the political party of the president "can make a difference" when the president is deciding whom to nominate. Interest groups, too, spend money to affect the appointment process for ambassadors. According to a senior staff member of the Senate Foreign Relations Committee, much of this money is spent at the agency level (in the case of ambassadorial nominees, at the State Department), where interest groups will try to lobby the committee responsible for screening all prospective foreign affairs nominations. If they are unsuccessful at the agency level, they may spend time and money at the grassroots level to influence confirmation outcomes, as the Hormel case illustrates.

Conclusion

This chapter has explored the dynamics of interest group participation in the confirmation process for two groups of nominees—nominees to fill vacancies on the president's cabinet and nominees to fill vacant ambassadorships abroad. Although the available data are not as complete as those available for evaluating the role of interest groups in the confirmation process for federal judges, it is possible to draw some important conclusions.

First, with regard to cabinet secretaries, interest groups are active participants in the confirmation process. Between 1977 and 1998, interest groups participated in 72.7 percent of all confirmation hearings for cabinet nominees. This compares with a participation rate of just 12.8 percent for judicial nominees. Interest groups' formal participation in the confirmation process for cabinet secretaries-designate has decreased steadily since 1980. While groups participated in more than half of the confirmation hearings for President Bill Clinton's cabinet nominees, that represents a substantial decrease from a high of 84.2 percent participation in hearings during the Carter administration.

Evidence from the 105th Congress suggests that interest groups are now using informal techniques in cabinet confirmations, although they seem less reliant on informal techniques than do the interest groups who participate in the confirmation process for judicial nominees. This is most likely because the formal avenues for participation have not been closed off from interest groups wishing to participate in cabinet confirmations in the way they have been with regard to judicial confirmations.

It is also clear that the same factors that influence interest group participation in the confirmation process for judicial nominees do not affect their participation in the confirmation process for cabinet secretaries-designate. This suggests that policy concerns rather than political circumstances dominate interest groups' calculations in deciding to participate in the confirmation process for cabinet nominees. The exception to this is the finding above that interest groups were most likely to participate during President Carter's administration. Like the confirmation process for judicial nominees, interest groups' formal participation in the confirmation process for cabinet nominees peaked in the late 1970s. They are less formally involved in confirmation politics for cabinet secretaries-designate today than they were two decades ago.

In contrast to cabinet confirmations, interest groups are not yet consistent participants in ambassadorial confirmations. The available evidence suggests that participation by interest groups during the confirmation process for James Hormel was an anomaly; interest groups do not generally follow ambassadorial appointments. Yet their departure from their standard practice by participating in the Hormel confirmation may be the most important finding of this chapter. In opposing Hormel's nomination to be the ambassador to Luxembourg, groups such as the Family Research Council waged a costly and intense public relations war against Hormel at the grassroots level. It is possible that with their success in forcing Hormel's rejection, interest groups will heighten their scrutiny of ambassadorial nominees as they engage in the omnipresent struggle to have an impact on the policy process.

6

Looking to the Future:
Interest Group Participation
and the Confirmation Process

> The Constitution begins with the words 'We, the people of the United States,' and in recent years, We the people have taken an unprecedented role in the process of nominating and confirming the public servants who govern in our name. This is, in the abstract, all to the good. But the sound-bite campaigns against nominees that are now a regular feature of our politics play to the worst in the American character.
>
> Stephen L. Carter, *The Confirmation Mess*, 1994

Margaret Morrow was the poster child for the far right. Nominated to fill a vacancy on California's Central District Court, conservative interest groups seized upon a statement she had made in 1988 that was critical of California's ballot initiatives procedure. First nominated in May 1996, Morrow's nomination languished for nearly two years as conservative senators responded to the interest groups' call to oppose her confirmation. Like Morrow, Frederica Massiah-Jackson's confirmation was undone by Pennsylvania law enforcement and criminal justice organizations. David Satcher's nomination was opposed by the Christian Coalition and other pro-life interest groups. The Human Rights Campaign battled for James Hormel's confirmation from the left, while the Family Research Council pushed against it from the right. Mike Schattman's nomination was undone by his home state senators. Hispanic groups protested outside of the Supreme Court, while the Judicial Selection Monitoring Project produced a videotape urging conservative activists to contribute to the organization to help keep President Clinton's nominees off the federal bench.

While many presidential nominees continue to be confirmed without controversy, in recent years an increasing number have been subject to intense Senate and interest group scrutiny, delay, and in some cases, rejection. By nearly all assessments, the Senate's confirmation process has moved away from its constitutional underpinnings toward something that only vaguely resembles the process the framers designed. What Common Cause called a "rubber stamp machine" in the 1970s is now criticized for being too slow, too unpredictable, and too disrespectful of the president and his nominees. In 1994, Stephen Carter declared that the United States was suffering from a "confirmation mess." In 1996, the Twentieth Century Fund called the appointment process an "obstacle course." When asked about the confirmation process that approved her to be a federal district judge in Massachusetts, Judge Nancy Gertner declared: "It's all so profoundly irrational."[1] And former U.S. Senator Howard Metzenbaum thinks "it's a tragedy what they're doing to these nominees."[2]

How did things get so bad in such a short period of time? Chapter 2 suggested several explanations, including changes in the Senate's role in the confirmation process, changes in internal Senate norms, and interest group participation. It is this last explanatory variable that appears to be most fruitful; despite changes to the Senate and its internal norms, most nominees move through the confirmation process smoothly and without problem. But in the contemporary confirmation process, interest groups participate in ways once reserved for only the most important of legislative initiatives. And when they do, they are a powerful force in affecting confirmation outcomes, reducing the likelihood of confirmation by nearly half. Recognizing that appointees to the federal government are integrally involved in shaping public policy, interest groups now focus on the confirmation process in the hopes of influencing public policy.

Interest groups are now nearly coequal actors with agency heads and the presidential personnel staff in the contemporary confirmation process. As the White House has decentralized its selection process and the president has exercised less responsibility in choosing nominees, interest groups have taken on an important new role. They now are an integral part of both choosing nominees and determining whether or not presidential nominees are confirmed. In the late 1970s, one observer described the steps interest groups go through in the late 1970s when trying to influence presidential selection: "The decentralized approach has meant that the interest groups have had to concentrate on the departments instead of the White House. Lists of applicants have been compiled. Meetings with secretaries have been arranged. Cabinet and agency officials have often turned to the groups for consultation and advice. Congress has been one rallying point for some of the groups, such as the blacks and Hispanics."[3]

Interest Groups in the Confirmation Process

Interest groups are strategic actors. They do not participate in all, or even the vast majority of, confirmation hearings for individuals nominated by the president. The president nominates hundreds of individuals every year to fill vacancies in offices considered to be major appointments. Most interest groups have neither the time nor the resources to review very many of these nominees. With the exception of cabinet nominees, most of the president's major appointments are ignored by interest groups. Instead, groups focus the vast majority of their scarce resources on targeting prominent nominees to important positions.

Interest groups participate more often in confirmations for high-level appointments than they do for lower-level positions. They are more likely to participate in the confirmation process when they believe that the vacancy to be filled is of serious consequence. For example, they are present more often in Circuit Court of Appeals confirmations than they are in district court confirmations and more often participate in cabinet confirmations than ambassadorial confirmations. Interest groups with strong views on specific matters of public policy are likely to participate in confirmation hearings for cabinet secretaries-designate whose agencies are charged with monitoring the programs that the groups care about. By participating in confirmation hearings for nominees to important positions, interest groups hope to influence lower-level positions that the high-level nominees have some responsibility in filling. In addition, interest groups hope to affect public policy in ways that are beneficial to their groups' members. As Robert Shogan writes: "Interest groups have learned that confirmation battles can help advance and protect their objectives."[4]

Interest groups are also inspired to participate in the confirmation process when the nominee is hostile to the groups' goals. Although the analysis of interest groups' formal participation demonstrates that interest groups more frequently testify or submit materials in support of nominees to federal judgeships and cabinet agencies, this finding is misleading. When considered in the context of groups' informal participation, it is clear that interest groups are more often mobilized against nominees than for them. As Stephen Carter writes: "The cruelest comments about Robert Bork came outside the hearing rooms."[5] Lawrence Baum adds: "Group opposition to a nominee is more common than support."[6] Segal and Spaeth conclude that "supportive interest-group mobilization arises largely in reaction to interest-group mobilization against nominees."[7]

As the preceding chapters have demonstrated, interest groups are active participants in the confirmation process for federal political officers. Sometimes their participation is sought by the White House or the Senate; other times they inject their opinions into the confirmation process without being asked. These groups often provide valuable information to senators concerning a nominee's background, expertise, and record. But sometimes they distort a nominee's past, reveal a nominee's secrets, and cast doubt on a nominee's fitness to serve. They are important actors in the confirmation process, but they are at least partly responsible for the "confirmation mess" that exists today.

When interest groups do decide to participate in the confirmation process, their participation may take one of two forms. First, interest groups can participate in the formal mechanisms of the Senate's confirmation process by attending hearings and providing testimony, either orally or in writing. Interest groups' formal participation began in earnest in the 1970s, as the aftermath of Watergate heightened Senate scrutiny of presidential nominees. As the Senate coordinated and centralized its advice and consent power in its committees during that period and began to assert a more active place in the appointment process, interest groups found new access points for their ideas and new pressure points to use against key senators. In the 1970s, interest groups began to use Senate confirmation hearings to practice organizational maintenance, to disseminate their message to senators, and to influence public policy by affecting confirmation outcomes. Senate committees frequently heard testimony from interest groups as they deliberated on the president's nominees.

Between 1979 and 1998, interest groups engaged in formal participation in 144 confirmation hearings (12.9 percent of the time) for judicial nominees. During those years, interest groups engaged in formal participation in sixty-four of eighty-eight (72.7 percent) cabinet nominations. Although the records of ambassadorial confirmations over the last two decades are incomplete, the available evidence suggests that interest group participation in confirmations for ambassadorial nominations is a rare event.

Since the late 1970s, interest group participation in the formal aspects of Senate confirmation has decreased. This is in part because Senate committees are now less willing to permit interest groups to have a formal role in the confirmation process. Scarred from the Bork experience, Senate committee chairs appear to be less interested in hearing from interest groups on the subject of presidential nominations. In addition, many Republicans blamed interest groups for Bork's defeat, as well as for the difficult confirmation experience had by Clarence Thomas, President Bush's nominee to the Supreme

Court in 1991. When the Republicans regained control of both the House and the Senate in 1995, they quickly moved to end any formal role for interest groups in the confirmation process, especially for judicial nominees.

With formal avenues of participation closed to them, interest groups participate in the contemporary confirmation process primarily through the informal avenues of influence available to them. They bring to bear a wide range of tactics, most adapted from their legislative strategies, to try to influence senators' confirmation decisions. As Segal and Spaeth (1993) point out in their study of interest group participation in Supreme Court confirmations, there is no way to measure this type of participation completely.[8] Yet the anecdotal evidence supplied by those individuals integrally involved with the confirmation process, including Senate staffers and interest group leaders, suggests that interest groups are extremely active behind the scenes. Interest groups write letters, organize grassroots campaigns, and lobby senators behind closed doors in order to influence confirmation outcomes.

In the contemporary confirmation process, interest groups use informal techniques much more frequently than they use formal techniques. This is especially true for judicial confirmations, where the Senate Judiciary Committee no longer is open to the formal participation of interest groups. As interest groups' opportunities to participate formally in the confirmation process have been reduced, they have retreated to more and more creative informal means of affecting the confirmation process. One such means of participation is the use of financial inducements to influence senators' votes through such activities as campaign contributions. Money has become intertwined with the confirmation in other ways as well, as interest groups have seized on the political nature of the confirmation process to generate much-needed revenue to fund their causes. The Judicial Selection Monitoring Project's fund-raising videotape, which was discussed in chapter 4, is but one example of the nexus of the interrelated nature of financial and political concerns in the confirmation process.

The finding of greatest consequence to the conventional wisdom surrounding the participation of interest groups in the confirmation process is that formal interest group participation has actually declined since Robert Bork's failed confirmation during the 100th Congress, in 1987. As was noted in both chapters 2 and 4, many previous studies of the role of interest groups in the confirmation process suggested that interest groups were emboldened by the successful group campaigns against Bork and that these newly emboldened groups took the confirmation process by storm. The reality, however, is much more complex than the conventional wisdom would indicate.

The evidence presented in this study indicates that formal interest group participation in the confirmation process—as measured by participation in confirmation hearings—has declined steadily since 1987 for judicial nominees. Formal interest group participation in judicial confirmations was more frequent prior to the 100th Congress, the congress in which Bork's nomination failed. Since 1995, interest groups have been shut out of judicial confirmation hearings altogether by Senate Judiciary Committee Chairman Orrin Hatch. The same finding holds true for cabinet nominees. Since the late 1970s, interest group participation in confirmation hearings for nominees to fill vacancies in the president's cabinet has declined substantially. In general, Senate committee chairs appear to have reacted to the spectacle of the Bork confirmation by being more selective in granting permission to interest groups to participate in the process. Regardless of the reason, however, the data clearly indicate a decline in the formal participation of interest groups in the confirmation process.

The data also indicate that informal interest group participation—behind-the-scenes lobbying by interest groups—has remained a constant presence and may have increased since 1987. Interest groups have increasingly moved toward media and grassroots strategies that take place far away from the Senate's hearing rooms. In the contemporary confirmation process, interest groups now use all avenues of influence available to them, not just the formal ones. Thus, it is clear that the conventional wisdom on the participation of interest groups since the Bork confirmation hearings must be revised; first, to indicate the dual nature of group participation, and second, to reflect the reality of diminished formal participation by interest groups in the confirmation process.

The interview data collected indicate that interest groups now use behind-the-scenes techniques to accomplish their policy goals through the confirmation process. The bottom line is that future studies making reference to the impact of the Bork confirmation hearings on interest group participation must recognize that there is an important distinction between formal and informal participation and must be clear about the extent to which both types have changed.

The Consequences of Interest Group Participation

As chapter 4 illustrated, when interest groups participate formally in the confirmation process for judicial nominees, their likelihood of being confirmed decreases significantly. Further, the case of James Hormel indicates that behind-the-scenes participation by interest groups also can affect outcomes in the confirmation process. In short, interest group participation introduces a dynamic into some confirmations that cannot be overcome by other systemic factors. When interest groups participate in the confirmation process, they create incentives for senators to oppose nominees and contribute to the overall contentiousness of the contemporary confirmation process.

Some consequences of interest group participation are readily evident from the analyses presented in chapters 4 and 5. First, interest group participation has a negative effect on confirmation outcomes. In the case of federal judges, interest group participation—regardless of the direction of that participation—reduces the probability of a nominee's confirmation by .48. Further, the direction of interest group participation—in favor of or in opposition to the nominee—is also a significant factor in determining confirmation outcomes. When interest groups appear before the Senate Judiciary Committee to testify against confirming a nominee, that individual's chances of being confirmed are again diminished.

Chapter 4 also demonstrates that interest groups are at least partially responsible for slowing the confirmation process, especially during 1996, 1997, and 1998. Such a slowing leads to additional consequences; the recruitment of individuals willing to accept a nomination to the federal courts may become more difficult, and long-term vacancies in the federal judiciary may cause delays in the administration of justice for those with cases pending in the federal courts.

Because nearly all cabinet nominees are confirmed, it is impossible to estimate statistically the impact of interest groups on these confirmations. However, as with judicial confirmations, antagonistic interest groups may have an impact on recruitment of individuals to serve on the president's team. And while interest group participation in confirmations for cabinet secretaries-designate does not appear to have an effect on confirmation outcomes for these nominees, groups have been able to force showdowns over nominees to other positions. For example, the evidence presented in chapter 5 suggests that interest groups were partially responsible for the return of James Hormel's ambassadorial nomination to President Clinton at the adjournment of the 105th Congress. Clearly, there are consequences of interest group participation in the confirmation process—especially when that participation is in opposition to a nominee.

Evidence from the Bork confirmation hearings and other studies indicates that interest group participation in the confirmation process can have a powerful effect on senators' confirmation decisions. With the new and increasing tactic of linking senators' confirmation votes to the electoral process through grassroots lobbying and campaign contributions, interest groups create new incentives for senators to lead the charge for or against some presidential nominations. Nominees who once would once have sailed through the Senate now may wait months or even years for confirmation. As Lawrence Baum has written: "If groups that are electorally important to a senator mount a campaign against a nominee, the senator may perceive a negative vote as politically advantageous. This is especially true, of course, if the groups' position seems to coincide with prevailing opinion in the senator's state. Further, substantial interest group opposition can overcome the assumption that a nominee will be confirmed and thus stir potential senate opponents to action."[9]

Interest group participation in the confirmation process has created a more contentious environment for presidential nominees. Recognizing that the confirmation process is another opportunity to push their policy agendas and appease their members, interest groups now use Senate confirmations to shape public policy and to punish or reward senators for their decisions. Interest groups opposed to nominees will engage in character attacks and the dissemination of misinformation about nominees. As former Senator Alan Simpson notes: "We have groups that rear up and gear up simply to smote a candidate between the eyes."[10] These groups share information with senators and work with members of the Senate to thwart the appointment of some nominees. Nominees now face the confirmation process with trepidation. In a phone conversation with members of the Senate Judiciary Committee staff, one nominee to the Ninth Circuit Court of Appeals even indicated that she was "terrified" of what would happen at her confirmation hearings.

Fear of Senate confirmation makes the process of recruiting individuals to serve as federal judges more difficult. Illinois Senator Dick Durbin notes in a piece for *Insight Magazine* that 120 people applied to fill a judicial vacancy in Illinois in 1994. But when another vacancy occurred in the fall of 1997, only eight people applied for the job. Durbin writes: "I can only guess why people declined to apply for the job. But a dispassionate look at the situation would give anyone pause. . . . People who are being nominated to fill those positions are being put through a brutal hazing ritual known as Senate confirmation."[11] Former Senator David Boren sums up the consequences of interest group participation in this way: "The confirmation process now drives out the more capable people because they feel they're just going to be torn apart. It's now impossible to confirm anyone with a record."[12]

Decisions about agency personnel and federal judges have important consequences for the type and quality of legislation enacted into federal law.

With regard to judicial and ambassadorial confirmation hearings, interest groups only occasionally participate formally, while they almost always are a presence during confirmations for cabinet secretaries-designate, although they do not participate in all cabinet confirmations. Furthermore, the participation of interest groups is tightly controlled by the chair of the committee of jurisdiction. Time after time, Senate staff members declared "it's up to the chairman" when asked about whether interest groups would be allowed to attend or participate in a confirmation hearing.

In the contemporary confirmation process it takes fifty-one senators to confirm a nominee and only one to keep someone from being confirmed. Interest groups recognize this, and those who support a nominee often wage extensive public campaigns in support of a nominee, while those who oppose a nominee often move underground, targeting senators who are in sync with the organization's views. All the opponents need to do is to persuade one senator to put a hold on the nominee, and the nomination is effectively dead.

Interest groups pay attention to whom the president nominates because they know that the individuals serving in government's highest offices are integrally involved with shaping public policy. Recognizing this, interest groups are active participants in the confirmation process, both formally and informally. In and of itself, there is not necessarily anything inappropriate with regard to interest group participation in the confirmation process. In a democratic political system, interest groups represent real people whose views should be taken into consideration in the legislative and appointment processes. When interest groups participate formally, their participation functions as just one of a number of influences on a senator's confirmation decision calculus. As John Wright explains: "A[n] . . . important function of congressional hearings is to force organized interests to reveal their preferences and to state them publicly."[13] When they do so, senators have an opportunity to ask questions, to listen to their colleagues' questions, and to weigh the testimony of interest groups against the testimony of the nominee. In this respect, the presence of interest groups in the confirmation process can assist senators with structuring their confirmation decisions and may make the confirmation process more democratic.

However, the evidence presented above indicates that formal participation has been declining over time and that interest groups now use informal techniques more frequently than ever before. The result is that their participation can no longer be monitored, nor is it subject to public scrutiny. Participating informally allows groups to exercise complete control over their message without the interference of other interest groups or members of the Senate seeking to determine the veracity of the information being disseminated. The danger, of course, is that such participation also permits interest groups to be ruthless in their attacks on nominees, which may in turn cause some potential nominees to think twice about seeking an appointed office in the federal government.

In light of the successes that interest groups enjoyed during the 105th Congress, it is likely that they will be emboldened to challenge more and more presidential nominations as the twenty-first century begins. This may especially be the case should the Republicans and Democrats swap control of the White House and the Senate. Former Senator Paul Simon, author of *Advice and Consent,* notes that the judicial confirmation process in particular has changed in recent years as Republicans have imposed stricter standards for evaluating a nominee's fitness for confirmation. And Simon is concerned about what will happen in the future. He cautions: "The danger is, of course, that when Democrats take back the [Judiciary] Committee, which they inevitably will one day, that they will do the same thing when a Republican is in the presidency. No one gets served well. The lesson is when the pendulum swings too far in one way it will swing back too far the other way."[14] Further, if judicial confirmations and the case of James Hormel prove to foreshadow the future, interest groups will only be emboldened by past successes to increase their use of informal means of participating in the confirmation process.

Should the passage of time lead to an increase in behind-the-scenes participation by interest groups, there may be some important consequences. First, as has been noted repeatedly throughout this book, informal participation cannot be monitored in any systematic way. Second, informal participation cannot be regulated in any systematic way. While a committee chair may prevent interest groups from testifying at committee hearings, he or she has no power to prevent interest groups from engaging in direct lobbying of individual senators or mobilizing their grass roots.

The prospects for improvement in the confirmation process appear to be far away. It still takes only one senator's objection to force the rejection of presidential nominees. And without other fundamental changes to the confirmation process, there is no reason to believe that the process will change in the near future.

In the contemporary confirmation process, interest groups are important actors. They were successful in forcing the slowdown of the confirmation process during the 105th Congress, and in some cases, like that of the nomination of Judge Frederica Massiah-Jackson, interest groups were integrally involved in forcing the rejection of individual nominees. Based upon that level of success, it is doubtful that groups will retreat from their aggressive lobbying efforts during the confirmation process at the dawn of the twenty-first century. It is also not unlikely that interest groups will stop pushing senators to reject nominees whom the groups deem to be unfit. This is their prerogative, and in many respects, the democratic process is better off for it. What is in doubt, however, is whether the confirmation process can withstand the pressure.

Definitions

In this study, a number of terms and definitions appear repeatedly. When the following terms are used, their meanings are as follows:

Appointment process is used to refer to both presidential and senatorial involvement in filling vacancies in the federal government. The term includes all of the steps involved in filling a vacancy that falls under the process established in Article II of the United States Constitution. That language reads: "The president . . . shall nominate, and by and with the advice and consent of the Senate, shall appoint Ambassadors, other public ministers and consuls, Judges of the Supreme Court, and all other Officers of the United States whose appointments are not herein otherwise provided for, and which shall be established by law."

Although the president appoints individuals to positions ranging from independent government agencies to the Supreme Court, this study is primarily concerned with *major appointments*. The standard definition of major appointments is "those positions at the highest levels of the federal government."[1] These positions include: "Cabinet and subcabinet officers, the heads of independent agencies, the members of regulatory commissions, the directors of government corporations, ambassadors, and federal judges."[2] Although most of these, and even some minor appointed positions, are discussed in this study, primary emphasis is on federal judgeships, cabinet positions, and ambassadors and the role that interest groups play in the confirmation process for these officials. An *appointee* is someone who successfully navigated the confirmation process and was confirmed by the Senate.

The terms *nomination* and/or *nomination process* is used to encompass the procedures used by executive branch personnel to select an individual to fill a vacancy that has occurred. *Selection process* is also used to refer to the president's process of choosing an individual to fill a vacancy requiring

159

appointment. *Nominees* or *presidential nominees* are those individuals who have been selected by the president and whose names have officially been forwarded to the Senate for consideration.

Confirmation and/or *confirmation process* refers to the procedures used by the United States Senate and its committees and subcommittees to approve or disapprove of a president's nominees. Throughout this study, the term *advice and consent* is also used to refer to the Senate's role in the federal appointment process. *Vetting* refers to the process of conducting background checks on a nominee or potential nominee. It may occur prior to a nomination and during the Senate's consideration of a nominee. *Senatorial courtesy* refers to the long-standing tradition of senators deferring to one another during the confirmation process. By tradition, if a senator objects to confirmation of an individual who would serve in his or her home state, the Senate most likely will not confirm the nominee.

Finally, for the purposes of this study, an *interest group* is defined as any nongovernmental, nonparty organization having multiple members and seeking to influence political outcomes. A *lobbyist* is an individual who works for an interest group, whose primary function is to make contact with policy makers. The term *grass roots* refers to those individuals in the mass public who share an attachment to an interest group, either by geography or by ideology. *Interest group activity/interest group participation* refers to the activities interest groups engage in as they attempt to influence outcomes in the legislative and confirmation processes.

A Note on Methodology

Two distinct methodologies are employed in this project. First, quantitative data analysis is the backbone of many of the conclusions in this study. Much of chapter 4 is based on a quantitative analysis of 1,242 judicial nominations and 1,112 confirmation hearings of nominees to the lower federal courts occurring between 1979 and 1998. This large-scale study of the lower federal courts is unusual in that previous studies of judicial confirmations tend to be focused on single case studies as a means of telling the judicial confirmation story. As Silverstein (1994, 5–6) points out: "The principal genre for the study of judicial confirmations has been the case study. . . . This micro-analysis reveals a wealth of valuable detail about a single nomination. . . . At the same time, the case study may focus the reader's attention too narrowly, resulting in an uncomfortable failure to appreciate the wonders of the forest for concentrating attention on a single, albeit dazzling tree." In this analysis, however, the emphasis is on the "forest," rather than the "dazzling trees." Such a large number of cases permits more sophisticated analysis of the role of interest groups in the confirmation process, and permits generalizeable conclusions to be drawn.

In addition to the quantitative analysis of interest groups in the confirmation process for lower federal court nominees, the first part of chapter 5 bases its conclusions on the role of interest groups in the confirmation process for cabinet secretaries-designate on a quantitative analysis of eighty-eight confirmation hearings for cabinet positions between 1977 and 1998. Although not nearly as large a sample as that which was used to analyze judicial confirmation, the data provide a broad look at the dynamics of interest group participation in the confirmation process for cabinet secretaries-designate.

Throughout this project, qualitative interview data and participant observation were used to provide corroborating information and examples

161

of the ways in which interest groups participate in the confirmation process. The qualitative data come from interview data gathered from twenty-eight separate interviews with U.S. senators, Senate staffers, interest group leaders, former senators, and nominees. In addition to formal interviews, many observations are taken from participant observation of the confirmation process from the vantage point of the Senate Judiciary Committee. Between November 1997 and August 1998, I served as an American Political Science Association Congressional Fellow in Washington D.C., where I worked for Senators Kennedy and Leahy on the Judiciary Committee. My primary responsibility was to assist both senators in preparing for their confirmation responsibilities, which gave me firsthand insights into the dynamics of interest group participation in the confirmation process. Both the quantitative and qualitative methodologies described briefly above are discussed in greater detail in the remainder of this appendix.

Quantitative Methodology

Much of the analysis presented in chapters 4 and 5 is based upon data collected from 1,242 judicial nominations and from 88 cabinet secretary nominations between 1977 and 1998. For those nominees granted hearings (1,112 judicial nominees and all 88 cabinet secretaries-designate), additional data were compiled from their hearing transcripts. (Hearing transcripts were compiled with the assistance of the Senate Committee on the Judiciary and the University of Maryland's McKeldin Library.) Each hearing was read and the following data were recorded: the nominee's name, the date of the hearing, the committee chair, the party leadership of the Senate, the position for which the nominee was nominated, whether interest groups were present at the confirmation hearing, the number of groups testifying, the number of groups submitting materials for the hearing record, the committee chair, whether government was divided or unified, and the direction (pro or con) of interest group participation. Then, data on whether the nominee ultimately was confirmed was compiled from Congressional Research Service and the Congressional Record.

The Data Sets

Once the data collection was completed, data were compiled into two separate SPSS (Statistical Package for the Social Sciences) data sets. The first data set categorized multiple data points for 1,242 nominees to the lower federal courts (1,112 of whom were granted hearings). The second data set recorded data on 88 confirmation hearings for cabinet secretaries-designate between 1977 and 1998. Appendix 2 records the sources of information that were used to compile both of these data sets.

Data Set One: Judicial Nominees Data Set (1979–1998)

The following list gives a description of each variable contained in the data set of lower federal court nominees, followed by the variable label (in parentheses). Then, for numeric variables, the value labels assigned follow:

Name of the Nominee: (NAME)
Congress in Which Nominated: (CONGRESS)
96th Congress = '96'
97th Congress = '97'
98th Congress = '98'
99th Congress = '99'
100th Congress = '100'
101st Congress = '101'
102nd Congress = '102'
103rd Congress = '103'
104th Congress = '104'
105th Congress = '105'

Date of Confirmation Hearing: (DATE)
(input from 01/01/79 to 10/30/98)
Year in Which Confirmation Hearing Was Held: (YEAR)
1979 = '1979'
1980 = '1980'
1981 = '1981'
1982 = '1982'
1983 = '1983'
1984 = '1984'
1985 = '1985'
1986 = '1986'
1987 = '1987'
1988 = '1988'
1989 = '1989'
1990 = '1990'
1991 = '1991'
1992 = '1992'

1993 = '1993'
1994 = '1994'
1995 = '1995'
1996 = '1996'
1997 = '1997'
1998 = '1998'

Position for Which an Individual Was Nominated: (POSITION)
Court of International Trade = '0'
Federal District Courts = '1'
Circuit Court of Appeals = '2'

Whether Interest Groups Were Present at Confirmation Hearings:
    (GROUPS)
Yes = '1'
No = '0'

Whether Interest Groups Testified at Confirmation Hearings: (TESTIFY)
Yes = '1'
No = '0'

Whether Interest Groups Submitted Materials at Confirmation Hearings:
    (SUBMIT)
Yes = '1'
No = '0'

Whether the Nominee Was Confirmed by the Senate: (CONFIRM)
Yes = '1'
No = '0'

Chair of the Judiciary Committee: (CHAIR)
Edward M. Kennedy = '1'
Strom Thurmond = '2'
Joseph Biden = '3'
Orrin Hatch = '4'

Partisan Control of the Senate: (PARTY)
Republican = '1'
Democrat = '0'

Divided or Unified Government: (DIVIDED)
Divided = '1'
Unified = '0'

Direction of Interest Group Participation: (DIRECTION)
Unanimously in favor of nominee = '1'

Majority of groups in favor of nominee = '2'
Mixed = '3'
Majority of groups oppose nominee = '4'
Unanimously opposed to nominee = '5'
Groups participated but took no position = '0'
No groups participated = '9'

Data Set Two: Cabinet Nominees Data Set (1977–1998)

The following list gives a description of each variable contained in the data set compiled for cabinet secretaries-designate, followed by the variable label (in parentheses). Then, for numeric variables, the value labels assigned follow.

Name of Nominee: (NAME)
Congress in Which Nominated: (CONGRESS)
96th Congress = '96'
97th Congress = '97'
98th Congress = '98'
99th Congress = '99'
100th Congress = '100'
101st Congress = '101'
102nd Congress = '102'
103rd Congress = '103'
104th Congress = '104'
105th Congress = '105'

Date of Confirmation Hearing: (DATE)
(input from 01/01/79 to 10/30/98)
Year in Which Confirmation Hearing Was Held: (YEAR)
1979 = '1979'
1980 = '1980'
1981 = '1981'
1982 = '1982'
1983 = '1983'
1984 = '1984'
1985 = '1985'
1986 = '1986'
1987 = '1987'
1988 = '1988'
1989 = '1989'
1990 = '1990'

1991 = '1991'
1992 = '1992'
1993 = '1993'
1994 = '1994'
1995 = '1995'
1996 = '1996'
1997 = '1997'
1998 = '1998'

Position for Which an Individual Was Nominated: (POSITION)
Secretary of State = 'state'
Secretary of Defense = 'defense'
Secretary of the Treasury = 'treasury'
Attorney General= 'ag'
Secretary of Agriculture = 'agricult'
Secretary of the Interior = 'interior'
Secretary of the Dept. of Health and Human Services = 'hhs'
Secretary of Commerce = 'commerce'
Secretary of the Dept. of Housing and Urban Development = 'hud'
Secretary of Labor = 'labor'
Secretary of Energy = 'energy'
Secretary of Education = 'ed'
Secretary of Veteran's Affairs = 'va'
Secretary of Transportation = 'trans'

Whether Interest Groups Were Present at Confirmation Hearings:
    (GROUPS)
Yes = '1'
No = '0'

Whether Interest Groups Testified at Confirmation Hearings: (TESTIFY)
Yes = '1'
No = '0'

Whether Interest Groups Submitted Materials at Confirmation Hearings:
    (SUBMIT)
Yes = '1'
No = '0'

Whether the Nominee Was Confirmed by the Senate: (CONFIRM)
Yes = '1'
No = '0'

President of the United States: (PRESIDE)
Jimmy Carter = '1'
Ronald Reagan = '2'
George Bush = '3'
Bill Clinton = '4'

Partisan Control of the Senate: (PARTY)
Republican = '1'
Democrat = '0'

Divided or Unified Government: (DIVGOV)
Divided = '1'
Unified = '0'

Direction of Interest Group Participation: (DIRECTIO)
Unanimously in favor of nominee = '1'
Majority of groups in favor of nominee = '2'
Mixed = '3'
Majority of groups oppose nominee = '4'
Unanimously opposed to nominee = '5'

A Note on Measurement

While most of the variables are self-explanatory, a note on the coding of a view of the variables may be useful to the reader. In both data sets, interest group presence or absence is measured as whether groups are present, through oral or written testimony, at confirmation hearings for lower court nominees. A group is defined as a nongovernmental, nonparty, multimembered organization seeking to influence public policy outcomes. (While there are instances in which private citizens testified against a nominee, their participation was not considered to be group participation, because they represented only themselves.) In order to determine the number of groups participating at the confirmation hearings for lower federal court judges and for cabinet secretaries-designate, I recorded the number of groups that either actually appeared at the confirmation hearings of each nominee, or that submitted materials to the hearing record. When at least one interest group either presented testimony or submitted materials for the hearing record, interest groups were recorded as being present during formal Senate consideration of a nominee.

Similarly, in both data sets, the direction of interest group participation is measured on a Likert scale, from '1' (unanimously in favor of a nominee) to '5' (unanimously opposed to a nominee). In cases where more than one organization participated in a confirmation hearing, the direction variable was coded based on the direction of the majority position of all the groups. If there was no majority in favor or opposed to a nominee, the variable was coded '3' for mixed participation. Divided government is measured as split party control of the presidency and the Senate. The variable was coded '0' when the president and Senate were controlled by the same party (1979–1980, and 1993–1994) and was coded '1' when the president and Senate were controlled by different parties (1987–1992).

The method noted above is consistent with the methodology used by Segal and Spaeth (1995) in their study of factors influencing the staffing of the Supreme Court. As they point out, this method of coding interest group participation clearly cannot comprehensively identify interest group lobbying of individual senators; but Segal and Spaeth also note that there is no way to obtain such information. They state:

> In the best of all possible situations, we would have senator-level data on the amount of lobbying by organized interests. . . . Obviously, such data are unavailable. Thus, while recognizing that some senators will be lobbied more than others, we chose a variable that measures lobbying activity with respect to each nominee, the number of organized interests presenting testimony for . . . and against the nominee . . . at the Senate Judiciary Committee hearings. . . .[W]e presume that the more opposition a nominee has, the less support he or she will have, and alternatively, the more organized support for a nominee, the more support he or she will have (Segal and Spaeth 1993, 150).

In the analyses described below, the data collected from committee hearings, with regard to interest group participation and the direction of that participation, by necessity acts as a proxy for senator-level data on group lobbying efforts.

Hypothesis Testing

In chapter 4, three main hypotheses were tested. First, the hypothesis that interest groups had become more involved in the confirmation process for federal judges since Robert Bork's failed confirmation in 1987 was explored. Using frequency distributions to determine the number of individuals nominated, the number of confirmation hearings held, and the number of instances of interest group participation during confirmation hearings between 1979 and 1998, it became clear that formal interest group participation had actually declined substantially since 1987. (These results appear in table 4.1). Then, descriptive statistics and logistic regression were used to test two additional hypotheses. Logistic regression is an appropriate methodology, because in both hypothesis tests the dependent variable is dichotomous (Agresti 1996; Menard 1995; Agresti 1984).

The second additional hypothesis tested in chapter 4 is that political factors influence whether interest groups participate in the confirmation process for federal judges. First, chi-square analysis was conducted to determine whether there were significant associations between variables in both models. When it became apparent that there were significant associations between interest group participation in confirmation hearings and a series of environmental variables, a model of group participation was developed. In order to operationalize the model, two variables were recoded into dichotomous independent variables. First, the POSITION variable was recoded to reflect a circuit court nomination versus a non–circuit court nomination. Thus a new variable was created:

Circuit Court of Appeals Nomination: (CIRCUIT)
Yes = '1'
No = '0'

Then, the CHAIR variable was recoded. Because its initial coding suggested some kind of ordinal ranking among committee chairs, it was recoded as a series of dummy variables to show that a confirmation hearing took place during the chairmanship of a particular individual. The new variables are as follows:

Was Edward Kennedy the Chairman? (KENNEDY)
Yes = '1'
No = '0'

Was Strom Thurmond the Chairman? (THURMOND)
Yes = '1'
No = '0'

Was Orrin Hatch the Chairman? (HATCH)
Yes = '1'
No = '0'

It should be noted that there was no new variable computed to reflect Joseph Biden's chairmanship of the Senate Judiciary Committee, since those confirmation hearings that took place during Biden's chairmanship are determined by a negative response to the three other chairmanship variables.

Once the key variables needed to test whether the political environment affects the likelihood of formal interest group participation, a logistic regression analysis was performed. The analysis was modeled as follows:

GROUPS = Constant + DIVGOV + CIRCUIT + KENNEDY + THURMOND + HATCH

The results of this hypothesis test appear in chapter 4. An examination of the results indicates that multicollinearity between the chairmanship variables and the divided government variable is highly problematic. Thus, a new model was tested, which did not include the divided government variable. This model is as follows:

GROUPS = Constant + CIRCUIT + KENNEDY + THURMOND + HATCH

Finally, to test the third hypothesis—that interest group participation, and the direction of that participation, are important determinants of confirmation outcomes—logistic regression analysis again is used. Again, it became necessary to recode one of the variables in the analysis. In order to appropriately specify the direction of interest group participation, the DIRECTIO variable was recoded into a new variable:

What Was the Direction of Interest Group Participation? (DIRECT2)
Groups took no position on the nominee = '0'
Groups unanimously supported the nominee = '1'
Majority of groups supported the nominee = '2'
Groups' opinions were mixed = '3'
Majority of groups opposed the nominee = '4'
Groups unanimously opposed the nominee = '5'

Once the new variable was created, it was possible to proceed with the hypothesis test. This time, the model is specified as follows:

CONFIRM = Constant + GROUPS + DIRECT2 + KENNEDY + THURMOND + HATCH

In each table of results, an impact-assessment calculation also is included. The impact of each independent variable on the dependent variables in question (group participation and confirmation outcome, respectively) is calculated based upon the method specified by Segal and Spaeth (1993) in their study of influences on confirmation outcomes for Supreme Court nominees. They explain that in order to "determine the influence of a one (or more) unit change in any independent variable from any prior probability level," a researcher must:

1. Choose a prior probability level.
2. Determine the odds ratio OR=(Pi/1—Pi) for that prior probability level.
3. Take the log of the OR of the prior probability level.
4. For a one-unit change in the independent variable, determine the new log of the odds ratio by adding or subtracting the estimated B for the coefficient of interest. This is the new log of the odds ration after the influence of the variable in question.
5. Take the anti-log of the new OR. This is the new odds ratio.
6. Divide the OR by 1 + OR. This is the new probability of an event happening.
7. Compare the new probability with the prior probability of the event happening. (Segal and Spaeth 1995, 371–72).

Once the calculations were completed, the difference in probability of the phenomenon measured by the dependent variable occurring when the independent variable is included in the analysis appears in the "Impact" column of the analysis tables.

In chapter 5, the data collected on cabinet secretaries-designate was used to compile table 5.1, which examined the extent to which interest groups participated in confirmation hearings for these nominees between 1979 and 1998. In order to compile this table, frequency distributions drawn from the data were used. Because the majority of the data compiled regarding cabinet appointees was nominal data, no further quantitative tests were performed on the data. Instead, qualitative data were used to supplement the remainder of the analysis and discussion in chapter 5.

Qualitative Methodology

In addition to the quantitative analysis of confirmation hearings for judicial nominees and cabinet nominees, this project uses qualitative evidence to support the findings of the logistic regression analysis. Most significantly, this project relies on data gathered through participant observation. Fenno (1978) pioneered the use of qualitative "participant observation" in *Home Style*, his 1978 examination of how members of Congress behave in their districts. Although Fenno's research focused on interviews with members of Congress, his notes on methodology are useful for understanding the qualitative methodology employed in this study. He notes: "Research based on participant observation is likely to have an exploratory emphasis. Someone doing this kind of research is quite likely to have no crystallized idea of what he or she is looking for or what questions to ask when he or she starts. Researchers typically become interested in some observable set of activities and decide to go have a firsthand look at them."

By spending ten months immersed in confirmation politics, I was able to observe several phenomena related to interest group participation. In addition to participant observation, I conducted thirty-one interviews and conversations with individuals who are or have been integrally involved in the confirmation process. All of these were all open-ended interviews, although similar questions were asked of all interviewees. Interview subjects were selected based upon research into the important players in the confirmation process. All were contacted personally via telephone, e-mail, or personal visit, and formal interviews were set up. Subjects were told that they were being interviewed for a dissertation on the role of interest groups in the Senate confirmation process. Interviewees were also told that their comments would be on the record but that at any time they could specify that they preferred their comments to be kept anonymous. Four individuals specifically requested that the entire interview be kept anonymous. The interview subjects and affiliations at the time of the interviews are as follows:

Alex Acosta—Director, Project on the Judiciary

Anonymous Congressional Research Service Specialist

Anonymous Democratic Senator

Anonymous Republican Senators (2)

Anonymous Senate Foreign Relations Committee Staffer

Nan Aron—Director, Alliance for Justice

Melody Barnes—Chief Counsel to Senator Edward M. Kennedy (D-MA)

Victoria Bassetti—Former Chief Counsel to Senator Richard Durbin (D-IL)

Linda Berg—National Organization for Women (via telephone)

David Boren (D-OK)—Former Senator and Judiciary Committee Member, President, The University of Oklahoma

Tracy Hahn-Burkett—Legislative Aide, People for the American Way and former staffer to Senator Herb Kohl (D-WI)

Michael Carrasco—Former Minority Nominations Clerk, Senate Committee on the Judiciary

Bruce Cohen—Minority Chief Counsel, Senate Committee on the Judiciary

Rhett DeHart—Former Counsel to Senator Jeff Sessions (R-AL) and current Counsel to Senator Orrin Hatch (R-UT)

Mary DeOrco—Investigator, Senate Committee on the Judiciary

Mark Fox—Legislative Assistant to Senator Daniel Inouye (D-HI)

Rogelio Garcia—Congressional Research Service Specialist

Nancy Gertner—Federal Judge, District of Massachusetts

Tom Jipping—Executive Director, People for the American Way

Stephan Kline—Former Director, Judicial Selection Project, Alliance for Justice

Howard Metzenbaum (D-OH)—Former U.S. Senator

Eliot Mincberg—Legal Director, People for the American Way

Scott Olson—Common Cause

Edward Perkins—Former Ambassador to Liberia, South Africa, the United Nations, and Australia

Warren Rudman (R-NH)—Former U.S. Senator

Mary Ellen Schattman—Wife of Michael Schattman and independent researcher

Michael Schattman—Nominee to the Federal District Court of North Texas

Steve Schwalm—Family Research Council

Paul Simon (D-IL)—Former Senator and member of the Senate Committee on the Judiciary

Ronald Weich—Former Chief Counsel to Senator Edward M. Kennedy

Although the interviews were open-ended, subjects were asked similar questions. The former senators and the Senate staffers that I interviewed were asked about the extent to which they utilize information from interest groups, the extent to which they seek out information from interest

groups, their view about the involvement of interest groups in the confirmation process, and their views about the proper role of interest groups in
the confirmation process. Former nominees were asked about their impres-
sions of the confirmation process in general, the extent to which interest
groups participated in their confirmation process, and their views about the
proper role of interest groups in the confirmation process. Interest group
leaders were asked to comment on whether they attempt to influence the
confirmation process, the strategies they use, and their measures of success.
They also were asked to provide copies of any written materials they had
produced relative to the confirmation process.

Notes

Introduction

1. See *The Senate Rubber Stamp Machine,* published by Common Cause in 1977.

2. Mackenzie 1996, p. 61.

3. LeLoup and Shull 1999, p. 54.

4. O'Brien 1988, p. 65.

5. Author's calculation based on data in Mackenzie 1996, p. 55.

7. Rogelio Garcia, interview by author, November 26, 1997.

8. Fenno 1959, p. vii.

9. Mak and Kennedy 1992, p. 22.

10. Tribe 1986, p. 2.

11. Rehnquist 1998, p. 7.

12. Letter from Senator Phil Gramm to the Honorable Thomas Windham, Chief of Police, Fort Worth Police Department, April 5, 1996.

13. Letter from Senator Kay Bailey Hutchison to the Honorable Thomas Windham, Chief of Police, Fort Worth Police Department, April 17, 1996.

14. Letter from Senator Kay Bailey Hutchison to Ms. Trista Allen, October 17, 1997.

15. "The Inside Report: At Last Report, Nomination Still Up in the Air." Column in *The Fort Worth Star-Telegram,* June 7, 1998, p. 3; Ron Hutcheson, "GOP's Hutchison Blasts Democratic Nominee Coggins, *The Fort Worth Star-Telegram,* June 27, 1998, p. 16.

16. Michael Schattman, interview by author, November 13, 1998.

17. Ornstein 1997, p. 5.

18. Mackenzie 1998, p. 6.

19. Letter from Bob J. Nash to Trent Lott, June 4, 1998.

20. The Senate did confirm many nominees whose nominations were received after the date of Nash's letter but confirmed only 62.5 percent of those individuals whose nominations were pending on June 4, 1998.

21. Mackenzie 1998, p. 2.

22. Sinclair 1996, p. 4.

23. As quoted in Mintz 1998, p. 1663.

24. See Bork 1990; Silverstein 1994; and Simon 1992, *Advice and Consent,* among others.

25. Schlozman and Tierney 1986, p. 150.

26. Warren Rudman, interview by author, August 7, 2000.

27. See, for example, Caldeira and Wright 1998; Baum 1995; Maltese 1995; Overby et al. 1994; Guliuzza, Reagan, and Barrett 1994; Silverstein 1994; Gittenstein 1992; Overby and Henschen 1992; Abraham 1991; Bork 1990; Bronner 1989; and Watson and Stookey 1998.

28. Caldeira and Wright 1998; Hrebenar 1997; Carter 1994; Silverstein 1994; Bork 1990; Wolpe 1990; and Bronner 1989.

29. Hrebenar 1997, p. 4.

30. Wolpe 1990, p. 113.

31. Berry 1997, p. 179.

32. See, for example, Carney 1998b.

33. Between November 1997 and August 1998, I worked as an American Political Science Association congressional fellow for the minority staff of the Senate Judiciary Committee. I worked most directly for Senator Edward M. Kennedy of Massachusetts and Senator Patrick J. Leahy of Vermont. My primary responsibility was to monitor judicial and Department of Justice confirmations, and this job provided me ample opportunities to evaluate firsthand interest group participation.

34. Rutkus 1991, p. 3.

35. Ibid., p. 7.

36. Ibid., p. 11.

37. Ibid., p. 19.

38. Ibid.

39. Sanford 1997, p. 1.

40. One CRS researcher summed it up this way: "Look, if there's no ambassador, it's not like the embassy shuts down. Work goes on. The ambassador is just a figurehead." (Author's interview with anonymous CRS researcher, 1997).

41. Former senator David L. Boren, interview with author, June 26, 1997.

Chapter 1

1. Farrand 1966b, p. 419.

2. Fisher 1991, p. 51.

3. Lowi and Ginsburg 1996, p. 18.

4. Farrand 1966a, pp. 20–22. All quotations from members of the Constitutional Convention have been left intact and have not been corrected for spelling or grammatical "errors." This is done to preserve the style of the speaker and is intentional.

5. Farrand 1966a, pp. 20–22.

6. Ibid., p. 116.
7. Ibid., p. 119.
8. Ibid.
9. Ibid., p. 120.
10. Ibid., p. 128.
11. Ibid., p. 230.
12. Ibid., pp. 282–83.
13. Ibid., pp. 294, 301.
14. Farrand 1966b, p. 44.
15. Ibid., pp. 44, 83.
16. Ibid., pp. 392–98.
17. Ibid., p. 473.
18. Rakove 1996, p. 264.
19. Ibid., p. 266.
20. Farrand 1966c, p. 150.
21. Ibid., p. 159.
22. Ibid., p. 162.
23. Harris 1953, pp. 37–38.
24. Ibid., p. 40.
25. Ibid., p. 36.
26. Arnold 1996, p. 477.
27. Ibid.
28. Ibid.
29. Ibid., pp. 477–78.
30. Ibid., p. 479.
31. Ibid., p. 481.
32. Ibid., p. 488.
33. Prince 1977, p. 4.
34. Abraham 1991, p. 71.
35. Harris 1953; Abraham 1996.
36. Harris 1953, p. 44.
37. Ibid., p. 46.
38. Mackenzie 1981, p. 94.
39. Harris 1953, pp. 49–50.
40. Ibid., pp. 51–52.
41. Silbey 1990, p. 9.
42. Mackenzie 1996, p. 39.
43. Harris 1953, p. 53.
44. Ibid.
45. Ibid., p. 59. The great irony, of course, is that Taney would later be confirmed to the position of Chief Justice of the United States and would later preside over the infamous Dred Scott case.

46. Ibid., p. 65.
47. Polk, as quoted in Harris 1953, p. 65.
48. Wayne et al. 1996, p. 516.
49. Ibid.
50. Harris 1953, pp. 79–80.
51. Ibid., p. 90.
52. Ibid., pp. 92–93.
53. Ibid., p. 94; Morganston 1976, p. 99.
54. Harris 1953, p. 94.
55. Maltese 1995, pp. 56–69.
56. Maltese 1998, pp. 52–53.
57. Harris 1953, pp. 133–34.
58. Maltese 1995, p. 118.
59. Harris 1953, p. 195.
60. Mackenzie 1981, p. 12.
61. Harris 1953, pp. 196–97.
62. Mackenzie 1981, p. 11.
63. Ibid., pp. 19–20.
64. Ibid., pp. 27–29.
65. Ibid., pp. 29–30.
66. Ibid., p. 36.
67. Ibid., p. 39.
68. Mackenzie 1996, p. 62.
69. O'Brien 1988, p. 73.
70. Nan Aron, Alliance for Justice President, interview by author, January 1998.
71. Carter 1994, p. 126.
72. Maltese 1995, pp. 137–38.
73. Prior to the Ninety-ninth Congress, the resume of congressional activity did not distinguish between civilian nominations to major positions and civilian nominations to less major positions. Because this study explores the confirmation process for nominees to major positions, data prior to the 99th Congress would be unreliable.
74. Presidential Appointees Initiative Report, April 2000.
75. Ibid.
76. From statistics routinely compiled for the Senate Judiciary Committee, minority staff.

Chapter 2

1. See Wayne et al. 1996, p. 516.
2. Rutkus 1997, pp. 7, 11.

3. Lenhart 1991, p. 3.

4. Mackenzie 1998, p. 21.

5. Heclo 1977, p. 82.

6. Presidential Appointees Initiative Report, April 2000.

7. Hertzke and Peters 1992, p. 4.

8. Loomis 2000, p. 27.

9. Ibid., pp. 27–28.

10. Weisberg, Heberlig, and Campoli 1999, p. 199.

11. Baumer, in Hertzke and Peters, eds. 1992, p. 294.

12. Sinclair 2000, p. 85.

13. Bach 1997, "Minority Rights and Senate Procedures," p. 2.

14. Binder and Smith 1997, p. 203.

15. Anecdotal evidence supports this view. However, it is impossible to know for certain how many hold requests are made per congress, as prior to the 106th Congress, holds were generally kept secret by the majority leader.

16. Silverstein 1994, p. 19.

17. For a discussion of changes to Senate norms beginning in the 1960s, see Hibbing and Peters (1990) and Sinclair (1989).

18. Silverstein 1994, pp. 27.

19. Eliot Mincberg, interview by author, July 13, 1998.

20. Among judicial nominees, these nominees include Margaret Morrow to be a District Court judge on California's Central District Court; Frederica Massiah-Jackson to be a District Court judge on Pennsylvania's Eastern District Court; Michael McCuskey and G. Patrick Murphy to serve on the Central and Southern Illinois District Courts, respectively. Nominees to other positions also were subject to holds. For example, Jim Dial's nomination to the Federal Communication Commission was held up in 1998 by a hold placed by Senator Carol Moseley Braun (D-IL). In 1998, James Hormel's nomination to become ambassador to Luxembourg was the victim of anonymous holds by at least four senators. Oklahoma Senator Jim Inhofe (R-OK) placed a hold on all pending Clinton judicial nominees after Clinton appointed Sara Fox to another term on the National Labor Relations Board in December 1999.

21. Silverstein 1994, p. 23.

22. Senator Gorton allegedly told the White House that he would agree to vote in favor of William Fletcher's nomination to the Ninth Circuit Court of Appeals only if President Clinton agreed to nominate Durham for another vacancy in the Ninth Circuit (See Callaghan 1998, sec. B, p. 1; Postman and Grimaldi 1998).

23. Author's interview with anonymous Foreign Relations committee staffer, August 9, 2000.

24. Silverstein 1994, p. 147.

25. Ibid., p. 153.

26. Flemming, MacLeod, and Talbert 1998; Caldeira and Wright 1998; Berry 1997; Ornstein 1997, pp. 5, 14; Shogan 1996; Maltese 1995; Fisher 1991; Mackenzie 1981; Cross 1977; and Mann 1964.

27. Silverstein 1994, p. 91.

28. Mintz 1998, p. 1663.

29. Maltese 1995, pp. 137–38.

30. Silverstein 1994, p. 10.

31. Shogan 1996, p. 152.

32. Baum 1995, p. 126.

33. Mincberg, interview, 1998.

34. Shogan 1996, p. 91.

35. Mackenzie 1981, pp. 15, 18.

36. Goldman 1997, pp. 238–39.

37. Author's interviews in 1997 and 1998 with various staff members from the Committee on Judiciary, United States Senate.

38. Burford 1986, p. 49.

39. Edward Perkins, interview by author, October 27, 1997.

40. Mackenzie 1998, p. 19.

41. Mincberg, interview, 1998.

42. As quoted in Shogan 1996, p. 146.

43. Mackenzie 1981; O'Brien 1988.

44. Davidson and Oleszek 1997, pp. 308–9.

45. *CBS This Morning*, March 19, 1997.

46. Neil Lewis, 1998. "GOP, Its Eyes on High Court, Blocks a Judge." *New York Times*, June 13, 1998, sec. A, p. 1.

47. Shogan 1996, p. 121.

48. Rhett DeHart, interview by author, February 1998.

49. Segal and Spaeth 1993, p. 125.

50. Bronner 1989, p. 98.

51. Gest and Lord 1997, p. 24.

52. Mincberg, interview, 1998.

53. Hatch, Speech to the Federalist Society, 1996.

54. CRS researcher, interview by author, November 26, 1997.

55. Victoria Bassetti, interview by author, March 1998.

56. Shapiro 1997, sec. A, p. 8.

57. Dewar 1997, A10.

58. McCarty and Razaghian 1998, p. 24.

59. Ashcroft 1998b, p. S. 649.

60. Weisberg 1997.

61. Suro 1997, sec. A, p. 1.

62. Shapiro 1997, sec. A., p. 8.

63. Sinclair 2000, p. 83.

64. Silverstein 1994, p. 154.

Appendix to Chapter 2

1. Key 1964, p. 688.
2. Ripley 1969, p. 168.
3. Broder, as quoted in Shogan 1996, p. 155.
4. Rogelio Garcia, interview by author, November 26, 1997.
5. Yalof 1999; Krutz, Fleisher, and Bond 1998; Hartley and Holmes 1997; Katzmann 1997.
6. Katzmann 1997, p. 19.

Chapter 3

1. Shogan 1996, p. 144.
2. Dahl 1956, p. 137.
3. Dahl 1961, p. 5.
4. For the purposes of this research, an interest group is defined as any nongovernmental, nonparty organization having multiple members and seeking to influence policy outcomes. Such a definition encompasses a wide range of organizations, including political action committees (PACs), labor unions, trade associations, multigroup coalitions, and public interest and consumer groups.
5. Carter 1994, p. 78.
6. Maltese 1995, p. 37.
7. Flemming, MacLeod, and Talbert 1998, p. 620.
8. Shogan 1996, p. 152.
9. Boren, interview, 1997.
10. Silverstein 1994, p. 154.
11. For more information on policy subgovernments, see Wayne et al. 1999; Davidson and Oleszek 1998; Campbell and Davidson 1998; Uslaner 1998, "Lobbying the Presidency and the Bureaucracy"; Browne 1998; and Hrebenar 1997.
12. Wilson 1991, p. 214.
13. Silverstein 1994, p. 62.
14. Anonymous CRS staff member, interview by author, 1997.
15. Boren, interview, 1997.
16. Dewar, March 23, 1997.
17. Schwalm, interview, 1998.
18. Linda Berg, interview by author, December 1997.
19. Burford 1986, p. 58.
20. Katzmann 1997, p. 35.
21. See the ABA's Report, "Standing Committee on Judiciary."
22. Hatch 1997, "There's No Vacancy Crisis in the Federal Courts." There is little evidence to indicate that senators are using ABA ratings any less than they did prior to Hatch's declaration that their official role had been revoked. Instead of sending its review to the Chairman of the Senate Judiciary Committee, the

ABA now sends a letter to each member of the Judiciary Committee directly, which gives judicial nominees a rating and describes the ABA's rating system.

23. House Republican Policy Committee, 1996. "Policy Statement on the Judicial Selection Process," p. 1.

24. It appears that Hatch's severing of ties to the ABA was more symbolic than substantive, at least in its effect. In a March 24, 1998, "Dear Colleague" letter, Missouri Senator John Ashcroft criticized the White House for continuing to consider the ABA's views: "Despite the Senate's decision to limit the ABA's influence on the nomination process, the Clinton Administration continues to rely on the ABA to help review and rate prospective judges."

25. Flemming, MacLeod, and Talbert 1998, p. 629.

26. Ronald Weich, interview by author, January 8, 1998.

27. Shogan 1996, p. 91.

28. Mincberg, interview, 1998.

29. Senator Gorton allegedly told the White House that he would agree to vote in favor of William Fletcher's nomination to the Ninth Circuit Court of Appeals only if President Clinton agreed to nominate Durham for another vacancy in the Ninth Circuit. (See Callaghan 1998, sec. B, p. 1; and Postman and Grimaldi 1998.) The Alliance for Justice began circulating its report on Durham in July 1998.

30 Alliance for Justice, 1998; Draft Report on Judge Barbara Durham, p. 12.

31. Mary DeOreo, interview by author, January 14, 1998.

32. Michael Carrasco, interview by author, November 4, 1998.

33. Ibid.

34. Hall 1996, p. 10.

35. Carrasco and Melody Barnes, interview by author, November 4, 1998.

36. Barnes, interview, 1998.

37. Carrasco, interview, 1998.

38. Weich, interview, 1998.

39. Tom Jipping, via the Judicial Selection Monitoring Project's Web site at http://www.4judicialrestraint.org.

40. The 1998 and 1996 Christian Coalition U.S. Senate Scorecards are available at the Christian Coalition's Web site at http://www.cc.org.

41. National Hispanic Leadership Agenda press release, June 24, 1998.

42. DeHart, interview, 1998.

43. Carrasco, interview, 1998.

44. Boren, interview, 1997.

45. Acosta, interview, 1998.

46. Sources: Lobbying Disclosure reports filed under the Lobbying Disclosure Act of 1995; Center for Responsive Politics.

47. Although it is impossible to know for certain whether any of the senators participating in the video actually received a copy of the Heritage Foundation mailing list, the practice of making available interest group mailing lists was wide-

spread during 1996 and 1997. Further, it was widely believed among Democratic staff in the Senate that the Republican senators who lent their time or support to the JSMP video had, in fact, been offered copies of the mailing list.

48. Rudman, interview, 2000.

49. Michael Schattman, interview, 1998.

50. Thomas Jipping, interview by author, December 16, 1997.

51. Scott Olson, telephone conversation with author, July 6, 2000.

52. Anonymous staffer, interview, 2000.

53. Latham 1965, pp. 35–36.

54. Katzmann 1997, p. 52.

55. Both of these examples are explained in greater detail in chapter 4.

Chapter 4

1. See, for example, Caldeira and Wright 1998; Maltese 1995; Overby et al. 1994; Guliuzza, Reagan, and Barrett 1994; Silverstein 1994; Overby et al. 1992; Simon 1992; Advice and Consent; Abraham 1991; Bronner 1989; and Watson and Stookey 1988.

2. Maltese 1995, p. 7.

3. Boren, interview, 1997.

4. Caldeira and Wright 1998, p. 501.

5. In "Witnesses at the Confirmation" (1998, p. 629), Flemming, MacLeod, and Talbert whether interest group participation in judicial confirmation hearings has increased over time. However, their study does not discuss the *effects* of interest group involvement on the confirmation process.

6. Note that the nominees included in this data set are those individuals selected by the president to fill vacant Article III judgeships. An Article III judgeship is one that meets the criteria specified in Article III of the United States Constitution. According to Rutkus (1991, "Judicial Nominations by President Bush," p. 1): "the 'Article III courts' consist of the U.S. Courts of Appeals, the U.S. Court of International Trade, and the U.S. District Courts in the 50 States, the District of Columbia, and Puerto Rico."

7. Senate Committee on Foreign Relations, 1997; Garcia 1996a, p. 1; Garcia 1996b, p. 1.

8. O'Brien 1988, p. 65.

9. Abraham 1991; Watson and Stookey 1988; and Matthews 1960.

10. Kozinski, as quoted in O'Brien 1997, pp. 75–76.

11. Rodriguez 1994, p. 6.

12. Reske 1997, p. 28.

13. *Congressional Record,* March 19, 1997, p. S. 2529.

14. Neil Lewis 1997, sec. A, p. 1.

15. Victor 1998, p. 742.

16. Henry 1997, p. 1.

17. Pines (1996) notes that during a presidential election year, the rate and pace of judicial nominees slows as the Senate waits to see whether there will be a shift in presidential leadership.

18. Alvord 1998, sec. B, p. 3.

19. Unpublished statistics compiled by the Senate Judiciary Committee, minority staff.

20. Carney 1998a, p. 1065.

21. Olin 1998, p. 5.

22. Carney 1998a, p. 1660.

23. Conservative interest groups were mentioned as a cause of the slowdown not only by the leaders of more liberal interest groups (author's interviews with People for the American Way's Eliot Mincberg and Tracy Hahn-Burkett, and Alliance for Justice's Nan Aron, all in 1998) and a nominee to the federal courts who was forced to withdraw, Michael Schattman (interview, 1998), but also by Tom Jipping, director of the Judicial Selection Monitoring Project (interview, 1997) who stated that he measured success by how many Clinton nominees his organization could delay or prevent from being confirmed.

24. For example, former Senator David L. Boren discussed the ways in which many groups use the confirmation process as another fund-raising enterprise (interview, 1997).

25. These conclusions are drawn from an examination of all confirmation hearings for federal judicial nominees between 1979 and 1998.

26. Shogan 1996, p. 153.

27. Jacobs 1997, sec. B, p. 7; Ornstein 1997, pp. 5, 14; Schwartz 1997 "One Man's Activist. . .: What Republicans Really Mean When They Condemn Judicial Activism"; and Biskupic 1997, sec. A, p. 1.

28. "Quit Stalling," 1997, sec. A, p. 24.

29. Neil Lewis 1994.

30. Jacobs 1997.

31. Jipping, interview, 1997.

32. The Hatch Pledge reads as follows: "Those nominees who are or will be judicial activists should not be nominated by the president or confirmed by the Senate, and I personally will do my best to see to it that they are not." As of September 1997, eleven senators had signed the pledge. They are: Senator Wayne Allard (R-CO), Senator John Ashcroft (R-MO), Senator Christopher Bond (R-MO), Senator Paul Coverdell (R-GA), Senator Larry Craig (R-ID), Senator Lauch Faircloth (R-NC), Senator Jesse Helms (R-NC), Senator Tim Hutchinson (R-AR), Senator James Inhofe (R-OK), Senator Bob Smith (R-NH), and Senator Charles Grassley (R-IA).

33. Rees 1997, p. 14.

34. Weyrich, as quoted in Victor 1998, p. 741.

35. Mary Ellen Schattman, interview by author, 1998.

36. For example, see Anthony Lewis 1998, sec. A, p. 15.

37. Carrasco, interview, 1998.

38. O'Brien 1988, p. 73.

39. Because he presided over the greatest number of judicial confirmations during the period of study, Senator Joe Biden's chairmanship is the control variable in the analysis of committee chairmanship on interest group participation.

40. Segal and Spaeth 1993, p. 144.

41. Ibid.

42. Aron, interview, 1998.

43. Mincberg, interview, 1998.

44. Rudman, interview, 2000.

45. Weich, interview, 1998.

46. DeOreo, interview, 1998.

47. Bassetti, interview, 1998.

48. Barnes and Carrasco, interviews, 1998.

49. DeHart, interview, 1998.

50. Michael Schattman, interview, 1998.

51. Law Enforcement Alliance of America letter, 1998.

52. Confirmation Hearing of Frederica Massiah-Jackson, February 22, 1998.

53. Letter from Judge Frederica Massiah-Jackson to President Bill Clinton, 1988.

54. Mincberg, interview, 1998.

55. Tracy Hahn-Burkett, interview by author, July 10, 1998.

56. Author's interviews with Tom Jipping (1997), Nan Aron (1998), and Alex Acosta (1998).

57. Ashcroft 1998b.

58. Hahn-Burkett, interview, 1998.

59. Judicial Selection Monitoring Project. "Judge the Judges," 1997.

60. JSMP Fund-raising Pledge Sheet, 1997.

61. Indeed, Flemming, MacLeod, and Talbert's 1998 article in *Political Research Quarterly* makes strides toward debunking this long-held myth about interest group participation.

62. Brown and Rodriguez 1996, p. 8.

63. Rehnquist 1998, pp. 7–8.

64. Hahn-Burkett, interview, 1998.

Chapter 5

1. Mackenzie 1981, p. 3.

2. Ibid., p. 6

3. Fenno 1959, p. 11.

4. Ibid., pp. 14, 54.

5. Carter 1994, pp. 31–32.

6. Weyrich, as quoted in Mackenzie 1996, p. 152.

7. Clerk of the Senate 1954, p. 2.

8. Reich 1997, p. 37.

9. Ibid., p. 38.

10. Anonymous staffer, interview, 2000.

11. Data are taken from the Cabinet Nominees Data Set, compiled by author. See appendix 2.

12. Mackenzie 1998; Shapiro 1997, sec. A, p. 8; Mackenzie 1996; Shogan 1996; Segal and Spaeth 1993; and Mackenzie 1981.

13. J. Cohen 1988, p. 19.

14. The agency to which an individual was nominated is coded as a dichotomous variable, reflecting whether the agency is one that is generally open to interest groups or closed to interest groups, per J. Cohen's 1988 study of cabinet agencies. See discussion above of Cohen's theory.

15. Anonymous staffer, interview, 2000.

16. See Committee on Labor and Human Resources, United States Senate, 1997. *Nomination (Alexis Herman)*. March 19, 1997. Washington, D.C.: Government Printing Office.

17. Mak and Kennedy 1992, p. 5.

18. Ibid., p. 3.

19. Lenhart 1991, p. 1.

20. Mak and Kennedy 1992, p. 3.

21. Washington Report, 1997.

22. Sanford 1997, p. 2.

23. Lenhart 1991, p. 27.

24. "Nominations." Congressional Research Service Memorandum. 1997, p. 1.

25. Ibid.

26. Schwalm, interview, 1998.

27. Perkins, interview, 1997.

28. Anonymous staffer, interview, 2000.

29. Mills 1998, p. 7.

30. "Qualified to Serve," 1998.

31. Schwalm, interview, 1998.

32. See Bayer 1998; "D'Amato Criticizes GOP Hold on Hormel Nomination."

33. Holland 1998b, sec. A, p. 1.

34. "Approve Hormel for Post," sec. A, p. 38.

35. Torricelli and Feinstein. "Sexual Orientation is *Not* a Job Qualification," sec. B, p. 9.

36. In interviews with the Alliance for Justice's Nan Aron, People for the American Way's Tracy Hahn-Burkett, and Steve Schwalm of the Family Research Council, none of the interview subjects could recall another instance of interest group participation in the confirmation process for ambassadorial nominees.

37. Bayer 1998, sec. A, p. 12.

38. Schwalm, interview, 1998.

39. Ibid.

40. Ibid.

41. Holland 1998a, sec. A, p. 7.
42. Schwalm, interview, 1998.

Chapter 6

1. Nancy Gertner, conversation with author, 1998.
2. Howard Metzenbaum, conversation with author, 1998.
3. Cross 1977, p. 805.
4. Shogan 1996, p. 95.
5. Carter 1994, p. 193.
6. Baum 1995, p. 36.
7. Segal and Spaeth 1993, pp. 153–54.
8. Ibid., p. 150.
9. Baum 1995, p. 53.
10. Transcript from the launch event of Citizens for Independent Courts, 1998.
11. Durbin 1998, p. 24.
12. Boren, interview, 1997.
13. Wright 1995, p. 42.
14. Simon, interview, 1998.

Appendix 1

1. Mackenzie 1981, p. xii.
2. Ibid.

Bibliography

Abraham, Henry J. 1991. *Justices and Presidents: A Political History of Appointments to the Supreme Court.* New York: Oxford University Press.

Acosta, Alex. 1998. Interview by author, March 1998. Project on the Judiciary, Washington, D.C.

Adminstrative Office of the United States Courts. 1997. "Judicial Vacancies As Of [various dates]" (Unpublished data provided by the Senate Judiciary Committee).

Agresti, Alan. 1984. *Analysis of Ordinal Categorical Data.* New York: John Wiley and Sons.

———. 1996. *An Introduction to Categorical Data Analysis.* New York: John Wiley and Sons.

Alliance for Justice. 1993. *Justice in the Making: A Citizen's Handbook for Choosing Federal Judges.* Washington: D.C.: Alliance for Justice.

———. 1997. "Judicial Selection Project: Annual Report 1997." Washington, D.C.: Alliance for Justice.

———. 1998. Draft Report on Judge Barbara Durham. July 1998. Washington, D.C.: Alliance for Justice.

Alvord, Valerie. 1998. "Nominee for Federal Judgeship Withdraws Name; After Two-Year Wait, S.D. Attorney Lasry Frustrated by Politics in U.S. Senate." *San Diego Union-Tribune.* February 5, 1998.

American Bar Association. Undated. "Standing Committee on Judiciary." Washington, D.C.: American Bar Association.

American Jewish Congress. 1998. "AJ Congress Calls on Senate to Reject Partisanship and to Act on Clinton's Nominations for Federal Judgeships." January 29, 1998.

Anonymous Congressional Research Service Senior Staff Member. 1997. Interview by author, November 26, 1997. Congressional Research Service, Washington, D.C.

Anonymous Staff Member, U.S. Senate Committee on Foreign Relations. Author's interview, August 9, 2000.

"Approve Hormel for Post." *Rocky Mountain News* (Denver, CO). April 21, 1998.

Arnold, Richard S. 1996. "Judicial Politics under President Washington." *Arizona Law Review* (38): 473–90.

Aron, Nan. 1998. Interview by author, January 1998. Washington, D.C.

Aron, Nan, Stephan Kline, and David Kennedy. 1997. Memo regarding "Misleading Fund-raising Campaign by Conservative Group." (Memo from The Alliance for Justice.) November 6, 1997.

Ashcroft, Sen. John. 1998a. "Dear Colleague" Letter Concerning the Role of the American Bar Association in Judicial Selection. March 24, 1998.

———. 1998b. "Statement on the Withdrawal of Frederica Massiah-Jackson." March 16, 1998.

Bach, Stanley. 1997. "Minority Rights and Senate Procedures." *CRS Report for Congress.* August 7, 1997.

Balz, Dan. 1997. "Clinton Pushes for Rights Nominee, Examines Strategy to Preempt Senate." *Washington Post.* December 10, 1997, sec. A, p. 8.

Barnes, Melody C. 1998. Interview by author, November 4, 1998, Washington, D.C.

Bassetti, Victoria. 1998. Interview by author, March 1998, Washington, D.C.

Baum, Lawrence. 1990. *American Courts: Process and Policy* (2nd edition). Boston: Houghton, Mifflin.

———. 1995. *The Supreme Court* (5th ed.). Washington, D.C.: Congressional Quarterly Press.

Baumer, Donald C. 1992. "Senate Democratic Leadership in the 101st Congress," in *The Atomistic Congress: An Interpretation of Congressional Change,* Allen D. Hertzke and Ronald M. Peters, eds. Armonk, New York: M. E. Sharpe.

Bayer, Amy. 1998. "Gay Nominee Poses Dilemma for GOP; Bigotry Alleged—Critics Claim It's a Matter of Issues." *San Diego Union-Tribune.* May 31, 1998.

Berg, Linda. 1997. Interview by author (via telephone), December 1997. National Organization for Women, Washington, D.C.

Berry, Jeffrey M. 1997. *The Interest Group Society* (3rd edition). New York: Longman Press.

Biden, Joseph R. 1989. Letter to President George H. W. Bush regarding the Senate Judiciary Committee's Blue Slip policy, June 6, 1989.

Binder, Sarah A. and Steven S. Smith. 1997. *Politics or Principle: Filibustering in the United States Senate.* Washington, D.C.: Brookings Institute Press.

Biskupic, Joan. 1997. "Hill Republicans Target Liberal Judges." *Washington Post.* September 13, 1997.

Boren, David L., former U.S. Senator. 1997. Interview by author, June 26, 1997. The University of Oklahoma, Norman, Oklahoma.

Bork, Robert H. 1990. *The Tempting of America: The Political Seduction of the Law.* New York: Simon and Schuster.

———. 1997. Letter soliciting contributions for the Judicial Selection Monitoring Project, September 9, 1997.

Bronner, Ethan. 1989. *Battle for Justice: How the Bork Nomination Shook America.* New York: Doubleday.

Brown, Bruce D., and Eva M. Rodriguez. 1996. "A Judicial Legacy Can Now Be Written," *New Jersey Law Journal.* November 18, 1996.

Browne, William P. 1998. "Lobbying the Public: All-Directional Advocacy," in *Interest Group Politics* (5th ed.). Allan J. Cigler and Burdett A. Loomis, eds. Washington D.C.: Congressional Quarterly Press.

Burford, Anne, with John Greenya. 1986. *Are You Tough Enough?* New York: McGraw Hill.

Caldeira, Gregory A. 1989. "Commentary on Senate Confirmation of Supreme Court Justices: The Roles of Organized and Unorganized Interests." *Kentucky Law Journal* 77: p. 531.

Caldeira, Gregory A., and John R. Wright. 1998. "Lobbying for Justice: Organized Interests, Supreme Court Nominees, and the United States Senate." *American Journal of Political Science* 42:2.

Callaghan, Peter. 1998. "Judge Isn't Packing up Gavel Yet: State Justice Durham Says She Has 'No Idea' When Appointment to Federal Court Might Occur." *News Tribune* (Tacoma, WA). May 6, 1998.

Campbell, Colton C., and Roger H. Davidson. 1998. "Coalition Building in Congress: The Consequences of Partisan Change," in *The Interest Group Connection: Electioneering, Lobbying, and Policy Making in Washington.* Paul S. Herrnson, Ronald G. Shaiko, and Clyde Wilcox, eds. Chatham, N.J.: Chatham House.

Campbell, Linda P. 1997. "Political Squabbles Delay Nominations to Federal Judiciary." *Fort Worth Star-Telegram.* June 25, 1997.

Carney, Dan. 1998a. "Agreement on Judgeships No Guarantee of Quick Confirmations." *Congressional Quarterly Weekly Report,* 56:19. May 9, 1998.

———. 1998b. "Congress v. Courts: A Conflict Fueled By Politics and Mistrust," in *Congressional Quarterly Weekly Report.* June 20, 1998.

Carrasco, Michael. 1998. Interview by author, November 4, 1998. Washington, D.C.

Carter, Stephen L. 1994. *The Confirmation Mess: Cleaning up the Federal Appointment Process.* New York: Basic.

CBS This Morning. 1997. "Anthony Lake"s Blasting of the Senate Confirmation Process." CBS News transcripts. March 19, 1997.

Christian Coalition. 1996. "U.S. Senate Scorecard 1996." Washington, D.C.: Christian Coalition.

Christian Coalition. 1998. "U.S. Senate Scorecard 1998." Christian Coalition Web site: http://www.cc.org/scorecards.

Cigler, Allan J. and Burdett A. Loomis, eds. 1983. *Interest Group Politics.* Washington D.C.: Congressional Quarterly Press.

Citizens for Independent Courts. 1998. Transcript from Launch Event. New York: Twentieth Century Fund.

Clerk of the Senate. 1954. *Civilian Nominations.* Washington, D.C.: Government Printing Office.

Cohen, Bruce. 1998. Interview by author, January 14, 1998. Senate Committee on the Judiciary, Washington, D.C.

Cohen, Jeffrey E. 1988. *The Politics of the U.S. Cabinet: Representation in the Executive Branch, 1789–1984*. Pittsburgh: University of Pittsburgh Press.

Cohen, Richard. 1998. "Gay Nominee for Ambassador May Not Even Get a Hearing." *Dallas Morning News*. April 5, 1998.

Committee on Agriculture, Nutrition, and Forestry. U.S. Senate. *Nomination of John R. Block to Be Secretary of Agriculture*. January 6, 1981. Washington, D.C.: Government Printing Office.

———. U.S. Senate. *Nomination of Richard E. Lyng*. March 4, 1986. Washington, D.C.: Government Printing Office.

———. U.S. Senate. *Nomination of Clayton Yeutter*. February 2, 1989. Washington, D.C.: Government Printing Office.

———. U.S. Senate. *Nomination of Edward R. Madigan*. March 5, 1991. Washington, D.C: Government Printing Office.

———. U.S. Senate. *Nomination of Hon. Mike Espy*. January 14, 1993. Washington, D.C.: Government Printing Office.

———. U.S. Senate. *Dan Glickman Nomination*. March 28, 1995. Washington, D.C.: Government Printing Office.

———. U.S. Senate. *Nomination Hearing of Daniel R. Glickman*. March 21, 1995. Washington, D.C.: Government Printing Office.

Committee on Armed Services. U.S. Senate. *Nominations: Harold Brown and Charles W. Duncan Jr*. January 11, 1977. Washington, D.C.: Government Printing Office.

———. U.S. Senate. *Nomination of Caspar W. Weinberger to Be Secretary of Defense*. January 6, 1981. Washington, D.C.: Government Printing Office.

———. U.S. Senate. *Nominations before the Senate Armed Services Committee, First Session, 100th Congress [Frank Carlucci]*. January 28, February 25, April 6, May 20, June 10, 24, August 4, September 29, October 9, 14, 16, November 12, 19, 24, December 1, 10, 11, 15, 18, 1987. Washington, D.C.: Government Printing Office.

———. U.S. Senate. *Nominations before the Senate Armed Services Committee, First Session, 101st Congress. [Richard Cheney]*. March 14, 16, April 5, 18, 19, May 3, 4, 16, 18, June 22, July 31, August 3, September 7, 8, 20, October 6, 17, November 7, 9, 20, 1989. Washington, D.C.: Government Printing Office.

———. U.S. Senate. *Nominations before the Senate Armed Services Committee, First Session, 103rd Congress*. January 7, 20, February 16, 25, March 4, 11, 30, April 28, May 13, 18, 19, 25, June 11, 30, July 13, 20, 30, September 22, 23, October 7, November 10, 18, 1993. Washington, D.C.: Government Printing Office.

———. U.S. Senate. *Nominations before the Senate Armed Services Committee, First Session, 105th Congress*. January 22, February 5, March 6, July 9, 17, 24, September 9, 16, October 1, 23, 30, November 8, 1997. Washington, D.C.: Government Printing Office.

Committee on Banking, Housing, and Urban Affairs. U.S. Senate. *Nomination:*

Patricia Roberts Harris. January 10, 1977. Washington, D.C.: Government Printing Office.

———. U.S. Senate. *Nomination of Moon Landrieu.* September 6, 1979. Washington, D.C.: Government Printing Office.

———. U.S. Senate. *Nomination of Samuel R. Pierce Jr.* January 13, 1981. Washington, D.C.: Government Printing Office.

———. U.S. Senate. *Nomination of Jack Kemp.* January 27, 1989. Washington, D.C.: Government Printing Office.

———. U.S. Senate. *Nomination of Henry Cisneros.* January 12, 1993. Washington, D.C.: Government Printing Office.

——— . U.S. Senate. *Nomination of Andrew M. Cuomo.* January 22, 1997. Washington, D.C.: Government Printing Office.

Committee on Commerce, Science, and Transportation. U.S. Senate. *Nominations: Secretaries Departments of Transportation and Commerce.* January 7, 10, 1977. Washington, D.C.: Government Printing Office.

———. U.S. Senate. *Nomination: Secretary of Commerce [Malcolm Baldrige].* January 6, 1981. Washington, D.C.: Government Printing Office.

———. U.S. Senate. *Nomination: Secretary of Transportation [Andrew Lewis].* January 7, 1981. Washington, D.C.: Government Printing Office.

———. U.S. Senate. *Nomination: DOT.* January 26, 1983. Washington, D.C.: Government Printing Office.

———. U.S. Senate. *Nomination: Department of Commerce [C. William Verity].* September 10, 1987. Washington, D.C.: Government Printing Office.

———. U.S. Senate. *Nominations: DOT [James Burnley].* November 17, 1987. Washington, D.C.: Government Printing Office.

———. U.S. Senate. *Nominations: Department of Commerce [Robert Mosbacher].* January 24, 1989. Washington, D.C.: Government Printing Office.

———. U.S. Senate. *Nominations: DOT [Samuel K. Skinner].* January 25, 1989. Washington, D.C.: Government Printing Office.

———. U.S. Senate. *Nomination of Ronald Harmon Brown to Be Secretary of Commerce.* January 6, 1993. Washington, D.C.: Government Printing Office.

———. U.S. Senate. *Nomination of William Daley to Be Secretary of Commerce.* January 22, 1997. Washington, D.C.: Government Printing Office.

———. U.S. Senate. *Nomination of Hon. Rodney E. Slater to Be Secretary of Transportation.* January 29, 1997. Washington, D.C.: Government Printing Office.

Committee on Energy and Natural Resources. U.S. Senate. *Nomination of Dr. James R. Schlesinger to Be the Nation's First Secretary of Energy.* August 3, 1977. Washington, D.C.: Government Printing Office.

———. U.S. Senate. *Charles William Duncan Jr. Nomination.* July 30, 1979. Washington, D.C.: Government Printing Office.

———. U.S. Senate. *Nomination—Secretary of Transportation [Neil Goldschmidt].* September 5, 1979. Washington, D.C.: Government Printing Office.

———. U.S. Senate. *Nominations—Department of Commerce and Federal Maritime*

Commission. December 19, 1979. Washington, D.C.: Government Printing Office.

———. U.S. Senate. *James G. Watt Nomination, Part 1.* January 7, 8, 1981. Washington, D.C.: Government Printing Office.

———. U.S. Senate. *James B. Edwards Nomination.* January 12, 1981. Washington, D.C.: Government Printing Office.

———. U.S. Senate. *Hodel and Hesse Nominations.* December 1, 1982. Washington, D.C.: Government Printing Office.

———. U.S. Senate. *William P. Clark Nomination.* November 1, 2, 1983. Washington, D.C.: Government Printing Office.

———. U.S. Senate. *Donald Paul Hodel Nomination.* February 1, 1985. Washington, D.C.: Government Printing Office.

———. U.S. Senate. *John S. Herrington Nomination.* January 31, 1985: Washington, D.C.: Government Printing Office.

———. U.S. Senate. *James D. Watkins Nomination.* February 22, 1989. Washington, D.C.: Government Printing Office.

———. U.S. Senate. *Hazel R. O'Leary Nomination.* January 19, 1993. Washington, D.C.: Government Printing Office.

———. U.S. Senate. *Bruce Babbitt Nomination.* January 19, 21, 1993. Washington, D.C.: Government Printing Office.

———. U.S. Senate. *Federico F. Pena Nomination.* January 30, 1997. Washington, D.C.: Government Printing Office.

Committee on Finance. U.S. Senate. *Blumenthal Nomination.* January 12, 1977. Washington, D.C.: Government Printing Office.

———. U.S. Senate. *Nominations: Joseph A. Califano Jr. and Laurence N. Woodworth.* January 13, 1977. Washington, D.C.: Government Printing Office.

———. U.S. Senate. *Nomination of G. William Miller.* July 27, 1979. Washington, D.C.: Government Printing Office.

———. U.S. Senate. *Nomination of Patricia Harris.* July 25, 26, 1979. Washington, D.C.: Government Printing Office.

———. U.S. Senate. *Nomination of Donald T. Regan.* January 6, 1981. Washington, D.C.: Government Printing Office.

———. U.S. Senate. *Nomination: Richard S. Schweiker.* January 6, 1981. Washington, D.C.: Government Printing Office.

———. U.S. Senate. *Nominations of Margaret M. Heckler and John A. Svahn.* February 25, 1983. Washington, D.C.: Government Printing Office.

———. U.S. Senate. *Nomination of James A. Baker III.* January 23, 1985. Washington, D.C.: Government Printing Office.

———. U.S. Senate. *Nomination of Dr. Otis R. Bowen.* December 10, 1985. Washington, D.C.: Government Printing Office.

———. U.S. Senate. *Nomination of Nicholas F. Brady.* September 13, 1988. Washington, D.C.: Government Printing Office.

———. U.S. Senate. *Anticipated Nomination of Hon. Lloyd Bentsen.* January 12, 1993. Washington, D.C.: Government Printing Office.

———. U.S. Senate. *Anticipated Nomination of Donna E. Shalala.* January 14, 1993. Washington, D.C.: Government Printing Office.

———. U.S. Senate. *Nomination of Robert E. Rubin.* January 10, 1995. Washington, D.C.: Government Printing Office.

Committee on Foreign Relations. U.S. Senate. *Vance Nomination.* January 11, 1977. Washington, D.C.: Government Printing Office.

———. U.S. Senate. *Nomination of Edmund S. Muskie.* May 7, 1980. Washington, D.C.: Government Printing Office.

———. U.S. Senate. *Nomination of Alexander M. Haig Jr., Part 1.* January 9, 10, 12, 13, 1981. Washington, D.C.: Government Printing Office.

———. U.S. Senate. *Nomination of Alexander Haig, Part 2.* January 14, 15, 1981. Washington, D.C.: Government Printing Office.

———. U.S. Senate. *Nomination of Warren M. Christopher to Be Secretary of State.* January 13, 14, 1993. Washington, D.C.: Government Printing Office.

———. U.S. Senate. *Nomination of Secretary of State [Madeleine Albright].* January 8, 1997. Washington, D.C.: Government Printing Office.

Committee on Interior and Insular Affairs. U.S. Senate. *Interior Nomination.* January 17, 18, 1977. Washington, D.C.: Government Printing Office.

Committee on the Judiciary. U.S. Senate. 1977. *Griffin Bell.* January 11–14, 17–19, 1977. Washington, D.C: Government Printing Office.

———. 1979. *Confirmation Hearings on Benjamin R. Civiletti, Nominee, Attorney General.* July 25–27, 1979. Washington D.C.: Government Printing Office

———. 1980a. *Confirmation Hearings on Federal Appointments.* 96th Cong., 1st sess. Washington, D.C.: Government Printing Office.

———. 1980b. *Legislative and Executive Calendar.* 96th Cong. (final edition).

———. 1981a. *Confirmation Hearings on Federal Appointments.* 96th Cong., 2nd sess. Washington, D.C.: Government Printing Office.

———. 1981b. *Confirmation Hearing on William French Smith, Nominee to Be Attorney General.* January 15, 1981. Washington, D.C.: Government Printing Office.

———. 1982a. *Confirmation Hearings on Federal Appointments.* 97th Cong., 1st sess. Washington, D.C.: Government Printing Office.

———. 1982b. *Legislative and Executive Calendar.* 97th Cong. (final edition).

———. 1983. *Confirmation Hearings on Federal Appointments.* 97th Cong., 2nd sess. Washington, D.C.: Government Printing Office.

———. 1984. *Confirmation Hearings on Federal Appointments.* 98th Cong., 1st sess. Washington, D.C.: Government Printing Office.

———. 1985a. *Confirmation Hearings on Federal Appointments.* 98th Cong., 2nd sess. Washington, D.C.: Government Printing Office.

———. 1985b. *Confirmation of Edwin Meese III.* January 29–31, 1985. Washington, D.C.: Government Printing Office.

———. 1986. *Confirmation Hearings on Federal Appointments.* 99th Cong., 1st sess. Washington, D.C.: Government Printing Office.

———. 1987. *Confirmation Hearings on Federal Appointments.* 99th Cong., 2nd sess. Washington, D.C.: Government Printing Office.

———. 1988. *Confirmation Hearings on Federal Appointments.* 100th Cong., 1st sess. Washington, D.C.: Government Printing Office.

———. 1989a. *Confirmation Hearings on Federal Appointments.* 100th Cong., 2nd sess. Washington, D.C.: Government Printing Office.

———. 1989b. *Confirmation Hearings on Federal Appointments, Part 8 [Richard Thornburgh].* July 27, 28, August 5, Sept. 8, 1988. Washington, D.C.: Government Printing Office.

———. 1990. *Confirmation Hearings on Federal Appointments.* 101st Cong., 1st sess. Washington, D.C.: Government Printing Office.

———. 1991a. *Confirmation Hearings on Federal Appointments.* 101st Cong., 2nd sess. Washington, D.C.: Government Printing Office.

———. 1991b. *Confirmation Hearings on Federal Appointments. Part 2: William P. Barr.* November 12, 13, 1991. Washington, D.C.: Government Printing Office.

———. 1992. *Confirmation Hearings on Federal Appointments.* 102nd Cong., 1st sess. Washington, D.C.: Government Printing Office.

———. 1993. *Confirmation Hearings on Federal Appointments.* 102nd Cong., 2nd sess. Washington, D.C.: Government Printing Office.

———. 1994. *Confirmation Hearings on Federal Appointments.* 103rd Cong., 1st sess. Washington, D.C.: Government Printing Office.

———. 1995. *Confirmation Hearings on Federal Appointments.* 103rd Cong., 2nd sess. Washington, D.C.: Government Printing Office.

———. 1996. *Confirmation Hearings on Federal Appointments.* 104th Cong., 1st sess. Washington, D.C.: Government Printing Office.

———. 1997. *Confirmation Hearings on Federal Appointments.* 104th Cong., 2nd sess. Washington, D.C.: Government Printing Office.

———. 1998a. *Confirmation Hearings on Federal Appointments.* 105th Cong., 1st sess. Washington, D.C.: Government Printing Office.

———. 1998b. U.S. Senate. *Nomination of Janet Reno to Be Attorney General of the U.S.* March 9, 10, 1993. Washington, D.C.: Government Printing Office.

Committee on Labor and Human Resources. U.S. Senate. *Nomination of F. Ray Marshall.* January 13, 1977. Washington, D.C.: Government Printing Office.

———. U.S. Senate. *Joseph A. Califano Jr. to Be Secretary of Health, Education and Welfare: Additional Consideration.* January 13, 1977. Washington, D.C.: Government Printing Office.

———. U.S. Senate. *Patricia Roberts Harris to Be Secretary of Health, Education, and Welfare: Additional Consideration.* July 26, 1979. Washington, D.C.: Government Printing Office.

———. U.S. Senate. *Nomination [Shirley Hufstedler].* November 27, 1979. Washington, D.C.: Government Printing Office.

———. U.S. Senate. *Nomination: Terrel H. Bell.* January 15, 1981. Washington, D.C.: Government Printing Office.

———. U.S. Senate. *Nomination: Raymond J. Donovan.* January 12, 27, 1981. Washington, D.C.: Government Printing Office.

———. U.S. Senate. *Margaret M. Heckler to Be Secretary, Department of Health and*

Human Services, Additional Consideration. March 3, 1983. Washington, D.C.: Government Printing Office.

———. *Nomination (William Emerson Brock III).* U.S. Senate. April 23, 1985. Washington, D.C.: Government Printing Office.

———. U.S. Senate. *Nomination (Otis R. Bowen).* December 11, 1985. Washington, D.C.: Government Printing Office.

———. U.S. Senate. *Nomination (William J. Bennett).* January 28, 1985. Washington, D.C.: Government Printing Office.

———. U.S. Senate. *Nomination (Elizabeth Hanford Dole).* January 19, 1989. Washington, D.C.: Government Printing Office.

———. U.S. Senate. *Nomination (Lynn Martin).* January 30, 1991. Washington, D.C.: Government Printing Office.

———. U.S. Senate. *Nomination (Andrew L. Alexander).* February 6, 1991. Washington, D.C: Government Printing Office.

———. U.S. Senate. *Nomination (Robert Reich).* January 7, 1993. Washington, D.C.: Government Printing Office.

———. U.S. Senate. *Nomination (Richard W. Riley).* January 12, 1993. Washington, D.C.: Government Printing Office.

———. U.S. Senate. *Nomination (Donna E. Shalala).* January 15, 1993. Washington, D.C.: Government Printing Office.

———. U.S. Senate. *Nomination (Alexis M. Herman).* March 18, 1997. Washington, D.C.: Government Printing Office.

Committee on Veterans' Affairs. U.S. Senate. *Nomination of Hon. Edward J. Derwinski.* March 1, 2, 1989. Washington, D.C.: Government Printing Office.

———. U.S. Senate. *Nomination of Jesse Brown to Be Secretary of Veterans Affairs.* January 7, 1993. Washington, D.C.: Government Printing Office.

Common Cause. 1977. *The Senate Rubber Stamp Machine.* Washington, D.C.: Common Cause.

Cross, Mercer. 1977. "Interest-Group Doubts Rise on Top Jobs." *Congressional Quarterly Weekly Report.* April 30, 1977. Pp. 805–9.

Dahl, Robert. 1956. *A Preface to Democratic Theory.* Chicago: University of Chicago Press.

———. 1961. *Who Governs? Democracy and Power in an American City.* New Haven, Conn.: Yale University Press.

Davidson, Roger H., and Walter J. Oleszek. 1998. *Congress and Its Members* (6th edition). Washington, D.C.: Congressional Quarterly Press.

DeHart, Rhett. 1998. Interview by author, February 1998. U.S. Senate Committee on the Judiciary. Washington, D.C.

Democratic Policy Committee. 1998. "Judicial Vacancies Create a Crisis in America's Federal Court System." Washington, D.C.: Democratic Policy Committee, United States Senate. March 13, 1998.

———. 1998b. "The Judicial Vacancy Crisis: The Republican Strategy to Delay and Intimidate Threatens the Independence of the Judiciary." Washington, D.C.: Democratic Policy Committee, United States Senate. January 29, 1998.

DeOreo, Mary. 1998. Interview by author, January 14, 1998. U.S. Senate Committee on the Judiciary, Washington, D.C.

Dewar, Helen. 1997. "Nominees Now Face 'Trial By Fire': Senate Confirmation Process Has Evolved into Political Warfare." *Washington Post.* March 23, 1997. P. A10.

Durbin, Senator Richard. 1998. "Q: Is the GOP causing a vacancy crisis in the federal judiciary?" (Includes Counterpoint by Senator John Ashcroft.) *Insight on the News* (March 2, 1998). Vol. 14, No.8., p. 24.

Faircloth, Sen. Lauch. 1997. "Nomination of Merrick B. Garland, of Maryland, to be U.S. Circuit Judge for the District of Columbia." *Congressional Record.* March 19, 1997. P. S2529.

Farrand, Max, ed. 1966a. *The Records of the Federal Convention of 1787.* Vol. I. New Haven, Conn.: Yale University Press.

———. 1966b. *The Records of the Federal Convention of 1787.* Vol. II. New Haven, Conn.: Yale University Press.

———. 1966c. *The Records of the Federal Convention of 1787.* Vol. III. New Haven, Conn.: Yale University Press.

Fenno Jr., Richard F. 1959. *The President's Cabinet: An Analysis in the Period from Wilson to Eisenhower.* Cambridge, Mass.: Harvard University Press.

Fisher, Louis. 1991. *Constitutional Conflicts between Congress and the President* (3rd edition). Lawrence: University of Kansas Press.

Flemming, Roy B., Michael C. MacLeod, and Jeffrey Talbert. 1998. "Witnesses at the Confirmations? The Appearance of Organized Interests at Senate Hearings of Federal Judicial Appointments, 1945–1992." *Political Research Quarterly* 51, no. 3 (September 1998): 617–31.

Fox, Mark. 1998. Interview by author, June 24, 1998. Washington, D.C.

Garcia, Rogelio, 1996a. "Presidential Appointments to Full-Time Positions in Independent and Other Agencies, 104th Congress." *CRS Report for Congress.* December 3, 1996.

———. 1996b. "Presidential Appointments to Full-Time Positions on Regulatory and Other Collegial Boards and Commissions, 104th Congress." *CRS Report for Congress.* November 18, 1996.

———. 1997. Specialist in American National Government, Government Division of the Congressional Research Service. Interview by author, November 26, 1997. Congressional Research Service, Washington, D.C.

Gertner, Judge Nancy. 1998. Conversation with author. July 1998.

Gest, Ted, and Lewis Lord. 1997. "The GOP's Judicial Freeze: A Fight to See Who Rules over the Law." *U.S. News and World Report.* May 26, 1997.

Gittenstein, Mark. 1992. *Matters of Principle: An Insider's Account of Robert Bork's Nomination to the Supreme Court.* New York: Simon and Schuster.

Goldman, Sheldon. 1997. *Picking Federal Judges: Lower Court Selection from Roosevelt through Reagan.* New Haven, Conn.: Yale University Press.

Gramm, Phil. 1996. Letter to the Honorable Thomas Windham concerning the nomination of Michael Schattman, October 5, 1997.

Guliuzza III, Frank, Daniel J. Reagan, and David M. Barrett. 1994. "The Senate Judiciary Committee and Supreme Court Nominees: Measuring the Dynamics of Confirmation Criteria," in *The Journal of Politics* 56(3).

Hahn-Burkett, Tracy. 1998. Interview by author, July 10, 1998. People for the American Way. Washington, D.C.

Hall, Richard. 1996. *Participation in Congress.* New Haven, Conn.: Yale University Press.

Hamilton, Alexander. 1790. Federalist Papers #64, 65, and 78. *The Federalist Papers.*

Harris, Joseph. 1953. *The Advice and Consent of the Senate.* Berkeley: University of California Press.

Hartley, Roger E., and Lisa M. Holmes. 1997. "Increasing Senate Scrutiny of Lower Federal Court Nominees." *Judicature* 80:6.

Hatch, Orrin G. 1995. Letter to Hon. Abner A. Mikva, Counsel to the President, on the Senate Judiciary Committee's Blue Slip policy, February 3, 1995.

———. 1996. "Remarks of Senator Orrin Hatch Before the Federalist Society's 10th Annual Lawyers Convention." November 15, 1996.

———. 1997. "There's No Vacancy Crisis in the Federal Courts." Column in *The Wall Street Journal.* August 13, 1997. P. A15.

Heclo, Hugh. 1977. *A Government of Strangers: Executive Politics in Washington.* Washington, D.C.: Brookings Institution.

Henry, Ed. 1997. "His Power Being Judged, Hatch Beats back Leaders." *Roll Call,* May 1, 1997.

Hertzke, Allen D., and Ronald M. Peters, eds. 1992. *The Atomistic Congress: An Interpretation of Congressional Change.* Armonk, N.Y.: M. E. Sharpe.

Hibbing, John R., and John J. Peters, eds. 1990. *The Changing World of the U.S. Senate.* Berkeley, Calif.: Institute of Governmental Studies.

Holland, Judy. 1998a. "Hormel Backers to Strategize at White House Meeting." *San Francisco Examiner.* June 3, 1998.

———. 1998b. "Hormel Nomination Not Dead, Hatch Says." *San Francisco Examiner.* March 6, 1998.

House Republican Policy Committee. "Policy Statement on the Judicial Selection Process." September 13, 1996.

Hrebenar, Ronald J. 1997. *Interest Group Politics in America* (3rd edition). Armonk, N.Y.: M. E. Sharpe.

Hutcheson, Ron. 1998a. "Hopes Fade for Judicial Nominee." *Fort Worth Star-Telegram.* March 14, 1998.

———. 1998b. "GOP's Hutchison Blasts Democratic Nominee Coggins." *Fort Worth Star-Telegram.* June 27, 1998. P. 16.

Hutchison, Kay Bailey. 1996. Letter to Police Chief Thomas Windham concerning the nomination of Michael Schattman, April 17, 1996.

———. 1997. Letter to Ms. Trista Allen concerning the nomination of Michael Schattman, October 17, 1997.

"Inhofe Deserves Support." *Daily Oklahoman.* May 7, 1998.

Internal Memorandum to Senator Joseph Biden on the evolution of the Senate Judiciary Committee"s Blue Slip policy, July 26, 1993.

"The Inside Report: At Last Report, Nomination Still Up in the Air." *Fort Worth Star-Telegram.* June 7, 1998. P. 3.

Jacobs, John. 1997. "The GOP's Ideological War on the Federal Judiciary." *Sacramento Bee.* November 6, 1997.

Jipping, Thomas L., Director of the Judicial Selection Monitoring Project. 1997. Interview by author, December 16, 1997. Free Congress Foundation, Washington, D.C.

———. 1998. Statement on Susan Oki Mollway. Retrieved from Judicial Selection Monitoring Project Web site: http://www.4judicialrestraint.org.

"Judge the Judges." 1997. Fund-raising video for the Judicial Selection Monitoring Project. September 1997.

Judicial Selection Monitoring Project. 1997a. Fund-raising Pledge Sheet. Washington, D.C.: Judicial Selection Monitoring Project.

———. 1997b. Letter to Senate Majority Leader Trent Lott concerning judicial activism, January 27, 1997.

———. 1997c. Memorandum of Commitment to Paul Weyrich.

Katzmann, Robert A. 1997. *Courts and Congress.* Washington, D.C.: The Brookings Institution.

———. 1998. Letter opposing Frederica Massiah-Jackson's nomination, March 11, 1998.

Key, V. O. 1964. *Political Parties and Pressure Groups.* New York: Crowell.

Kline, Stephan. 1997. Interview by author, December 8, 1997. Alliance for Justice Judicial Selection Project, Washington, D.C.

Krutz, Glen S., Richard Fleisher, and Jon R. Bond. 1998. "From Abe Fortas to Zoe Baird: Explaining Why Some Presidential Nominations Fail in the Senate." *American Political Science Review,* January 7, 1998.

Latham, Earl. 1965. *The Group Basis of Politics.* Ithaca, N.Y.: Cornell University Press.

Law Enforcement Alliance of America. 1998. Letter to Senator Edward M. Kennedy concerning the nomination of Frederica Massiah-Jackson, March 10, 1998.

LeLoup, Lance T., and Steven A. Shull. 1999. *The President and Congress: Collaboration and Combat in National Policy Making.* Boston: Allyn and Bacon.

Lenhart, Warren W. 1991. "Ambassadorial Appointments: The Congressional Debate over Qualifications and Implications for U.S. Policy." *CRS Report for Congress.* May 1, 1991.

Lewis, Anthony. 1998. "Moving the Judges." *New York Times.* April 27, 1998.

Lewis, Neil. 1994. "GOP Heat Will Be on Hatch to Reshape Federal Judiciary." *Deseret News* (Retrieved from http://www.desnews.com). November 20, 1994.

———. 1997. "Republicans Seek Greater Influence in Naming Judges." *New York Times.* April 27, 1997.

Light, Paul. 1995. *Thickening Government: Federal Hierarchy and the Diffusion of Accountability.* Washington, D.C.: The Brookings Institution.

Lobbying Disclosure Reports. Obtained from the Center for Responsive Politics (retrieved from Web site: http://www.opensecrets.org), 2000.

Loomis, Burdett. 2000. *The Contemporary Congress* (3d ed.) Boston: Bedford/St. Martin's Press.

Lowi, Ted, and Benjamin Ginsburg. 1997. *American Government: Freedom and Power.* New York: W. W. Norton and Company.

Mackenzie, G. Calvin. 1981. *The Politics of Presidential Appointments.* New York: The Free Press.

———. 1996. Introduction. In *Obstacle Course: The Report of the Twentieth Century Fund on the Presidential Appointment Process.* New York: The Twentieth Century Fund.

———. 1998. "Starting Over: The Presidential Appointment Process in 1997." A Twentieth Century Fund White Paper. New York: The Twentieth Century Fund.

Mak, Dayton, and Charles Stuart Kennedy. 1992. *American Ambassadors in a Troubled World: Interviews with Senior Diplomats.* Westport, Conn.: Greenwood Press.

Maltese, John Anthony. 1995. *The Selling of Supreme Court Nominees.* Baltimore, Md.: Johns Hopkins University Press.

———. 1998. *The Selling of Supreme Court Nominees* (2d ed.). Baltimore, Md.: Johns Hopkins University Press.

Mann, Dean E. 1964. "The Selection of Federal Political Executives." *American Political Science Review* 58:1.

Massiah-Jackson, Frederica. 1998. Letter to William J. Clinton withdrawing her nomination to the federal district court for Western Pennsylvania, March 16, 1998.

Matthews, Donald R. 1960. *U.S. Senators and Their World.* New York: Vintage.

McCarty, Nolan, and Rose Razaghian. 1998. "Advice and Consent: Senate Responses to Executive Branch Nominations, 1885–1996." Paper Presented at the 1998 Annual Meeting of the Midwestern Political Science Association Meeting, Chicago, Illinois.

Menard, Scott. 1995. *Applied Logistic Regression Analysis.* Thousand Oaks, Calif.: Sage.

Metzenbaum, Senator Howard. Conversation with author. August 1998.

Mills, Kim. 1998. "Holding His Fate in Their Hands: Three Senators Block Hormel's Nomination to Be Luxembourg's Ambassador." *Human Rights Campaign Quarterly.* Spring 1998.

Mincberg, Eliot. 1998. Interview by author, July 13, 1998. People for the American Way, Washington, D.C.

Mintz, Elena. 1998. "From Reagan to Clinton, Interest Groups Refocus." In *Congressional Quarterly Weekly Report,* June 20, 1998.

Morganston, Charles Emile. 1976. *The Appointing and Removal Power of the President of the United States: A Treatise.* Westport, Conn.: Greenwood Press.

Morrison, James. 1998. "Hormel Foes Increasing." *The Washington Times*. March 10, 1998. P. A12.

Nash, Bob J. 1998. Letter from Bob J. Nash, Assistant to the President and Director of Presidential Personnel, to Senate Majority Leader Trent Lott, June 4, 1998.

National Hispanic Leadership Agenda. 1998. "National Hispanic Leadership Agenda Seeks House and Senate Accountability." (Press Release) June 24, 1998.

O'Brien, David M. 1988. *Judicial Roulette*. New York: The Twentieth Century Fund.

O'Brien, David M., ed. 1997. *Judges on Judging: Views from the Bench*. Chatham, N.J.: Chatham House.

Olin, Dirk. 1998. "The Radical Center: Ransoming the Bench." *The Recorder*. May 15, 1998.

Olson, Scott. 2000. Telephone conversation with author. August 9, 2000.

Ornstein, Norman J. 1997. "It's Time to Rethink How Senate Handles 'Advice and Consent'," in *Roll Call*. February 17, 1997.

Overby, L. Marvin, and Beth M. Henschen, 1992. "Courting Constituents?: An Analysis of the Senate Confirmation Vote on Justice Clarence Thomas," in *American Political Science Review* 86: 997–1003.

Overby, L. Marvin, Beth M. Henschen, Michael H. Walsh, and Julie Strauss. 1994. "African American Constituents and Supreme Court Nominees: An Examination of the Senate Confirmation of Thurgood Marshall," in *Political Research Quarterly* 47, no. 4: 839–56.

People for the American Way. 1997. *Judges Delayed, Justice Denied: The Right-Wing Attack on the Federal Judiciary*. Washington, D.C.: People for the American Way.

Perkins, Edward. 1997. Former ambassador to the United Nations, Australia, Liberia, and South Africa. Interview by author, October 27, 1997. The University of Oklahoma, Norman, Oklahoma.

Pines, Deborah. 1996. "Second Circuit Vacancy Stirs Speculation; Straub, Lewin, Sotomayor, Raggi Mentioned for Spot." *New York Law Journal*. March 13, 1996. P. 1.

Postman, David, and James Grimaldi. 1998. "Deal to Break Senate Logjam May Elevate State Justice—Gorton Said Key to Deal." *Seattle Times*. May 5, 1998. P. A1.

Presidential Appointee Initiative. "The Presidential Appointee Initiative Launched." (Presidential Appointee Initiative Launch Event Transcript). Washington, D.C.: The Brookings Institution. April 28, 2000.

Prince, Carl E. 1977. *Federalists and the Origins of the U.S. Civil Service*. New York: New York University Press.

"Qualified to Serve." Editorial in *The Washington Post*. May 12, 1998. P. A18.

"Quit Stalling: Ideologues in Congress Are Holding up Appointments of Qualified Federal Judges." Editorial in *New York Newsday*. February 24, 1997.

Rakove, Jack N. *Original Meanings: Politics and Ideas in the Making of the Constitution.* New York: Alfred A. Knopf.

Rees, Matthew. 1997. "Judging the Judges." *The Weekly Standard.* March 3, 1997.

Rehnquist, William H. 1998. "The 1997 Year-End Report on the Federal Judiciary." January 1, 1998.

Reich, Robert. 1997. *Locked in the Cabinet.* New York: Knopf.

Reske, Henry J. 1997. "Withholding Consent: Senate Judiciary Chair Says He Won't Approve Activist Judges." *ABA Journal.* February 1997, pp. 28–29.

"Resume of Congressional Activity—95th Congress." *Congressional Record Daily Digest.* October 14, 1978, p. D925. Retrieved from http://thomas.loc.gov/home/resume/095res.html.

"Resume of Congressional Activity—96th Congress." *Congressional Record Daily Digest.* December 30, 1980, p. D1593. Retrieved from http://thomas.loc.gov/home/resume/096res.html.

"Resume of Congressional Activity—97th Congress." *Congressional Record Daily Digest.* January 25, 1983. P. D835. Retrieved from http://thomas.loc.gov/home/resume/097res.html.

"Resume of Congressional Activity—98th Congress." *Congressional Record Daily Digest.* November 18, 1983, P. D861; December 14, 1983, P. D1603; December 12, 1984, P. D794. Retrieved from http://thomas.loc.gov/home/resume/098res.html.

"Resume of Congressional Activity—99th Congress." *Congressional Record Daily Digest.* January 6, 1987. P. D10. Retrieved from http://thomas.loc.gov/home/resume/099res.html.

"Resume of Congressional Activity—100th Congress." *Congressional Record Daily Digest.* November 10, 1988. P. D1399. Retrieved from http://thomas.loc.gov/home/resume/100res.html.

"Resume of Congressional Activity—101st Congress." *Congressional Record Daily Digest.* January 3, 1991. P. D1. Retrieved from http://thomas.loc.gov/home/resume/101res.html.

"Resume of Congressional Activity—102nd Congress." *Congressional Record Daily Digest.* January 5, 1993. P. D1; January 3, 1992. P. D1557; and October 9, 1992. P. D1332. Retrieved from http://thomas.loc.gov/home/resume/102res.html.

"Resume of Congressional Activity—103rd Congress." *Congressional Record Daily Digest.* December 20, 1994. P. D1275. Retrieved from http://thomas.loc.gov/home/resume/103res.html.

"Resume of Congressional Activity—104th Congress." *Congressional Record Daily Digest.* January 7, 1997. P. D1. Retrieved from http://thomas.loc.gov/home/resume/104res.html.

"Resume of Congressional Activity—105th Congress–First Session." *Congressional Record Daily Digest.* January 28, 1998. P. D15. Retrieved from http://thomas.loc.gov/home/resume/1051res.html.

Ripley, Randall B. 1969. *Power in the Senate.* New York: St. Martin's.

Rodriguez, Eva M. 1994. "Itchy Republicans Prepare for Power Role in Judge Picks; Conservative Senator Takes Helm of Judiciary Committee." *The Legal Times* 18.

Rudman, Senator Warren. 2000. Author's Interview (via telephone). August 7, 2000.

Rutkus, Denis Steven. 1984. "Nomination and Confirmation Actions: 98th Congress." *CRS Report for Congress.* December 31, 1984.

———. 1986. "Judicial Nominations by President Reagan during the 99th Congress." *CRS Report for Congress.* November 26, 1986.

———. 1988. "Judicial Nominations by President Reagan during the 100th Congress." *CRS Report for Congress.* December 22, 1988.

———. 1991. "Judicial Nominations by President Bush during the 101st Congress." *CRS Report for Congress.*

———. 1993. "Judicial Nominations by President Bush during the 101st and 102nd Congresses." *CRS Report for Congress.* March 29, 1993.

———. 1997. "Judicial Nominations by President Clinton during the 103rd and 104th Congresses." *CRS Report for Congress.* January 24, 1997.

———. 1998. "Judicial Nominations by President Clinton during the 103rd–105th Congresses." *CRS Report for Congress.* January 24, 1998.

Sanford, Jonathan. 1997. "Senate Disposition of Ambassadorial Nominations, 1987–96." *CRS Report for Congress.* September 19, 1997.

Schattman, Mary Ellen. 1998. Interview by Author. November 13–15, 1998. Fort Worth, Texas.

Schattman, Michael. 1998. Interview by author, November 13–15, 1998. Fort Worth, Texas.

Schlozman, Kay Lehman, and John T. Tierney. 1986. *Organized Interests and American Democracy.* New York: Harper and Row.

Schwalm, Steve. 1998. Interview by author, March 1998. Family Research Council, Washington, D.C.

Schwartz, Herman. 1997. "One Man's Activist . . . : What Republicans Really Mean When They Condemn Judicial Activism." *The Washington Monthly.* November 1997.

Segal, Jeffrey A., and Harold J. Spaeth. 1993. *The Supreme Court and the Attitudinal Model.* Cambridge: Cambridge University Press.

Segal, Jeffrey A., Charles Cameron, Lee Epstein, and Harold J. Spaeth. 1995. "Ideological Values and the Votes of U.S. Supreme Court Justices Revisited." *Journal of Politics* 57: 812–23.

Shapiro, Walter. 1997. "Acting is Now All the Confirmation Process Can Muster." *USA Today.* December 16, 1997.

Shogan, Robert. 1996. "The Confirmation Wars: How Politicians, Interest Groups, and the Press Shape the Presidential Appointment Process," in *Obstacle Course: The Report of the Twentieth Century Fund on the Presidential Appointment Process.* New York: The Twentieth Century Fund.

Silbey, Joel H. 1990. "Beyond Realignment and Realignment Theory: American Political Eras, 1789–1989," in *The End of Realignment: Interpreting Electoral Eras,* Byron E. Shafer, ed. Madison: University of Wisconsin Press.

Silverstein, Mark. 1994. *Judicious Choices: The New Politics of Supreme Court Confirmations.* New York: W. W. Norton.

Simon, Senator Paul. 1992. *Advice and Consent: Clarence Thomas, Robert Bork, and the Intriguing History of the Supreme Court's Nomination Battles.* Washington, D.C.: National Press Books.

———. 1998. Interview by author (via telephone), July 15, 1998. Washington, D.C.

Sinclair, Barbara. 1989. *The Transformation of the U.S. Senate.* Baltimore, Md.: Johns Hopkins Press.

———. 1996. *Unorthodox Lawmaking: New Legislative Processes in the U.S. Congress.* Washington, D.C.: Congressional Quarterly Press.

———. 2000. *Unorthodox Lawmaking: New Legislative Processes in the U.S. Congress* (2d ed.). Washington, D.C.: Congressional Quarterly Press.

Suro, Roberto. 1997. "Lee Nomination Fails as Panel Divides on Affirmative Action." *Washington Post.* November 14, 1997.

Torricelli, Sen. Robert, and Sen. Dianne Feinstein. 1998. "Nominee is a Victim of Gay Bias." *The Record* (Bergen Co., New Jersey). June 9, 1998. P. L9. (Also printed as "Sexual Orientation is *Not* a Job Qualification." *Los Angeles Times.* June 4, 1998.)

Tribe, Lawrence. 1986. *God Save This Honorable Court.* New York: Penguin.

Uslaner, Eric. 1998. "Lobbying the Presidency and the Bureaucracy," in *The Interest Group Connection: Electioneering, Lobbying, and Policy Making in Washington.* Ed. Paul S. Herrnson, Ronald G. Shaiko, and Clyde Wilcox. Chatham, N.J.: Chatham House Publishers.

Victor, Kirk. 1998. "Hatch on the High Wire." *National Journal.* April 4, 1998.

Washington Report. 1997. "Senate Hearing on Middle East Appointees." Retrieved from http://www.washington-report.org/backissues/1297/9712049.html. December 1997.

Watson, George, and John Stookey. 1988. "Supreme Court Confirmation Hearings: A View from the Senate." *Judicature* 71(4): 186–96.

Wayne, Stephen J., G. Calvin Mackenzie, David M. O'Brien, and Richard L. Cole. 1996. *The Politics of American Government: Foundations, Participation, Institutions, and Policy* (2d ed.). New York: St. Martin's.

Weich, Ronald, former Chief Counsel to Senator Edward M. Kennedy. 1998. Interview by author, January 8, 1998. Zuckerman, Spaeder, Goldstein, Taylor, and Kolker, Washington, D.C.

Weisberg, Jacob. 1997. "Payback Time: Should Agreeing with the President Cost You an Administration Job?" *Slate.* November 20, 1997. Retrieved from Web site: http://slate.msn.com/StrangeBedfellow/97-11-20/StrangeBedfellow.asp.

Weisberg, Herbert F., Eric S. Heberlig, and Lisa M. Campoli, eds. *Classics in Congressional Politics.* New York: Longman Publishers.

Weyrich, Paul M. 1997. Letter from Paul M. Weyrich, Director of the Free Congress Foundation, soliciting contributions for the Judicial Selection Monitoring Project, August 17, 1997.

Wilson, James Q. 1991. *Bureaucracy; What Government Agencies Do and Why They Do It.* New York: Basic.

Wolpe, Bruce C. 1990. *Lobbying Congress: How the System Works.* Washington D.C.: Congressional Quarterly Press.

Wright, John R. 1995. *Interest Groups and Congress: Lobbying, Contributions, and Influence.* Boston: Allyn and Bacon.

Yalof, David Alistair. 1999. *Pursuit of Justices: Presidential Politics and the Selection of Supreme Court Nominees.* Chicago: University of Chicago Press.

Index